A sociology of crime

Designed as an alternative to conventional correctional texts in criminology, *A Sociology of Crime* departs from the traditional concern with criminal behaviour and its causes to emphasize the socially constructed nature of crime. Adopting a radically sociological perspective, Stephen Hester and Peter Eglin argue that crime is a product of social processes which identify certain acts and persons as criminal.

In their exploration of this theme, Hester and Eglin use three leading approaches in contemporary sociological theory – ethnomethodology, symbolic interactionism, and structural conflict theory. They apply each of these perspectives to a detailed study of the anatomy of crime, at the same time reviewing other main criminological perspectives on both sides of the Atlantic, including the feminist one. They focus on three main topics: making crime by making criminal law; making crime by enforcing criminal law; and making crime by the administration of criminal justice in the courts.

International in outlook, *A Sociology of Crime* contains a wealth of empirical material from the USA, Britain and Canada which is closely linked to the theoretical approaches discussed. With its fresh and invigorating perspective on crime, it will be an invaluable text for students of criminology and sociology.

Stephen Hester is Associate Professor of Sociology at Wilfrid Laurier University, Canada, and Lecturer in Sociology at the University of Wales, Bangor. **Peter Eglin** is Associate Professor of Sociology at Wilfrid Laurier University, Canada.

A sociology of crime

Stephen Hester and Peter Eglin

Routledge
Taylor & Francis Group

LONDON AND NEW YORK

First published in 1992
by Routledge
2 Park Square, Milton Park, Abingdon, Oxon OX14 4RN

Simultaneously published in the USA and Canada
by Routledge
270 Madison Ave, New York, NY 10016

Transferred to Digital Printing 2008

Routledge is an imprint of the Taylor & Francis Group, an informa business

Typeset in Baskerville by LaserScript Limited, Mitcham, Surrey

Printed and bound in Great Britain by TJI Digital, Padstow, Cornwall

British Library Cataloguing in Publication Data
A catalogue record for this book is available from the British Library.

Library of Congress Cataloging in Publication Data
Hester, Stephen.
  A sociology of crime/Stephen Hester and Peter Eglin.
  p. cm.
  Includes bibliographical references and index.
  1. Crime – Sociological aspects. 2. Sociology – Methodology.
  I. Eglin, Peter. II. Title.
  HM210.H47   1992
  364 – dc20   91-41468
                                                CIP

ISBN 10: 0-415-07369-3 (hbk)
ISBN 10: 0-415-07370-7 (pbk)

ISBN 13: 978-0-415-07369-1 (hbk)
ISBN 13: 978-0-415-07370-7 (pbk)

Contents

Preface

This book originated when we were invited to write a new, replacement course in criminology for Telecollege at Wilfred Laurier University. In doing so, we wanted to offer a sociological version of criminology which avoided the standard preoccupations with correctionalism and causality. We had been teaching criminology in departments of sociology for fifteen years or more, and we had come to treat as a matter of sociological 'common-sense knowledge' the view that 'crime' is socially constituted through processes of law creation, law enforcement and the administration of justice. Accordingly, we designed as an alternative a series of twelve programmes which emphasized a sociological approach to crime which not only informs the student about 'crime' but about 'doing sociology' or 'thinking sociologically' as well. After several transformations, this series then became the basis of *A Sociology of Crime*.

As an alternative to the standard correctional text, our work can be seen to belong to a 'subversive' tradition within criminology. As in the work of others before us (Becker, Box, Kitsuse and Cicourel, Matza, Phillipson, Pollner, Rock, Scull, Sim, Spitzer) its subversion consists in its calling into question the correctional, consensual and causal orthodoxy and in considering instead how crime is social constructed. It is this subversive tradition which enables proponents of otherwise incommensurate sociological approaches to find, at least fleetingly, a common ground, namely an interest in the question of how crime is socially produced or constituted. In the chapters that follow (except for our last chapter where we include some of the insights of the otherwise now rather moribund structural consensus perspective) we have confined our attention to the structural conflict perspective, symbolic interactionism and ethnomethodology. (Since we do not regard feminist sociology or feminist criminology (Gelsthorpe and Morris 1990; Valverde 1991) as naming a unique sociological perspective, but rather as reflecting the impact of the women's movement across all perspectives in the disciplines of sociology and criminology, we have not tacked on a 'women's chapter' or a series of feminist chapters, but have tried to incorporate relevant viewpoints and studies throughout.) Common ground notwithstanding, our focus on symbolic interactionist, ethnomethodological and structural conflict perspectives on crime does not mean that we advocate integrationist or incorporationist notions of sociological enquiry in which the partial pictures afforded by different approaches can be added up with the prospect of obtaining a 'fuller picture' of some independent reality. We prefer the 'constitutive' conception of the role of sociological perspectives. As we argue in the last chapter there is no archimedean, perspectiveless point from which to engage in criminology or any other form of enquiry. It is the use of perspectives which constitutes the topics and phenomena they address, and so perspectives are valuable for just what they can show about the world. For this reason it is pointless to ask of them what they are incapable of providing. But it is a worse error to suppose that there is some way around them. If this work can contribute to the learning of this lesson in criminology and the sociology of crime, then the effort of writing it will have been worthwhile.

Each chapter consists of an explication of some relevant portion of the theoretical perspective assigned to it, together with a number of exemplary case studies. In selecting case studies for discussion we have sought to draw as fairly as possible on research from Britain, Canada and the United States. At the same time, so as not to overburden the text with material and because our aim is to *exhibit* the perspectives rather than survey the field, we have not dealt, except in passing, with a number of areas which we recognize are clearly relevant to our topic. These include the activation of the police by the public, especially in the form of the citizen's call to the police and the involvement of the mass media in the construction of crime. Our relative inattention to these topics does not mean we consider them unimportant in their own right, only that consideration of them was not essential to our task.

We wish to acknowledge with gratitude the involvement and support of Cliff Bilyea, Tom Fleming, Sunil Kuruvilla, Susan Lennard, Bruce Minore and Ken Morrison. Also greatly appreciated are the advice and encouragement of Elisabeth Tribe at Routledge, and the helpful comments of their anonymous reviewer. To acknowledge a list of influences is both a difficult and unfair task. However, in Hester's case particular mention should be made of Paul Rock and especially the late Steven Box. Richard Scase is also thanked for making facilities available at the University of Kent for Hester's sabbatical during which part of the text was written. On a more personal level, Eglin thanks Maria and John for good fellowship and liquid refreshment when working late at the office. We also wish to acknowledge our debt to the members of our respective 'families' – Joe, Joyce, Linda, Laura, Serena, Zandria, Kate, Laura and Daniel. Their support, encouragement and generosity in relieving us of the burdens of domestic labour figured crucially in the 'practical circumstances' and 'social conditions' of producing this text.

Chapter 1

Sociology and crime

In this opening chapter we are concerned to provide the foundation for the overall position we take in the book, including the selection of the sociological perspectives with which it deals. We begin by explaining the distinction between social and sociological problems. We then describe the 'face of the enemy', namely correctional or 'cause-and-cure' criminology/sociology, based as it is in a 'social-problems' conception of crime. Against this background we introduce the three sociological perspectives which we use and which address crime as a sociological problem. We specify the types of sociological questions they raise about crime. Finally we set out the key issues, organization and overall aims of the book.

SOCIAL AND SOCIOLOGICAL PROBLEMS

We begin by making a distinction between *social* and *sociological* problems. Following Spector and Kitsuse (1987 (1977)), we conceptualize social problems as those activities through which conditions and circumstances are claimed and defined as problems by governments, the media, the private and public welfare agencies, as well as problem spokespeople amongst the general public, that is:

> we define social problems as the activities of individuals or groups making assertions of grievances and claims with respect to some putative conditions. The emergence of a social problem is contingent upon the organization of activities asserting the need for eradicating, ameliorating, or otherwise changing some condition.
>
> (Spector and Kitsuse 1987: 75–76)

Social problems, then, reflect what persons are currently concerned about, what they claim something should be done about, what people find undesirable and in need of eradication. Such problems, depending on the concerns of the time and place, are subject to change. They range from wife battering to illiteracy, racial discrimination to environmental pollution, drugs to abortion, alcohol to sexual assault, gender inequality to juvenile delinquency. For example, as Pfohl (1977) has shown, it was only in the early 1960s that 'child abuse' became recognized as a 'problem' about which something should be done. Previously, although children were beaten and otherwise 'abused', this never became a matter of sustained public attention. Only when certain groups, in this case medical specialists such as radiologists, acted in such a way as to result in this being brought to widespread public attention was this condition defined as a major public problem. Various kinds of 'crime' have also been defined at various times as social problems. For example, robbery, that is theft with violence, has long been recognized as a crime but it was only in the early 1970s that a particular form of it became labelled as 'mugging' and became elevated to the status of a serious social problem. This occurred as a result of the activities of claims-makers such as politicians, police officers and journalists. It depended, too, on the nature of the routine operation of news gathering and production (Fishman 1980) and on the 'structural context' of political and economic relations at the time (Hall *et al.* 1978).

Sociological problems are those which are derived from the concerns which motivate sociological inquiry. These concerns reflect the different theoretical perspectives which are used by sociologists. Perhaps the most fundamental of these concerns is the problem of social order: how is society possible? Other pre-occupations of sociologists include: understanding social action, locating social practices and cultures within changing structural environments, describing social processes, including the forma-tion of social identities and identifying organizational structures of social interaction; they also include methodological debates about the problems of theory and practice, structure and agency and objectivity and meaning.

It is our view, sociologically speaking, that 'crime' is interesting only in so far as it provides a pretext for asking sociological questions rather than those motivated by a concern to 'do something about it'. This means that our interest in 'crime' is sociological rather than correctional or ameliorative. Much inquiry into crime appears to presuppose that the fundamental questions are 'what causes crime?' and 'what can be done to cure it?' For us, however, these questions reflect a view which is itself in need of sociological investigation.

Some of the concerns of those who claim that crime is a *social* problem include: crime is not only increasing but becoming increasingly violent; that these increases are occurring despite increased public expenditure; that harsher penalties, a return to traditional values and an expansion of law enforcement personnel are needed to deal with the failure of the criminal justice system to deal effectively with the problem of crime. These are views that, while widespread in society, tend to be articulated by particular interest or value groups such as associations of chiefs of police or correctional officers or government departments or grass-roots organizations such as Victims of Violence (see Amernic 1984). The propagation of such views is a classical example of the construction of a social problem through claims-making.

CORRECTIONAL CRIMINOLOGY AND SOCIOLOGY

Some sociologists have been coopted into viewing crime as a social problem. The story of Irvin Waller's involvement in the propagation of 'Victims of Crime' as a social problem through his work for the Ministry of the Solicitor General of Canada is elegantly told by Paul Rock (1986) in *A View from the Shadows*. Both in such applied work, and more fundamentally in their theoretical formulations, such sociologists have become part of the process through which crime is constructed as a problem. This has arisen in part through the historical connection of sociology with the practical discipline of criminology, a discipline which has defined itself in 'cause-and-cure' terms. For example:

> Criminology, in its narrow sense, is concerned with the study of the phenomenon of crime and of the factors or circumstances . . . which may have an influence on or be associated with criminal behaviour and the state of crime in general. But this does not and should not exhaust the whole subject matter of criminology. There remains the vitally important problem of combating crime . . . To rob it of this practical function, is to divorce criminology from reality and render it sterile.
>
> (Radzinowicz 1962: 168)

The scholarly objective of criminology is the development of a body of knowledge regarding this process of law, crime, and reaction to crime . . . The practical objective of criminology, supplementing the scientific or theoretical objective, is to reduce the amount of pain and suffering in the world.

(Sutherland and Cressey 1978: 3, 24)

Research in criminology is conducted for the purpose of understanding criminal behaviour. If we can understand the behaviour, we will have a better chance of predicting when it will occur and then be able to take policy steps to control, eliminate, or prevent the behaviour.

(Reid 1985: 66)

Let us state quite categorically that the major task of radical criminology is to seek a solution to the problem of crime and that of a socialist policy is to substantially reduce the crime rate.

(Young 1986: 28; quoted in Sim *et al.* 1987: 42, and Smart 1990: 72)

Following Matza (1969), such sociology can be regarded as correctional. The central components of correctional criminology and sociology are as follows: (1) the equivalence of social and sociological problems; (2) the derivation of sociological questions from social concerns; (3) the objective of sociological inquiry as the amelioration of social problems; (4) an 'overwhelming' preoccupation with questions of etiology or causation in relation to criminal *behaviour*; (5) a commitment to the methodological principles of positivistic social science.

In order to exemplify this process of cooptation we review briefly some of the major positivistic theories of criminal behaviour (see, for example, Wilson and Herrnstein 1986). We begin with the non-sociological theories the focus of which has been on the biological and psychological causes of criminal behaviour. For an exhaustive review of current work of this type see Eysenck and Gudjonsson (1989) *The Causes and Cures of Criminality*.

Biological and psychological theories of criminal behaviour

From the biological criminology of Lombroso in the nineteenth century to the psychological criminology of Eysenck in the twentieth, as Box (1981) points out, the concern has been with isolating the criminal *individual* by identifying those characteristics which differentiated him or her from the 'normal' person. For the biological criminologist, these differentia were to be found in the human body; that is, it was assumed that there were physiological differences between criminals and normals. Early work in this field, for example, that stemming from an 1876 pamphlet of Lombroso (1972 (1911); Sutherland and Cressey 1978: 58–59), argued that criminals were distinguished by their 'head shapes, peculiarities in their eyes, receding foreheads, weak chins, compressed faces, flared nostrils, long ape-like arms and agile and muscular bodies' (Box 1981: 2). Since then it has been claimed and continues to be claimed (by the likes of Dr Sarnoff Mednick (Sim *et al.* 1987: 10)) that criminality is caused by or at least correlated with such factors as biological inferiority (Hooton 1939), body shape (Glueck and Glueck 1950, 1956; Sheldon 1949; Kretschmer 1925), nutritional deficiency (Hippchen 1977), chromosome abnormality (West 1969) and, when averaged out for 'racial' groups, the size of the genitals, buttocks and brain (Rushton 1989). Rushton's work, which has achieved some notoriety in Canada, is a straight revival or continuation of nineteenth-century 'race science', down to the 'anthroporn' of one of its principal sources (French Army-Surgeon 1972 (1898)).

For the psychological criminologist, the determinants of individual criminality, in contrast, are to be found in various aspects of the human personality. These include extreme intraversion and extraversion (Eysenck 1964, 1977), a weak super-ego and riotous id (Alexander and Ross 1952), insanity (Menninger 1969; Prins 1980) and 'a commitment to bureaucratic detail coupled with an opportunistic belief in a Messianic identity' (Kuttner 1985: 35). This last pair of features is said to characterize 'the genocidal mentality' as exhibited by Phillip the Second of Spain, Sultan Abdul Hamid the Second of Turkey and Adolf Hitler, although the author acknowledges that '[s]orting criteria that can identify and separate invisible mental lesions of individuals prone to mass violence remain unknown' (ibid: 42). During the Gulf Massacre (January–March 1991) Saddam Hussein was credited with exhibiting the pathological condition called by its inventors 'malignant narcissism'. Comment should be superfluous.

Sociological theories of criminal behaviour

Sociological theories of criminal behaviour locate the difference between the criminal and the normal person in the character of the social environment to which the person is exposed. Early work by the Chicago School of Sociology, for example, correlated criminality with urban 'social disorganization' or 'social pathology' in terms similar to Durkheim's concept of anomie, that is, a lack of moral regulation brought about by rapid social change. Merton (1938) also employed the concept of anomie, though rather differently (see now Hilbert 1989), linking deviant behaviour with the disjunction between institutionalized aspirations and the availability of access to legitimate opportunity structures. The prime candidates for criminal behaviour such as property theft, for example, were those whose class position prevented them from realizing material success through school, work and other legitimate means. For Sutherland (1939) in his theory of differential association the link between society and criminal behaviour was related to exposure to 'definitions favourable to the violation of law'. In particular, Sutherland proposed that 'a person becomes delinquent because of an excess of definitions favourable to violation of law over definitions unfavourable to violation of law' (quoted in Box 1981: 110). Later, in the work of subcultural theorists such as Cohen (1955), Cloward and Ohlin (1960) and Young (1971a), attempts were made to combine the Mertonian emphasis on structural disjunctures and the Sutherlandesque focus on cultural transmission. The major, though not exclusive, focus of these studies was on lower-class delinquency. Finally, control theory has examined the connection between criminal behaviour and the weakness or absence of certain social bonds such as commitment to conformity, attachment to conventional others, involvement in conventional activities and belief in the legitimacy of particular rules.

   Whether explicitly derived from his work or not the sociological theories considered above may be said to stand in the tradition of theorizing established by Durkheim in such works as *Suicide* (1951 (1897), and *The Rules of Sociological Method* (1982 (1895)). The behaviour in question, here criminality, is to be explained in terms of the principles of social–structural differentiation and determinism. Moreover:

   Although we set out primarily to study reality, it does not follow that we do not wish to improve it; we should judge our re-searches to have no worth at all if they were to have only a speculative interest. If we separate carefully the theoretical from the practical problems, it is not to the neglect of the latter; but, on the contrary, to be in a better position to solve them.

(Durkheim 1964 (1893): 33)

A critique of correctional criminology and sociology

We see the failures of this correctional, social-problems-oriented approach to the study of crime as residing in three errors. Firstly, the attitude towards the study of crime is shaped from the outset and throughout the inquiry by an overriding concern to 'do something about crime'. This concern is founded in an anxiety about the state of civil society which arose in the wake of the industrial revolution. 'Positivistic' social science in general and criminology in particular was conceived against the background of this anxiety about the perceived 'evil consequences' of industrialization. For example, what came to be known as 'juvenile delinquency' was problematic because it was taken as portending the greater evil of adult crime and that, in turn, was seen to threaten the very fabric of civil society with the prospect of anarchy (Houston 1978). The development of scientific inquiry into these phenomena was explicitly conceived as directed towards their amelioration (and thus to the relief of this anxiety). In the words of Comte, '*savoir pour prévoir, prévoir pour prévenir*'. Lukes has this to say about Comte's most famous follower:

> Durkheim's notions of 'egoism' and 'anomie' were rooted in a broad and all-pervasive tradition of discussion concerning the causes of imminent social disintegration and the practical measures needed to avoid it – tradition ranging from the far right to the far left. His own approach was distinctive . . . The remedy lay neither in outdated traditionalist beliefs and institutions, nor in speculative and utopian social schemes; the only way to solve 'the difficulties of these crucial times' . . . was the scientific way.
>
> (Lukes 1975: 198–199)

The anxiety expressed in positivistic social science persists in the correctional criminological studies reviewed above as well as in sociology more generally. Correctional criminology and sociology thus equate social and sociological problems, deriving the latter from the former and making sociological objectives serve broader social ends. At its most extreme such sociology becomes merely the servant of the state, the current atheoretical version of which Young (1986) calls 'administrative criminology', though the term was applied earlier by Vold (1958) to the eighteenth-century 'classical' school of criminology (Bottomley 1979: 2). For us the presumed equivalence of sociological and social problems in this tradition indicates an endorsement by the sociologist of the norms, values and beliefs which give rise to the 'problems' in the first place. We question this endorsement! For us such grounds are to be treated as topics of inquiry rather than as resources for generating 'sociological problems'. We are interested in the use of values, norms and beliefs by members of society as means for constructing social order, and so we see no justification for subscribing to that which we want to treat as problematic.

Secondly, correctional criminology deploys assumptions about human beings which display a failure to appreciate the socially meaningful character of crime both as a form of social action and as a description of human behaviour. Thus, in its preoccupation with the cause-and-effect relations between various 'factors' and criminal behaviour, correctional criminology contains a view of human beings as objects rather than as subjects, treatable for the practical purposes of 'scientific inquiry' just like the objects of natural science. Against this we take the view that humans are more appropriately viewed as subjects because their behaviour is 'subjectively meaningful' to them. As Schutz puts it:

> This state of affairs is founded on the fact that there is an essential difference in the structure of the thought objects or mental objects formed by the social sciences and those formed by the natural sciences. It is up to the natural scientist and to him alone to define, in accordance with the procedural rules of his science, his observational field, and to determine the facts, data, and events within it which are relevant for his problem or scientific purpose at hand. Neither are those facts and events pre-selected, nor is the observational field pre-interpreted. The world of nature, as explored by the natural scientist, does not 'mean' anything to the molecules, atoms and electrons. But the observational field of the social scientist – social reality – has a specific meaning and a relevance structure for the human beings living, acting, and thinking within it. By a series of common-sense constructs they have pre-selected and

pre-interpreted this world which they experience as the reality of their daily lives. It is these thought objects of theirs which determine their behaviour by motivating it. The thought objects constructed by the social scientist, in order to grasp this social reality, have to be founded upon the thought objects constructed by the common-sense thinking of men [sic], living their daily life within their social world.

(Schutz 1967: 58–59)

Similarly, as Matza says:

The confusion began when primitive social scientists – many of whom are still vigorous – mistook the phenomenon under consideration – man [sic] – and conceived it as object instead of subject. That was a great mistake. Numerous theories appeared positing man as merely reactive and denying that he is the author of action, but none were convincing . . . These minimizations of man persisted as presumptions which guided research and shaped operative theory. They were maintained despite classic repudiations of the objective view by Max Weber and George Herbert Mead . . . The initial mistake continues to plague sociology, as well as the other human disciplines.

(Matza 1969: 7–8)

Thirdly, correctional criminology takes for granted the 'objectivity' of crime rather than recognizing that 'crime' is socially defined and relative. Following Becker's (1963: 9) foundational statement (see Chapter 2) it may be said that 'crime' is constructed in two senses. Firstly, it is constructed through the processes whereby certain kinds of acts come to be defined as crimes, that is, through the making of some criminal law. Secondly, it is constructed through the processes of law enforcement whereby particular instances of those acts are selected and identified by the police as falling under the categories of the criminal law. We would want to add a third sense of crime construction to take account of the work of the courts in making the fit between police selection/ identification and legal definition, and in attaching the status 'criminal' to particular actors. Preoccupation with the question, 'what are the causes of crime', necessarily takes for granted these processes.

This failure to consider the constructed character of crime is evident in correctional criminology's reliance on official and other statistics about crime. Thus, in the Durkheimian tradition crime rates are treated as if they are things and amenable to variable analysis. It is not recognized that such measures and the analyses built on them are the product of a series of interpretive and judgmental practices, as we shall see. In short:

> The whole *raison d'etre* of criminology is that it addresses crime. It categorizes a vast range of activities and treats them as if they were all subject to the same laws – whether laws of human behaviour, genetic inheritance, economic rationality, development or the like . . . The thing that criminology cannot do is deconstruct crime. It cannot locate rape or child sexual abuse in the domain of sexuality or theft in the domain of economic activity or drug use in the domain of health. To do so would be to abandon criminology to sociology; but more importantly it would involve abandoning the idea of a unified problem which requires a unified response – at least, at the theoretical level.
>
> (Smart 1990: 77)

WHAT IS CRIME? THREE SOCIOLOGICAL APPROACHES

In the light of our critique of correctional criminology, we hold the following two features to be fundamental axioms in the study of crime: (1) social action is intersubjectively meaningful, and (2) 'crime' is socially constructed. The sociological approaches used in this book take these two axioms seriously. We therefore pay no further attention to theories of crime causation except in so far as societal members' use of the theories themselves may be seen to play some part in the process through which crime is created in society. We shall be drawing on the sociological approaches of symbolic interactionism, ethnomethodology and structural conflict theory. As we make clear below, we use only that part of structural conflict theory that provides 'interpretative–historical' accounts of crime construction; we do not engage the larger structural–determinist or causal framework of this approach. We shall occasionally make reference to the structural consensus approach as this serves as a useful foil to the structural conflict approach but also because, when it was not concerned with issues of crime causation, this approach did have some things to say which have proved both interesting and instructive.

Symbolic interactionism

According to Herbert Blumer, symbolic interactionism rests on three simple premises:

1 The first premise is that human beings act toward things on the basis of the meanings that the things have for them.
2 The second premise is that the meaning of such things is derived from, or arises out of, the social interaction that one has with one's fellows.
3 The third premise is that these meanings are handled in, and modified through, an interpretative process used by the person in dealing with the things he encounters.

(Blumer 1969: 2)

As far as the study of crime is concerned, the first premise entails the view that whether a given act is criminal or not depends on the meanings which are attributed to it. Acts are not criminal in themselves; their criminality is a property or meaning conferred upon them (Erikson 1962). From a symbolic interactionist point of view, crime is a matter of social definition. The second premise means that these conferred meanings arise interactionally, whether in interaction with others or with oneself. Thus, in the course of direct social interaction persons may construe each other's behaviour as criminal. Similarly, in the process of self-interaction a person may take the standpoint of others towards his or her behaviour and thereby identify it as criminal. The third premise means that what particular meaning is conferred or construed depends upon how the act is interpreted by the parties to the interaction. This also implies that how an act is interpreted depends on how the interactional setting or situation is defined by participants. Interactionists have paid particular attention to the face-to-face, situational and organizational aspects of the contexts of symbolic interaction.

In accordance with these premises symbolic interactionist studies of crime focus on the examination of the processes (and contexts) of social interaction whereby (and in which):

1 certain forms of behaviour become prohibited by criminal law, that is, the process of crime definition through legislation;
2 certain acts and persons become subject to law enforcement, that is, the process of crime selection by the police;

3   certain acts and persons become fitted with the label 'criminal',
    that is, the process of crime interpretation by the courts;
4   criminal identity is developed, maintained and transformed.

There is a fifth line of inquiry that examines the (subjectively)
meaningful character of criminal behaviour for 'criminals' themselves. Symbolic interactionists have conducted 'ethnographic'
studies of the social organization and meaning of 'crime' as far as
those who engage in it are concerned. Dating back to the work of
the Chicago School of Sociology, such studies have produced a
wealth of ethnographic sociological literature in the fields of crime
and deviance from, for example, Anderson (1923) through Whyte
(1943), Carey (1968), Adler (1985) to Prus and Sharper (1991).
However, since these studies do not make problematic how the
forms of crime and deviance they so carefully and faithfully describe are defined as 'crime' (or 'deviance') they will not concern
us here. Instead, we shall draw on that strand of symbolic interactionist theory whose concerns consist of questions (1), (2), (3)
and (4) listed previously (although we give only cursory treatment
to the last). This strand has come to be known as the 'labelling
perspective' or, more narrowly, 'labelling theory' (see Chapter 5).

The aim in such work is with analytically inducing formal gen-
eralizations about the meanings of crime and the interactional
(and organizational) processes through which they are generated.
This quest for generalization and the necessarily entailed decon-
textualization of meaning constitution is a feature which
distinguishes symbolic interactionism from ethnomethodology, as
we shall see.

Furthermore, symbolic interactionism in general and labelling
theory in particular have been the subject of considerable controversy. This is, in part, due to the fact that there is not one
interactionist position but several (Plummer 1991). Some varieties
may be described as quite radically interpretive whilst others are
open to mergers with other approaches, notably positivism on the
one hand and the structural conflict perspective on the other. It is
arguable that the 'Iowa' school of symbolic interactionism is
simply misnamed, for its methodology is indistinguishable from
the 'abstracted empiricism' of mainstream American positivistic
sociology (Meltzer *et al.* 1975: 55–67). The same can be said
of 'social structural symbolic interactionism' (Stryker 1980).
However, it is unfortunate that the labelling position associated

with the central 'Chicago' stream of symbolic interactionism has
been persistently misread by orthodox positivistic sociologists as
making essentially causal claims (see Plummer 1979). Nevertheless, it has been noticed that even more 'interpretive' formulations
of interactionism and labelling theory retain elements of causal
theorizing, common-sense 'realism' and variable analysis. Thus, in
their foundational article, 'A note on the uses of official statistics',
Kitsuse and Cicourel declare:

> a sociological theory of deviance would focus on three inter-
> related problems of explanation:
> (1) How different forms of behavior come to be defined as
> deviant by various groups or organizations in the society,
> (2) how individuals manifesting such behaviors are organiza-
> tionally processed to produce rates of deviant behavior among
> various segments of the population, and
> (3) how acts which are officially or unofficially defined as
> deviant are generated by such conditions as family organization,
> role inconsistencies or situational 'pressures'.
> (Kitsuse and Cicourel 1963: 135)

That is, to the classical interactionist focus on (1) the definition
and (2) the selection of deviance, they add (3) the incongruous
traditional interest of positivistic sociology in structural–causal
explanation. (This ambivalence has persisted throughout
Cicourel's work (for example, 1964, 1976) and can be found also
in Douglas's (1967) interactionist study of suicide (Eglin 1987:
206-207).)

Similarly, despite his seminal statement of the central tenets of
the labelling approach to deviance in *Outsiders*, Becker (1963)
incorporated the common-sense distinction between 'obedient'
and 'rule-breaking' behaviour into his model of deviance in contradiction of his own claim that 'deviant behavior is behavior that
people so label' (Becker 1963: 9). Consequently, 'four of the five
empirical chapters' in *Outsiders* 'do not present research on the
societal reaction to deviance, but are concerned with the deviants
themselves' (Spector and Kitsuse 1987: 98). We examine this
problem in detail in Chapter 10 via Pollner's ethnomethodological
critique.

Furthermore, in *Making the Grade*, a study of student life in an
American university, Becker (with Geer and Hughes 1968) resorts
to quantitative measurement, presenting 'tables which classify and

count the number of observed occurrences which support his
hypothesis' and which 'also show the number of negative cases'
(Cuff and Payne 1979 (1984): 210). Quantitative measurement is,
of course, a cardinal feature of the variable analysis that is a
mainstay of positivistic methodology, one which Blumer (1956
(1969)) had so trenchantly criticized from a symbolic interactionist perspective in 'Sociological analysis and the "variable"'.

For some sociologists of crime and deviance, interactionism/
labelling theory has been something of a passing phase on the way
to a more 'radical' position within the structural conflict perspective (and sometimes on the way from a traditional positivistic
position). (Others, such as Atkinson (1978), record a journey from
positivism through interactionism to ethnomethodology.) This
has been noted by a number of commentators (for example,
Klockars 1979; Downes and Rock 1982: 213; Hinch 1985) and
appears to be true, for example, of Chambliss, Quinney (see p. 21),
Platt (compare the first and second editions of *The Child Savers*
(1969, 1975)), Cohen (compare the first and second editions of
Folk Devils and Moral Panics (1972, 1980)), Young (see p. 21–23)
and to a lesser extent of Box (compare the first and second
editions of *Deviance, Reality and Society* (1971, 1981)). For some this
shift crystallized half way in the form of a 'radical interactionism'
(for example, Carlen 1976); McBarnet's (1981) study of conviction
occupies similar transitional ground. We characterize this position
in Chapter 9 and set it off from the ethnomethodological
perspective in Chapter 10.

Apart, then, from some attention to the 'radical' species of
interactionism, we restrict our treatment of the whole perspective
to its 'pure' interpretive form. We exhibit its analysis of crime
definition in Chapter 2, crime selection in Chapter 5, crime
interpretation in Chapter 9 and self-identification as criminal in
Chapters 5 and 11.

Ethnomethodology

Ethnomethodology is the study of members' methods of making
sense, that is their methods of producing and recognizing
'sensible' social actions and settings (Garfinkel 1967). When
persons produce actions they do so in such a way as to make the
actions 'accountable' as those actions, where 'accountable' means
'observable–reportable'. That is, persons design their actions so as

others may identify them as what they are. They make them observable for others' report. The 'design' comprises the methods used to produce the action. Similarly, recipients of action must use those same methods to recognize the identity of those actions. Thus, a first principle of ethnomethodology is that of 'recipient design', that is, that actions are designed for their recipients. From this point of view an action (or other object or social fact such as a setting) *is* its 'production and recognition apparatus' (Garfinkel and Sacks 1970).

A second principle of ethnomethodology is expressed in Garfinkel's (1967) injunction to 'treat social facts as *interactional accomplishments*' (cf. Pollner 1974b: 27, emphasis added). As Pollner says: 'Where others might see "things", "givens" or "facts of life", the ethnomethodologist sees (or attempts to see) *process*: the process through which the perceivedly stable features of socially organized environments are continually created and sustained' (ibid). Accordingly, ethnomethodology pays close attention to the production and recognition of social action in particular situations or settings. But it does so exclusively with reference to how the participants within the settings locally produce or accomplish them. That is, it is taken up with the 'local production of social order'. Moreover, its attention is less on the participants acting than on the actions and settings themselves. For ethnomethodology, participants are 'members', members are 'courses of action', settings are 'self-organizing' (Pollner 1979) and the identities of actions-and-settings are mutually constituted.

A third principle of ethnomethodology centres on the distinction between topic and resource (Zimmerman and Pollner 1970). Ethnomethodology is not concerned with sociologically predefining some phenomenon for explanation nor with seeking to employ members' meanings as resources for those explanations. Rather ethnomethodology endeavours to seek out what participants in particular settings are themselves oriented to and how those features enter into their perceptions, actions and accounts. In this way members' 'meanings' become a topic of inquiry rather than resources for mapping out a sociologically imposed set of relevances.

A fourth principle of ethnomethodological studies concerns a particular conception of the social actor. In contrast to structuralist views of the actor as one who has internalized his/her culture as a set of rules prescribing normative behaviour, and whose actions are then 'rule-governed' – a version of the actor described by Garfinkel as 'the pre-programmed cultural dope' – ethnomethodology treats the actor as a 'rule-using' creature, one who is oriented to rules in the course of action and who may design particular actions to be in accord with rules. This clearly has relevance for sociological investigations of any setting that may be said to be organized by rules, and has particular relevance for an understanding of the criminal law as a body of rules. (We examine the latter in Chapter 4.)

From its beginnings in Garfinkel's classic studies, ethnomethodology has since matured and diversified into a variety of strands held together not least by the aforementioned principles. For our purposes we shall draw, though not exclusively, on three of these strands each of which provides for a different type of analysis. The first is the analysis of 'mundane reason'. This involves the study of how members of society make use of assumptions about the objectivity and intersubjectivity of the features of their social worlds. The interest is in the use of these assumptions in fact production (as in the facts of crime, the facts of suicide, the facts of gender). Much influenced by Schutzian phenomenology and the early work of Garfinkel, the major work in this 'tradition' of ethnomethodology is that of Pollner (1974a, 1974b, 1975, 1978, 1987). Adaptations and extensions of this work can also be found in Smith (1978) and Hester (1991). The second strand is 'membership categorization analysis'. This originated in the work of Harvey Sacks in a series of unpublished lectures in the 1960s. Work deriving from, and some of the original lectures, have now been published (Sacks 1967, 1972a, 1974, 1989), and a collection of studies, building from Sacks's original insights has now been developed (e.g. Atkinson and Drew 1979; Drew 1978; Hester 1992; Jayyusi 1984; Payne 1976; Sharrock 1974; Watson 1976, 1978, 1983). The focus of this type of ethnomethodology is the use of 'membership categories' and what may be assumed about them ('category predicates') in producing and recognizing 'sensible' occasions (or scenes), actions and talk. The third strand is 'conversation analysis'. Once again, Harvey Sacks was a major figure in the establishment of this approach, both in his unpublished lectures and published work. Through his work and that of co-researchers such as Schegloff and Jefferson (for example, Sacks, Schegloff and Jefferson 1974; Schegloff 1968), conversation analysis has become one of the most well-known and influential forms of ethnomethodological inquiry. Its particular interest is in the sequencing and positioning of units of talk in ordinary conversation and other 'speech exchange systems' where the rules of turn-taking which are used by speakers to develop orderly talk are modified (as in ceremonies, classrooms and, as we show in Chapter 10, courtrooms). As with each of the other strands, conversation analysis is committed to uncovering those methods of social interaction to which members themselves are oriented.

With respect to the study of crime ethnomethodology, like symbolic interactionism, treats crime as a matter of definition or, more precisely, as a product of members' methods of practical reasoning. However, unlike symbolic interactionism ethnomethodology is concerned with the situated production and use of these definitions rather than treating these as given in the fabric of local settings. Accordingly, ethnomethodology directs our attention to such matters as:

1 the methods by which particular legal actions such as legislating, accusing, complaining, identifying 'suspicious' persons, arresting, plea negotiating, (cross-)examining, judging, sentencing and appealing are produced and recognized;
2 the methods by which legal settings and situations such as a call to the police, police interrogations and courts and trials are socially organized;
3 the methods by which legal and criminal identities such as lawyer, client, police, suspect, judge and defendant are achieved in social interaction.

The structural conflict perspective

The term 'conflict theory' is applied to a variety of approaches within criminology in particular and in sociology more generally. It is not our intention to survey this variety in this book but to exhibit the characteristics of what Cuff et al. (1990) call the 'structural conflict perspective', an approach founded principally in the works of Marx. We postpone describing the theoretical elements of Marx's political economy until Chapter 3, preferring here to outline the general features of the structural conflict perspective and distinguish it from the other perspectives. This perspective is itself broad enough, embracing as it does a diversity of positions. It may nevertheless be said that these positions share in common an orientation to the importance of the following four perspectival features:

1 any social fact (institution, practice, law . . .) is to be understood by seeing it in relation to the structure of society as a whole;
2 the structure of society is best described, ultimately, in terms of a conflict of interests rather than a consensus of values; thus power is the fundamental societal ingredient;
3 of various dimensions (class, status, party, gender, race . . .) of conflict over power, that between classes (in Marx's sense) is fundamental;
4 sociological analysis is intendedly critical of social arrangements, and directed towards social and political change, usually of a socialist nature; partly for this reason certain versions of the perspective (see Cuff *et al* 1990: Chapter 4) have become identified with the title 'critical' as in 'critical criminology'. The following statement from Taylor *et al* exhibits this critical stance:

> one of the central purposes of this critique has been to assert the possibility – not only of a fully social *theory* – but also of a society in which men [sic] are able to assert themselves in a fully social fashion. With Marx, we have been concerned with the social arrangements that have obstructed, and the social contradictions that enhance, man's chances of achieving full sociality – a state of freedom from material necessity, and (therefore) of material incentive, a release from the constraints of forced production, and abolition of the forced division of labour, and a set of social arrangements, therefore, in which there would be no politically, economically, and socially-induced need to criminalize deviance.
>
> (Taylor *et al* 1973: 270)

Furthermore, 'It should be clear that a criminology which is not normatively committed to the abolition of inequalities of wealth and power, and in particular of inequalities in property and life-chances, is inevitably bound to fall into correctionalism' (ibid: 281).

We may use this set of features to distinguish both those perspectives which share one or more features with the structural conflict perspective, and sometimes employ the term 'conflict theory', and those positions within the structural conflict perspective which vary in the emphasis or interpretation they give to the elements comprising particular features.

Thus, firstly, the structural consensus perspective shares the structural feature 1 but not 2, 3 or 4. In so far as it has adopted the 'cause-and-cure' attitude of correctional criminology then it takes on the ameliorative feature (4) also, but this has standardly been construed in terms of liberal-democratic or social-democratic reform rather than socialist transformation of society. There is a version of 'conflict theory' associated with Lewis Coser and others, but it interprets such forms of conflict as that embedded in collective bargaining between employers and trades unions as expressing a consensual value (competitiveness) that contributes to overall societal cohesion. It thus remains within structural-consensus premises.

Secondly, symbolic interactionism largely shares the conflict feature 2 with the structural conflict perspective. Indeed, Hagan (1991), among others, treats labelling theory as a species of conflict theory. However, both the interactionist perspective and labelling theory (and what Spector and Kitsuse (1987: Chapter 3) call 'value-conflict theory') depart from the structural conflict perspective in not sharing features 1 and 3: they do not standardly have recourse to the wider structural context of society, and they do not privilege class among the various dimensions of conflict. Where the feature 4 is not altogether absent it amounts usually to the advocacy of pluralism and a concern for liberalizing the criminal law, its administration and enforcement by recommending, for example, 'radical non-intervention' in the primary deviance of the young (Schur 1973).

Thirdly, what has been identified as 'Weberian conflict theory' (Cuff et al. 1990: 97–103; Caputo et al. 1989: 5) occupies a position half inside and half outside the structural conflict perspective. While it shares with the latter features 1 and 2 of structure and conflict, it does not privilege class as a source of power nor necessarily espouse socialist-transformative ends, and so does not share features 3 and 4. Hinch (1987: 182–188) uses the title 'liberal conflict' to describe this approach. According to him and to Caputo et al. (1989: 5) such works as those of the early Quinney (1970) and of Turk (1969, 1976) are examples of studies in Weberian conflict because they identify class power as only one among a variety of forms of power used in the struggle between competing groups. In contrast Marxist conflict theorists see class power as central. It is this feature that marks their work as the paradigmatic exemplar of the structural conflict perspective (see also Hinch 1985).

Fourthly, feminist sociological studies can be found across the entire range of sociological perspectives. 'There never has been nor is there one feminist movement . . . Nor is there one feminist criminology or feminist approach to law' (Edwards 1990: 145). Again, it is not our intention, nor do we have the competence, to survey this entire body of work (see Downes and Rock 1982 (1988); Smart 1990; Valverde 1991). Rather we confine our attention to those positions that share at least features 1, 2 and 4 of the structural conflict perspective; where, in the examples we consider, a particular study treats gender as theoretically independent of class, posing patriarchy as its own, not to say primary, form of power, we note it as a 'feminist-conflict' position (Kleck and Sayles 1990) within the overall perspective.

Recent work tends to speak of 'structures of dominance' in which capitalism (class), patriarchy (gender) and neo-colonialism (race) are treated as at least analytically separate domains of power, among which the exact empirical relationship at any historical moment remains to be analysed. We restate this point in Chapter 3, and introduce one feminist's modification of Marxist political economy below.

We now turn to characterizing variation within the structural conflict perspective as it is applied to the study of crime/criminal law. As Hinch contends:

> There is a strong tendency among non-Marxist scholars to assume that there is only one Marxian theory of crime and criminality, when in fact there are several. Furthermore, it is assumed that this one Marxian theory is an extreme example of a style of argument known as *economic determinism* when, in fact, this type of argument is a highly contentious issue within Marxism. If there is one issue or factor which seems to be common to the . . . examples of Marxian analysis . . . , it is that they all begin with the assumption that class relations are the most significant factor affecting the definition of crime and criminalization . . . however, . . . they assess the issue of class relations differently, and give varying levels of significance to noneconomic factors.
>
> (Hinch 1987: 189)

Hinch goes on to distinguish four styles of Marxian analysis of crime. We modify his useful classification by retaining the distinction between 'instrumentalist' and 'structuralist' accounts of the role of the state in capitalist societies, incorporating his third type (which emphasizes the role of 'contradictions') into the structuralist type, and substituting for his fourth type (which emphasizes 'socialist praxis') the distinction between left-realist and left-idealist positions. As we explain at greater length in Chapter 3, neo-Marxist theory has elaborated Marx's own analysis of the state as the 'executive committee of the bourgeoisie', in terms of three functions the state performs for capital. It provides social and economic conditions that foster capital accumulation, it provides the means of coercion against the system's opponents, and it supplies legitimation of the system itself. The criminal laws, the courts and the police are elements of the state that may then be involved in performing these tasks.

Instrumentalist accounts are those that emphasize the use of these means by the state as coercive tools for more or less directly serving the interests of particular capitalist elements if not the whole capitalist class. The state and the capitalists are said to comprise a single ruling class with common interests, often common social backgrounds, and current social, economic and cultural ties – in short they comprise a 'power elite' (Mills 1956; Miliband 1969). Chambliss's analyses of the British vagrancy statutes and the African poll tax laws which we review in Chapter 3, and the analysis of changes in police methods in the USA in the 1960s and 1970s by the Center for Research on Criminal Justice which we review in Chapter 7, are examples of such instrumentalist accounts. The paradigmatic exemplar is perhaps Quinney's (1974) study, in which he moves away from his earlier 'liberal', not to say 'interactionist', position (Hinch 1987: 189–190, 187).

Fellow Marxists have evaluated such studies as inadequate because they fail to explain why a biased and coercive legal system appears to many in society as fair and just. Structuralist accounts attempt to meet this criticism by bringing out the state's use of the legal system (among other means) as a way to legitimate the structure of capitalist social relations as a whole, even where that may mean on some occasion acting against the immediate, direct interests of some capitalists. Such accounts reveal the extent to which the state develops interests of its own, acts relatively independently of the capitalist class and, indeed, becomes a site on which the 'contradictions' of capitalism – for example, the built-in conflict between capital and labour – are themselves played out. This kind of emphasis is captured through the frequent use of the expression, '*reproducing* capitalist social relations', to describe the role of the state in managing class conflict. It also recognizes the extent to which apparent consensus and working-class consent prevail in what structural-conflict analysts would still want to call 'class-divided societies'. Comack's (1985) analysis of the origins of Canada's narcotic drugs laws in Chapter 3 is an example of structural Marxist accounts. Such studies are indebted to the structural Marxism of Gramsci, Althusser and Poulantzas and the 'poststructuralism' of Foucault (see Cuff *et al.* 1990: Chapter 4; Scraton 1985): for example, Gramsci's 'concept of hegemony . . . demonstrates how dominance can be achieved and maintained without the use of direct coercion' (Scraton 1990: 15). A clear and instructive comparison of instrumentalist and structuralist accounts is afforded by Smandych's (1985) analysis of the origins of Canadian anti-combines legislation in the period 1890 to 1910, a 'modified instrumentalist' position is developed in McMullan and Ratner (1983) and a strong critique of instrumentalist analyses of corporate crime can be found in Sargent (1990). (To head off confusion we note here that the meaning of the term structural in 'structural Marxism' derives from linguistics where it refers to the system of contrasts (of sounds and sense) from which any sign gets its meaning, and which then comprise 'an underlying framework of language and meanings whose symbolic systems shape up or "structure" what individuals can do, albeit unconsciously and unbeknownst to them' (Cuff *et al.* 1990: xv); whereas 'structural' in 'structural conflict perspective' refers to 'how the organization of the whole society shapes or structures individual behaviour' (Cuff *et al.* 1990: 128–129, xv); see Williams (1983: 301).)

The same form of structuralist analysis has been applied to gender relations under patriarchy. Thus, as we shall see when considering Snider's study of the reform of Canada's rape law in Chapter 3, feminists remain sceptical of the efficacy of state action to produce justice for women through legal reform just because '[l]aw does not stand outside gender relations and adjudicate upon them. Law is part of these relations and is always already gendered in its principles and practices' (Smart 1990: 80). Legal, judicial and policing reform are said, then, to reproduce the gendered social relations of patriarchy and, Snider (1990) would add, of capitalism.

The second distinction, that between 'left realism' and 'left idealism', is related to the first, and like it has been used, chiefly by Young, as a way to distinguish earlier, 'idealist' work in 'radical' (Platt and Cooper 1974) or 'new' (Taylor *et al* 1973) criminology from more recent, 'realist' studies (Young 1979, 1986; Lea and Young 1984; Matthews and Young 1986; Kinsey *et al* 1986). By 'left idealism' its critics mean to refer to a combination of (1) an instrumentalist conception of the state's use of the legal system as a coercive tool for criminalizing and putting down working-class opposition (as above), and (2) what they consider a 'romanticized' image of the criminal and the deviant in which working-class street crime is seen as overt or incipient political rebellion. Against this view exponents of 'left realism' point out that members of the working class – notably women (see Fairweather, quoted in Edwards (1990: 148)) – are themselves the chief victims of working-class crime, and that their voices are among the loudest calling on the state to impose law and order via the standard means of the law, the courts and the police. We take up this argument in Chapter 8 and again in Chapter 12.

We conclude here, however, by returning to methodological considerations in order to indicate a curious anomaly. The last in the series of quotations in the section on correctional criminology above is by Young himself, the chief proponent of left realism. From being among the first (in the UK) to join, in the late 1960s, the interactionist critique of the structural consensus orthodoxy of the 1950s, he became a leader in the 1970s of the left idealism of the 'new' (that is, Marxist) critical criminology (see the quotation under feature 4 (p. 18)), only to take up left realism in the 1980s. In so doing he has completed a cycle which returns to the essentially cause-and-cure correctionalism from which this sequence of changes initially departed, a correctionalism with its attendant positivistic features of a reliance on official statistics, the large-scale social survey and variable analysis, and a corresponding return to reformist politics. As Smart (1990: 72) says, 'The problem of positivism is, therefore, not redeemed by the espousal of left politics. Positivism poses an epistemological problem; it is not a simple problem of party membership.' It is altogether a remarkable journey.

Thus the current state of affairs in critical criminology is one in which the earlier instrumentalist emphasis has given ground to two contrasting developments. The one, left realism, returns to cause-and-cure correctionalism and thereby moves beyond the purview of our concerns in this book, while the other, embodying a more structuralist emphasis, continues to provide analyses of the relations among changes in crime control, the state and the political economy of capitalism (Scraton 1985); furthermore, it finds itself expanding to take in the types of domination based on gender and race in addition to that founded in class. We note particularly the contributions to *Law, Order and the Authoritarian State* (Scraton 1987b), *The New Criminologies in Canada: State, Crime, and Control* (Fleming 1985) and *Feminist Perspectives in Criminology* (Gelsthorpe and Morris 1990) and draw on them in the structural-conflict chapters to follow. (See also Comack and Brickey (1991).)

It may seem incongruous to incorporate an avowedly structuralist approach into this book, given our strong endorsement of the interpretive positions of symbolic interactionism and ethno-methodology. It is generally acknowledged, however, that there is a tension between determinism and voluntarism in the body of Marxist thought that is the core of the structural conflict approach. For the purpose of the book we are appropriating only the voluntaristic elements, eschewing the cruder deterministic emphases associated with what is often described as 'vulgar' Marxism. We recognize that social conditions can have a 'constraining influence' on human action but we prefer to view those constraints as being not only reproduced but also produced in the first place through practical activity, as Marx well knew (Rose 1982). Of course, it is central to the Marxist paradigm that humans can be alienated from their products but these reifications are themselves sustained only through particular human social practices. The 'natural facts of economic life' and the class relations which sustain them are prime examples of these reifications which are ongoingly produced and reproduced by practical actions.

Through a long series of publications Dorothy Smith (1990) has been particularly influential in pressing this view against a Marxist political economy which in retaining capitalism's categories of capital and labour, public and private, remains ideological, determinist and sexist. This aspect of her ethnomethodologically informed Marxist feminism is well summarized by Hale in her very useful introductory text as follows:

What Smith advocates is a shift in focus from the description of class as 'empty places occupied by people' to the analysis of active processes, actual things that people do in organizing the relations of production so that the patterns that we see as 'class' emerge. The system of classes does not exist all by itself. People actually produce these relations, and they also change them. When questions about class are raised like this, what women do ceases to be a marginal topic and becomes central to the analysis. Women can be shown to be very active in the social construction of class relations through the work they do within the home, as well as in the myriad of offices where secretaries put together the work of their bosses.

(Hale 1990: 295)

We recognize, too, that criminology and this book itself are open to the same charge of sexism in so far as they found themselves on the distinction between crime and tort (that is, between criminal law and civil law), and between crime and mental illness, in order to deal only with crime. For to the extent that the crime/tort distinction marks a further distinction between public and private wrongs, and women's lives and actions are assigned to the private sphere (Smith 1977), then to deal with crime is to deal overwhelmingly with men's lives and actions, and to marginalize women's. Allowing for the regulation of women's occupational, reproductive and sex lives exercised traditionally by the criminal laws of prostitution, abortion and rape, then control of women, it may be argued, resides primarily in other areas of state jurisdiction, notably the laws and practices regulating employment, welfare, health and family and matrimonial life (see, for example, Brophy and Smart 1985; Smith 1990: Chapter 5). We try to compensate for this bias, at least partially, by taking up the crime/ tort distinction in Chapter 8 as one of the 'instruments' of class, and now patriarchal, rule.

Except, then, for work following such dictums as Smith's, structural conflict theory generally takes for granted the detail of the interactional processes through which social phenomena such as crime are constructed. Instead, it invites us to consider that which is defined as crime, both in law and in action, from a broader, collective vantage point, with particular reference to the interests or benefits which it serves and provides for certain social groups or classes and, as has been increasingly emphasized by recent critical criminologists, the state itself.

In summary, with respect to the study of crime, critical or structural-conflict theory considers the following issues:

1 What social relations and whose interests are served by the criminalization of certain forms of behaviour?
2 How are those relations and interests reproduced in the administration of justice through the courts?
3 How are those relations and interests served through the organization and operation of police work?

KEY ISSUES IN THIS BOOK

We shall then be using these three approaches to focus on three central issues in the study of crime:

1 Making crime by making law;
2 Making crime through law enforcement (the police);
3 Making crime through the administration of justice (the courts).

Each of these issues comprises a major section (three chapters) of the book. After this introductory chapter, each issue is approached from the three perspectives of symbolic interactionism, ethnomethodology and structural conflict theory, with one chapter each. The remaining two chapters deal with crime and punishment from all three perspectives (Chapter 11), and the functions of crime control from structural-consensus and structural-conflict points of view (Chapter 12). This last chapter also serves to summarize and conclude the book.

OVERALL AIMS OF THE BOOK

Overall, our aims are as follows:

1 At its broadest, our aim is to teach students to think sociologically about crime.
2 More particularly, our aim is to provide exemplifications of how to use the three sociological perspectives of symbolic interactionism, ethnomethodology and structural conflict theory.
3 In so doing, we wish to recommend a radically sociological approach to crime, one uncontaminated by passing correctional fads and fancies.
4 Finally, we wish to show how sociology can teach valuable insights into crime and how the study of crime can provide an interesting vehicle for learning about sociology.

Chapter 2

Constructing criminal law

We have five main aims in this chapter: firstly, to introduce the idea of the 'constructed' character of criminal law; secondly, to show the structural consensus view of criminal law; thirdly, to show, by comparison, the social constructionist view of criminal law, with reference to the concepts of value pluralism, rule creation and rule enforcement, claims and claims-making and moral, professional and organizational enterprise and entrepreneurs; fourthly, to illustrate the use of these concepts in an examination of the development of Canadian narcotics legislation, of recent changes in laws regulating drinking and driving, and of the new 'battered wife defence'; and fifthly, to present the argument that, for the case of drugs, criminalization might precede social problem formation and that both may facilitate further criminality.

CRIME AS A SOCIAL CONSTRUCTION

Without criminal law there would be no 'crime'. Virtually every form of human action – from taking others' property to taking others' lives – has in some time or place been deemed warranted, if not desirable. For example, until recently, slavery, non-consensual intercourse within marriage, and all forms of execution have been widely practised and have received official approval. This is not to say that people have not objected to these forms of behaviour, but until proscribed by criminal law they cannot be considered 'crimes'. Crime, then, is a relative or legalistic, rather than an absolute, concept (Douglas 1971). Criminal law is constructed within society. Hence, crime, too, is a social construction.

Consequently, a first question for the sociology of crime is the origin and development of criminal law. This question can be addressed from each of the three perspectives outlined in the previous chapter. In this chapter we shall be making use of the symbolic interactionist or, more precisely, the social constructionist perspective on the origin and development of criminal law. However, to throw into relief its distinctive features, we begin with a summary account of the structural consensus approach to criminal law. This is not only useful for expository purposes but it also corresponds to the chronology of the application of sociological theory to this issue.

THE STRUCTURAL CONSENSUS VIEW OF CRIMINAL LAW

The structural consensus perspective is so named because of the role it ascribes to moral or normative consensus in the explanation of social order. It assumes that socially organized life is not possible without widely shared fundamental values. Such values are said to underlie and be expressed in the norms that regulate the various institutional orders of society, such as the economy, the polity, kinship relations and cultural and community organizations. From this point of view, law in general and criminal law in particular assume a particular significance in so far as they embody an agreement on fundamental values. This is not to say that societies remain static but rather that change in one sector of society may ramify through the rest of society. Structural consensus theorists incorporate an evolutionary component into their theorizing, arguing that as societies change so do their values and systems of law. Durkheim, for example, claimed that forms of law were an expression of the forms of solidarity in society. As societies changed from 'mechanical' to 'organic' solidarity so their forms of law changed from being in the main repressive to being preponderantly restitutive.

For the structural consensus position the links among 'society', 'values' and 'law' are conceptual rather than empirical. Durkheim, for example, took the view 'that society is *in essence* its moral codes, the rules which govern the relations between its members' (Sharrock 1977: 486, emphasis is in original). Thus, in so far as it is assumed that society is possible only under conditions of human consensus about fundamental values, and that criminal law embodies those values, then only those laws which reflect that consensus will become established. Criminal law is thereby explained by its consequences, that is, teleologically.

Thus, while the structural consensus view may explain the persistence of criminal law, it does not explain its origins except by presumptive fiat. Moreover, whilst it is possible to argue that there is a consensus about some laws at the present time, such evidence cannot be used legitimately in support of the proposition that criminal law originated with a consensus on the value of criminal law. Criminology has yet to provide any convincing examples of criminal law as a product of consensus.

THE SOCIAL CONSTRUCTIONIST VIEW OF CRIMINAL LAW

The social constructionist view of criminal law became popular during the 1960s. During this period the structural consensus approach which had hitherto dominated sociological theory in North America came to be questioned. Sociologists began to see pluralism where they had previously seen uniformity, heterogeneity instead of homogeneity, conflict rather than consensus. It may well be that these changes in the discipline were related to changes in the wider society. Thus, as conflict in society became more visible, so sociologists incorporated a concern with it into their theorizing. For some, these developments were precursors of a later shift in criminological thought to a more 'radical' and fully fledged Marxist position, as we mentioned in Chapter 1. This is a development which we shall consider in the next chapter. In the period of the late 1950s and the 1960s, however, we see the application of the symbolic interactionist perspective to these matters and the resulting development of the social constructionist view of criminal law: the view that criminal law is a product of the activities of competing interest or value groups. The founding statement is that of Becker:

> the central fact about deviance [is that] it is created by society. I do not mean this in the way it is ordinarily understood, in which the causes of deviance are located in the social situation of the deviant or in 'social factors' which prompt his action. I mean, rather, that *social groups create deviance by making the rules whose infraction constitutes deviance*, and by applying those rules to particular people and labelling them as outsiders. From this point of view, deviance is *not* a quality of the act the person

commits, but rather a consequence of the application by others of rules and sanctions to an 'offender'. The deviant is one to whom that label has successfully been applied; deviant behaviour is behaviour that people so label.

(Becker 1963: 9, emphasis in original)

Similarly, as Quinney writes:

First, my perspective is based on a special conception of society. Society is characterized by diversity, conflict, coercion and change, rather than by consensus and stability. Second, law is a *result* of the operation of interests, rather than an instrument that functions outside of particular interests. Though law may control interests, it is in the first place *created* by interests. Third, law incorporates the interests of specific persons and groups; it is seldom the product of the whole society. Law is made by men [sic], representing special interests, who have the power to translate their interests into public policy.

(Quinney 1970: 35, emphasis in original)

As we saw above, given the assumption of the structural consensus perspective that 'society is in essence its moral codes', then society is inconceivable without moral consensus and, consequently, how the criminal law originates is not a problem that arises. Once, however, the presumptive link between society and moral consensus is removed, and it is recognized that societies may be, and in most modern cases are, a melange of differing value systems and rules defining what is deviant, then the problem of how the particular acts defined as deviant in the criminal law are established *does* arise. As the quotation from Becker (1963) shows, once this symbolic interactionist position is applied to the study of deviance two areas of inquiry appear, namely the problem of rule creation (defining what kinds of acts are going to be called crimes) and the problem of rule enforcement (identifying what particular instances of those acts will be selected as crimes). Recall from Chapter 1 our adding a third topic, that of the problem of rule fitting (making the links between definition and selection/ identification). It is with the first of these two areas, that of rule creation, that what has come to be called the 'social constructionist' approach, has concerned itself. (We consider the symbolic interactionist treatment of rule enforcement by the police in Chapter 5, and that of rule fitting by the courts in Chapter 9.) And as the quotation from Quinney (1970) indicates, the interests of those creating law will figure prominently in any such account.

In discussing examples of criminal law creation from this point of view we will employ the overarching conceptual framework contained in the work of Spector and Kitsuse (1987 (1977)), which applies to the whole field of social problem construction and incorporates the range of particular case studies of criminal law creation that we draw on here.

Following and modifying Blumer (1971), Spector and Kitsuse take the view that social problems including crime are not objective conditions or things, requiring measurement and explanation, but rather consist firstly of the activities of those 'individuals or groups making assertions of grievances and claims with respect to some putative conditions' (Spector and Kitsuse 1987: 75), and secondly of the activities of those who respond to these claims. '*The central problem for a theory of social problems is to account for the emergence, nature, and maintenance of claims-making and responding activities*' (ibid: 76, original emphasis).

With reference to the construction of social problems, a 'claim' may be regarded as an 'authoritative or challenging request' or a 'demand of a right or supposed right'. 'Claims-making' consists of a form of social interaction in the course of which demands are made 'that something be done about some putative condition' (ibid: 78). Examples of claims-making activities include: 'demanding services, filling out forms, lodging complaints, filing lawsuits, calling press conferences, writing letters of protest, passing resolutions, publishing exposés, placing ads in newspapers, supporting or opposing some governmental practice or policy, setting up picket lines or boycotts' (ibid: 78–79). Claims-makers include a great variety of persons:

> protest groups or moral crusaders who make demands and complaints; the officials or agencies to whom such complaints are directed; members of the media who publicize and disseminate news about such activities (as well as participate in them); commissions of inquiry; legislative bodies and executive or administrative agencies that respond to claims-making constituents; members of the helping professions, such as physicians, psychiatrists, social workers; and sometimes, social scientists who contribute to the definition and development of social problems.
>
> (Spector and Kitsuse 1987: 79)

We should add that governments not only respond to claims-makers but themselves initiate courses of claims-making that may result in the designation of some condition as a problem and in corresponding legislation that criminalizes the offending activity. This social constructionist perspective has been employed in studies of law creation with respect to several kinds of deviance, including drug use, cigarette smoking, drunkenness, drinking and driving, sexual psychopathy, homosexuality, prostitution, juvenile delinquency, child abuse, wife abuse and rape, amongst others. Rather than provide extended lists of references we recommend the reader consult Gladstone *et al.* (1991), the recent collection by Best (1989), Manning (1985), the text by Conrad and Schneider (1980), Hagan's (1980) very useful, if now somewhat dated, review, or such journals as *Social Problems, Law and Society Review, British Journal of Law and Society, Canadian Journal of Law and Society* and *International Journal of the Sociology of Law.*

CONSTRUCTING CRIME THROUGH MAKING LAW: THREE EXAMPLES

By way of illustration we shall consider three examples of the social constructionist approach to law creation. Firstly, we shall examine the construction of anti-narcotics legislation, as analysed in the work of Small (1978 (formerly Cook 1969, 1970)) on Canadian opium laws. There is a sizeable ancillary sociological and historical literature on this topic, much of it reviewed in Blackwell and Erickson (1988), Saunders and Mitchell (1990: 598–605) and Mitchell (1991). The case of the Marihuana Tax Act of 1937 in the United States has also been much discussed (Becker 1963; Dickson 1968; Galliher and Walker 1977). Secondly, we shall consider from a social constructionist perspective recent moves to stiffen penalties in the case of drinking and driving in Canada (cf. Gusfield (1981) and Ross (1982) on the United States). Thirdly, we shall review the recent adoption in Canada of the 'battered wife defence' to a charge of murder, in the context of Tierney's (1982) account of the 'battered women movement and the creation of the wife beating problem'.

Small: the development of Canadian narcotics legislation

Small (1978) poses the question: what led to the criminalization of narcotics use in the period 1908–23? Beginning with the Opium Act of 1908 a series of Acts were passed culminating in the Opium and Narcotic Drug Act of 1929 which together criminalized the import, manufacture, sale, possession and use for other than medical purposes of opium and its derivatives, and of cocaine and marihuana. This legislation is the foundation of the current Narcotic Control Act. Small accounts for this by appealing to the claims-making and other activities of various moral crusaders and to the favourable social context which shaped and was in turn shaped by them. The three important features of this context are (1) the racial conflict between 'whites' and 'orientals', (2) the status conflict between the high-status medical profession and its clients using narcotics for therapeutic purposes and the low-status users, particularly Chinese, using opium for pleasure and (3) the prevailing cultural beliefs and values about drugs and their link with sexual promiscuity and 'race mixing'.

The racism of the time was expressed in such claims as 'they [Asiatics] make the country of no value for the surplus population of Great Britain', uttered by Mr Duncan Ross of Vancouver (House of Commons Debates 1907–1908) and 'whatever their motive, the traffic [in drugs] always comes with the Oriental, and . . . one would, therefore be justified in assuming that it was their desire to injure the bright-browed races of the world (Murphy 1922)' (Small 1978: 37).

The criminalization was shaped by the differential power arising from status differences of different groups of users and producers of opium. Thus, while physicians created addicts among their often middle-class and maternal clientele by prescribing medicines containing opiates for a variety of complaints, neither they nor their practice was considered criminal. The 1908 Patent and Proprietary Medicines Act prohibited only indiscriminate use of medical opiates, backed up by only minor penalties. In contrast, there was virtually no opposition to the criminalization of 'non-therapeutic' opiate use associated in the public mind with the low-status immigrant Chinese population. Similarly, producers of the drugs, alcohol and tobacco, were often British, of high status and contributed useful taxes; their activities were not proscribed. The same was not true of the often Chinese low-status producers of smoking opium. Together with den proprietors and storekeepers who sold opium they could expect the exercise of the 'drastic right of search' without warrant of their 'non-dwelling houses' by police, no appeals for those with no fixed residence, 7-year maximum sentences and possible deportation for conviction for trafficking and whipping for giving drugs to minors.

Contemporary cultural beliefs were crystallized in the image of the 'dope fiend'. This, in turn, was founded on the thesis that drug use causes a change of personality which in turn causes criminal behaviour. While defined principally with reference to opiate use it was extended to characterize the users of cocaine, marihuana and tobacco. (We discuss its application to alcohol in the next section, on drinking-and-driving legislation.) Thus, Murphy (1922) had this to say about marihuana use:

> Persons using this narcotic, smoke the dried leaves of the plant, which has the effect of driving them completely insane. The addict loses all sense of moral responsibility. Addicts to this drug, while under its influence, are immune to pain, and could be severely injured without having any realization of their condition. While in this condition, they become raving maniacs and are liable to kill or indulge in any form of violence to other persons, using the most savage methods of cruelty without, as said before, any sense of moral responsibility.
>
> (cited in Small 1978: 33)

Sustaining this view was a nineteenth-century social philosophical belief in the 'natural depravity of man', a state held in check only by the institutions of church and family. Drug use was thought to break down the barriers maintained by these institutions, leaving people, especially the young (especially daughters), exposed to the vices of pre-marital, promiscuous and, 'God forbid', interracial sex.

These racial and status divisions and beliefs about dope fiends and the like were formulated and exploited in the claims-making and other activities of a number of moral crusaders or 'entrepreneurs'. These are persons or groups who engage in 'moral enterprise' designed to extend the scope of moral and, in particular, legal regulation (Becker 1963). Especially enterprising with respect to narcotics control in Canada was the then Deputy Minister of Labour, Mackenzie King. His involvement began when he was investigating compensation claims from the Chinese and Japanese victims of the Vancouver anti-Asiatic riots of 1907.

King was disturbed to find two claims from Chinese opium merchants who had lost their stocks of opium in the riots. He reacted by preparing a government report on the 'Need for the Suppression of Opium in Canada' which led to the Opium Act of 1908 which prohibited the import, manufacture and sale of opium for other than medical purposes. He then conducted an anti-narcotics campaign by attending and publicizing the results of international conferences on narcotics control, by soliciting testimonials from clergy, police officers and welfare workers and reading them in the House, and by appealing to newspaper articles on the subject of drug use. By 1911 King was ready to propose more punitive legislation, the passage of which was claimed by King to 'assist "a world wide movement which has for its object the suppression of this kind of evil in all countries" (House of Commons Debates, 1910–11)' (Small 1978: 29–30). As a result, the 1911 Opium and Drug Act was passed which extended the 1908 Act by defining possession for use as an offence, by including cocaine and by expanding police powers. (Marihuana was added to the list of proscribed drugs in 1923 for reasons nobody appears to know.)

King was not alone in his campaigning. He solicited and received support from individuals such as the conservative politician, H. H. Stevens, and leaders of the methodist and presbyterian churches, and from groups such as the Anti-Opium League of Vancouver and law-enforcement organizations. These latter included the Vancouver police, the Chiefs of the Division of Narcotic Control of the Department of Health and the Royal Canadian Mounted Police (RCMP). The involvement of these law-enforcement groups illustrates the importance of not only moral but also professional (Hagan and Leon 1977) and organizational (cf. Johnson 1981) interests and enterprise in the construction of the anti-narcotics laws. The Vancouver police, because of the difficulty of obtaining convictions under the 1908 law, which did not include possession, pressed for possession and smoking of opium to be added to the list of offences under the law. This demand was satisfied in the 1911 Act and 'the offence of possession remained a highly valued enforcement resource' (Small 1978: 40). Following the establishment of a national enforcement network in 1919, addicts were differentiated by the second Chief of the Division of Narcotic Control, Colonel Sharman, into three categories: medical addicts, professional addicts and criminal addicts. It was the last of these three who would receive criminal sanctions. Finally, the RCMP, which replaced the Royal

North-West Mounted Police (RNWMP) in 1920, saw in narcotics work a means of survival. Because of their role in strike breaking, as in the Winnipeg General Strike of 1919, they were in danger of being disbanded.

With the establishment of the specialised RCMP drug squads there came into being a branch of the police whose performance and morale depended entirely on their achieving high conviction rates under the Opium and Narcotic Drug Act. For the Mountie drug squads narcotics work became a moral crusade . . . The Mounties had a vested interest in narcotics legislation, ie. they had a great deal to lose if Parliament ever decided that a serious drug problem requiring their services did not exist in Canada.

(Small 1978: 41)

The creation of drug laws not only involves claims-making activities, it also reveals the use of certain values by the claims-makers. From a social constructionist perspective, values, as Spector and Kitsuse (1987: 93) point out, are not regarded as determinants of behaviour but rather as resources which have uses in social action. Thus, criminal law creation in general and drug laws in particular involve the use by their creators of values which it is claimed justify, warrant, demand and otherwise make desirable the criminalization of certain behaviours.

Becker (1963: 136) describes three values which he claims 'provided legitimacy for attempts to prevent the use of intoxicants and narcotics'. The first of these values is 'that the individual should exercise complete responsibility for what he does and what happens to him; he should never do anything that might cause loss of self-control'. The second value is that the individual should not engage in 'action taken solely to achieve states of ecstasy'. The third value is that of 'humanitarianism'; that is, 'reformers believed that people enslaved by the use of alcohol would benefit from laws making it impossible for them to give in to their weaknesses'.

Drinking-and-driving laws

In the case of drinking and driving, an offence to which considerable publicity has been given in recent years, it is possible to discern a similar collection of values being used by groups seeking to stiffen penalties for such an offence as well as to deter potential offenders.

In Canada in 1985, following the success of groups such as MADD (Mothers Against Drunken Driving) in the United States (Reinarman 1988), organizations such as PRIDE (People to Reduce Impaired Driving Everywhere) and SADD (Students Against Drinking and Driving) were set up and engaged in campaigns against drinking and driving. A primary objective of these groups was to increase public perception of the seriousness of this offence. As a result of this focus on the 'problem' of drinking and driving, in 1985 penalties under the Criminal Code and such provincial statutes as the Highway Traffic Act of Ontario were increased. For the 'impaired' driver the minimum fine for a first offence was increased from $50 to $300, with loss of licence for 3 months. For a second offence, the minimum period of imprisonment was increased to 14 days with 6 months' driving prohibition. For subsequent offences the minimum was increased to 90 days with a 1-year driving prohibition. The maximum penalty for impaired driving was set at 5 years' imprisonment for an indictable offence with 3 years' driving prohibition. For 'impaired driving causing death' the maximum penalty was increased to 14 years' imprisonment and 10 years' driving prohibition (Miller 1991: 44–48; Fritz 1991: 24–26).

The case of drinking and driving is an interesting one in so far as it is based upon not only certain values but also particular assumptions about the nature of alcohol, its effects and the related social behaviour of its users. Broadly speaking, there are two models available for understanding the effects of drugs in general and alcohol in particular. The first of these has been variously described as the physiological, pharmacological or medical model. It assumes that chemical stimuli such as drugs and alcohol produce certain behavioural effects when they are ingested. The behaviour of the individual 'under the influence' of the drug is understandable in terms of the effects of that drug. It is thus assumed that drugs have certain inherent effects and that users can expect to experience them if they take the drug and, as a result, to behave in ways typical for that type of drug. The second model is a sociological or cultural model of drug effects. This model assumes that something intercedes between the chemical stimuli and the experiences and behaviour of the drug user. This something is 'culture' – that set of beliefs, understandings, knowledge and ways of acting of which is particular to a group with respect to some item of conduct. The effects of drugs and alcohol are therefore regarded as being influenced and shaped by the culture of the group which uses them. There are, in other words, no automatic effects of any drug. Instead, what people experience when they take a drug and how they 'comport' themselves under the drug's influence depends on what they know about it, what they expect of it and what they culturally permit in the way of behaviour.

The presumption that a person with 0.08 mm alcohol in their blood is an 'impaired' driver clearly is in line with the first of these two models. It assumes that objectionable behaviour, especially behaviour which puts in jeopardy the safety of other members of the community, is a direct consequence of the ingestion of alcohol. This takes no account of the cultural influences on behaviour, as described in studies conducted under the auspices of the sociological model. The prevailing model assumes, in other words, that alcohol rather than culture is the cause of behaviour. However, it is readily apparent that different societies and indeed different groups within the same society consume alcohol and comport themselves very differently under its influence. The logic of the sociological model is that objectionable drinking and 'drunken' behaviour has less to do with the substance ingested than with the cultural context of that ingestion. Alcohol does not necessarily release inhibitions or lead to 'rowdy' and 'reckless' behaviour, but given the right cultural context it may be permitted and expected to do so (MacAndrew and Edgerton 1969).

Alcohol and its presumed inherent effects are also used as a way of accounting for traffic accidents. Frequently, accidents are 'blamed' on the fact that the parties to the accident had been drinking. The police routinely search for signs of drinking when they investigate accidents. Such a practice not only presumes that alcohol itself is responsible for the accident, it also diverts attention from other possible and plausible ways of accounting for the accident and any injuries and fatalities which may have occurred. Thus, given the highly complex character of vehicle construction and mechanical operation there exists a formidable array of possible causes of any accident, quite apart from the other variables such as the condition of the highway and the conduct of other drivers on the road. To what, then, do we owe this presumption or at least readiness to assume that alcohol is to blame? One possible answer, of the sort which we shall be attending to in greater depth in the following chapter, is provided by structural conflict theory, namely that it diverts attention from corporate malpractice in the manufacture of vehicles, that is, the failure of manufacturers, through their desire to maximize profit, to ensure that their vehicles are as safe as they can possibly be in the event of accidents. There is evidence which shows that the degree of injury and the extent of fatalities are both related to the type of vehicle, with the cheaper and smaller types of vehicles offering the most chance of the more serious consequences.

We shall take up the issue of the relationship between criminalization of drug and alcohol laws, amongst others, and certain structural and, in particular, social-class, considerations in the following chapter. (And a possible ethnomethodological interest in the question of the creation of the drunk-driver-as-the-cause-of-traffic-accidents is suggested in Chapter 4.) However, to conclude this section, what requires emphasis is not the putative 'functions' of criminalization, but rather the activities through which criminalization occurs. That certain unintended consequences may nevertheless flow from criminalization is something the social constructionist perspective alerts us to. We consider two of these unintended consequences in the final section of this chapter.

The women's movement and the battered wife defence

Like getting drunk, drinking-and-driving is a course of action engaged in predominantly by men. It is not unknown for both practices to be followed by the beating of women (and children). The criminalization of drugs, alcohol and prostitution, and the legal regulation of jazz (Gray 1989), that occurred in the first quarter of the twentieth century in North America (Hagan 1980) and, to a lesser degree, in the UK, were accompanied by the first phase of the modern women's movement. This was the phase of:

> maternal feminism . . . a feminism premised on moralism rather than the desire to free family-women from all sexual stereotypes and discrimination; family-centred as opposed to professional feminism. The cult of true womanhood and the assumption that the 'proper' sphere of women was the home were its central tenets.
>
> (Chunn 1988: 93)

Thus, the maternal feminist organizations found themselves quite comfortably ensconced in the male-dominated social and moral reform movement which emerged in the 1880s and declined throughout the 1920s. Concerned about the 'social disorganization' seemingly wrought by vice and immorality, urban, Protestant, middle-class men and women pushed for measures to eradicate the drunkenness, gambling, lewd public entertainments, adultery, bigamy, desertion, child abuse, prostitution, white slavery and opium dens which were undermining family life and, ultimately, social order. At the same time, reforms aimed at opening up the public sphere to women were not an issue. Even in relation to suffrage, for example, maternal feminist organizations and male suffragists were at one, embracing the demand for female enfranchisement not as a measure of democracy or women's rights but 'as an enabling tool for pet social reforms' (Roberts 1979: 22).

(Chunn 1988: 93)

For example, Emily Murphy, whom we encountered above as a moral crusader against drugs (and race and sex), was an advocate of women's rights in this maternal feminist sense. She became the 'first woman to be appointed Police Magistrate in the British Empire' (Mander 1985: 12), to be precise in Alberta in 1916, and was one of the five women to bring the 'persons case' that in 1929 succeeded in winning Canadian women the right to be members of the Senate. But, as she said at the time, 'It should be made clear that we . . . are not considering the pronouncement of the Privy Council as standing for a sex victory, but, rather, as one which will now permit our saying "we" instead of "you" in affairs of State' (Mander 1985: 124).

The beginning of the second, current phase of the movement is generally set in the mid-1960s. It is arguably the most significant social-problem-defining movement in recent history, being largely responsible for women's inequality or sexism coming to be seen as a problem of global proportions. There have been numerous 'submovements' devoted to particular issues. Several have focused on forms of violence against women. That is, women's groups have been active in getting rape (Rose 1977; Snider 1985 (see Chapter 3)), wife battering (see below), sexual harassment (Wise and Stanley 1987; Grahame 1985; MacKinnon 1987: Chapter 9) and pornography (Cole 1989) defined as problems; they have contributed significantly to the process by which child abuse (Lenton 1989) has come to be perceived as a problem, especially its offshoot, the problem of child sexual assault (for example, Mitchell 1985). In all these cases some degree of criminalization of the offending activities has resulted. Other submovements have fought for decriminalizing various practices, for example, abortion and prostitution (Jenness 1990; Bell 1987; Shaver 1985) while others have elevated women's inequality in employment (for example, pay inequity) and in family, matrimonial and welfare law to the status of major public issues (Brophy and Smart 1985).

New crimes have been created, notably the extension of sexual assault to cover the case of a husband raping his wife. (See Chapter 3 for a structural conflict account of this shift in definition.) Since 1990, the case of a wife killing her abusive husband has become in a sense decriminalized in Canada. In the United States as of the time of writing some fourteen states are reconsidering the cases of women convicted of murder in circumstances where the 'battered wife syndrome' was present (CBS, '48 Hours', 17 July 1991). (We touch on this from an ethnomethodological viewpoint in Chapter 4.) That is, there is now available to a woman charged with killing her husband the 'battered wife defence'. While we know of no constructionist study that yet addresses this development in criminal law, the prior period of claims-making activities focusing on the 'battered wife problem' has been the subject of considerable inquiry (see Walker 1990). Tierney's (1982) American study is a paradigmatic exemplar of the constructionist approach applied to this topic: 'In less than ten years, wife beating has been transformed from a subject of private shame and misery to an object of public concern' (Tierney 1982: 210). The quotation poses the sociological problem Tierney addresses. Given that in, say, 1970 there were no shelters for battered women, no programmes, no organizations, no news stories, no public concern, in short, no 'problem', and given further that there is no real basis for claiming that there had been any significant change in the incidence of wife beating in the following 10 years, what, then, accounts for the existence of all these things in 1980? In particular, we may ask, what accounts for the increased criminalization in this area, comprising increased penalties, more forceful prosecutorial policies (see Chapter 9) and tougher policing (McGillivray 1990), criminalization that has continued into the 1980s culminating, in Canada and the United States, in the battered wife defence?

Tierney seeks an answer in the activities of 'social movement organizations' (SMOs) in mobilizing resources to 'produce' the problem. Her analysis reveals the significance of a pre-existing organizational base, the movement's flexibility and the availability of incentives for sponsors, in accounting for the rapid emergence of the problem. Two related themes of the analysis are the attention given by the mass media to the issue, and the professional character of the SMO. Her study, then, focuses not on the actual claims made themselves, but on the organizational environment in which they were made. It especially provides an example of a point made by McCarthy and Zald (1973: 20): 'The professional social movement is the common form of recent movements and presents a sharp departure from the classical model' in which the activities of grass-roots groups are central. This is the point we will bring out in what follows. Readers more interested in the role of the media may wish to pursue the topic via Johnson (1989) and references therein.

The battered women's movement was able to take advantage of the pre-existing organizational base in the larger women's movement, and of the professional location of those in mental health and social work who took up the issue. The movement had access to full-time leaders and to support from such established sectors as the philanthropic foundations, governments and the media, and there was separation between supporters and beneficiaries. Flexibility was then afforded by the range of organizations available as sponsors, from churches, women's service organizations and different levels of government to local voluntary fund-raising bodies and individual group projects. The very variety of legal, financial and health troubles faced by battered women appealed to a range of potential providers. Movement activities were directed at making police, courts and the law more responsive, at counselling victims and at providing crisis support. Sponsoring organizations found the issue offered various incentives. Veterans' organizations, to cite a Canadian example not mentioned by Tierney (1982), saw an opportunity to change or increase their clientele. The professional profile of the movement was attractive to those sponsors – such as the Imperial Order of Daughters of the Empire – wanting to support moderate rather than radical feminist programmes. Legal agencies benefited from giving support by gaining the diversion of criminal cases from the courts. Social welfare agencies saw the 'problem' as an occasion for 'moral entrepreneurship', for 'capitalizing on feminist issues' and for 'maintaining the family unit' (ibid: 215). Tierney also cites Johnson (1981) who details cases of what he calls 'programme enterprise' (a variant of professional or organizational enterprise) by government agencies with budgets to spend, soliciting applications from movement organizations; this enables them 'to move into new domains as "old" social problems decline' (Tierney 1982: 215).

Such an analysis throws interesting light on the construction of wife beating as crime. On the one hand, as the movement generated public concern and public attention, it simultaneously generated data. Through a symbiosis with the mass media, more cases came to be reported and the class composition of the perceived problem broadened from a working-class to a classless phenomenon. The problem grew. At the same time its character became shaped by its organizational incarnation. As opposed to a radical feminist conception of wife beating as an expression of a structure of dominance, namely patriarchy, for which radical social change is the required preventive and criminal prosecution the required treatment strategy, Tierney saw two trends in evidence pointing in a different direction. Both stem from the relative success of the professional side of the movement in coming to 'own', in Gusfield's (1989) phrase, the problem. The provenance of practitioners in social work, mental health and law means that 'the wife beating problem will likely become increasingly "medicalized", professionalized, individualized, and de-politicized' (Tierney 1982: 216). The therapeutic-treatment-of-female-clients-in-bad-marriages will replace the feminist analysis, and domestic-violence programmes for offenders will replace prison. Similarly, the movement itself will become coopted by professionally staffed, social-service-oriented organizations who will sing to the tune of the moderate and reformist sponsors. The overall outcome, to extrapolate from Tierney's account, is ultimately less criminalization, and therefore less crime, than the rhetoric would lead us to expect. This outcome, though not necessarily Tierney's analysis, is confirmed by the British research of Edwards (1990) and the US research of Ferraro (1989). See Chapter 8 for a feminist-conflict analysis of this topic.

CRIMINALIZATION, SOCIAL PROBLEMS AND CRIME: THE CASE OF DRUG LAWS AGAIN

In the model for the development of social problems set out by Spector and Kitsuse and discussed earlier, criminalization of some putatively harmful act is one possible response of government to a course of claims-making by social movement personnel. However, as Small indicates for the case of drugs, criminalization may be in part the progenitor of a social problem, thus reversing the 'normal' train of events. The point is made forcefully by Green in the following quotation:

> Canadian narcotics control then, is not the product of con-
> flicting [economic] interests [the structural conflict view – see
> Chapter 3]. Nor does it represent a translation of public
> morality into legal norms [the structural consensus view – see
> above]. It is rather those legal norms that created the public
> morality that were responsible for the moral transformation of
> a private indulgence into a public crime. In time, through the
> efforts of zealous reformers and enforcers and the paucity of
> organized or influential opposition, the public came to share
> that drug ideology that motivated the initial anti-drug
> crusaders. One lesson at least to be drawn from this experience
> is that the relationship between criminal law and morality is not
> inevitably unidirectional, that the law is as likely to be a vehicle
> for social change as to precipitate legislative revision. The essen-
> tial consistency of Canadian narcotics legislation throughout
> those decades during which public moral attitudes toward drug
> users changed from one of tolerance to one of condemnation
> supports this thesis.
>
> (Green 1986: 38)

If creating a social problem is one possible unintended consequence of criminalizing some practice then facilitating further
criminality is a second such consequence. This is partly a result of
the transformation of identity from 'normal' to 'deviant' following
upon the application or enforcement of the law on particular
offenders: 'narcotics dependents – through the creation of an
extraordinarily restrictive and punitive control system – became
the very kind of criminally involved (and thus morally inferior)
persons the reformist interests always said they were' (Green 1986:
39). As 'secondary deviance' such criminality is best addressed in

connection with the symbolic interactionist analysis of police work in Chapter 5. But it is also partly a result simply of the change in the status or standing of the practice that prohibition through the criminal law entails. There is perhaps no stronger case for the position taken in this course – that to understand crime it is necessary first to understand the criminal law – than that of the extent of the crime made possible by the laws criminalizing drugs. We conclude this chapter with the following reflection by Sharrock on the possible consequences of de-criminalizing drugs:

Consider the case of marijuana smoking. This is an illegal activity, which some people regard as a serious problem. Although not serious in its own right, marijuana is bad, in their eyes, because it can lead to the use of hard drugs. Marijuana is a social problem too. Since it is illegal, many people who want to use the drug do so in defiance of the law and, therefore, engage in criminal activity. The implication of the argument which labelling theory [here subsumed under the social constructionist perspective] puts forward is clear. If people ceased to be concerned about marijuana, then the *problem* would disappear. Marijuana use would not cease: smoking it would stop being an illegal activity. One might speculate that the amount of marijuana use would also decline as a consequence of legalisation since some people might be smoking it now for the satisfaction to be obtained from a relatively harmless but illegal activity. The 'solution' to the marijuana problem is not the prevention of its use but a changing of attitudes towards it. Such a change could well have other consequences. If the cultivation, distribution and sale of cannabis were legalised, then one would do away with a lot of deviant activity. One would have put an end to the need to smuggle the drug and also the illegalities involved in the use of the profits from the trade. Whether marijuana is harmful is a complicated question, and whether it is more so than other drugs [tobacco and alcohol] in widespread and legal use is debatable. As to the suggestion that 'soft' drugs lead to the use of 'hard' drugs, this too might be contested. If it is the case that they do, then part of the reason may be that it is in someone's *economic* interest to move people from 'soft' to 'hard' drug use, together with the fact that because of its illegality, the marijuana trade and the 'hard' drug trade are tied up with one another. Last but not least, one can

point to the way that the treatment of narcotic use has given rise
to the development of organised crime and the formation of
criminal gangs which go on to break the law in a variety of ways
above and beyond the dealing in drugs. In much the same way,
the prohibition of alcohol in the USA led to murder and the
formation of gangs through the development of bootlegging.
Starting from the assumption that society makes deviant acts
possible by setting up prohibitions, the argument leads to the
conclusion that by setting up such rules, society also provides
people with the circumstances which will motivate them to
perform further deviant acts, to develop lifestyles and organi-
sations around the needs of the prohibited activity. This will
result in the formation of deviant groups. The effect of lifting
the proscription on the original deviant act might not be the
prevention of the act from occurring, but it would be the
elimination of the possibility of and the need for many other
illegalities arising from it. (Lemert 1967.)

(Sharrock 1984: 93–94, original emphasis)

As if confirmation of Sharrock's argument were needed, we ap-
pend this remark from a recent editorial in the *Globe and Mail*
about the effects of the rising price of cigarettes due to increased
taxation:

While measures to curtail an activity that is a major cause of
illness should be applauded, the tax increases can create social
problems of their own. Crime related to cigarettes has soared –
police complain that cigarettes are more popular with some
thieves than money.

(*Globe and Mail* 27 May 1991, p. A12)

Chapter 3

Criminalization and domination

It will never be a good world while knights and gentlemen make us laws, that are chosen for fear and do but oppress us, and do not know the people's sores.

From pamphlet of English seventeenth-century radical democrats (Hill 1975, cited in Chomsky 1991a: 358)

In this chapter our aims are, firstly, to describe the central concepts of the structural conflict approach (also known as the critical functionalist or Marxist approach) – political economy, forces and relations of production, social class, class conflict, legal and political superstructure, social consciousness, ideology, accumulation, coercion and legitimation – as they apply to the question of the origins and functions of criminal law; secondly, to compare and contrast this approach with the social constructionist perspective examined in the previous chapter; thirdly, to illustrate the use of this approach in explaining the origins and functions of laws criminalizing vagrancy, tax evasion in a colonial context, drugs, various forms of non-parliamentary political opposition and sexual assault; and fourthly, to consider, from a structural conflict point of view, the absence of a range of putatively harmful activities from the purview of criminal law.

THE STRUCTURAL CONFLICT APPROACH

In the Preface to *A Contribution to the Critique of Political Economy*, Marx outlines the rudiments of the structural conflict or Marxist approach as follows:

The general result at which I arrived and which, once won, served as a guiding thread for my studies, can be briefly

formulated as follows: In the social production of their life, men [sic] enter into definite relations that are indispensable and independent of their will, relations of production which correspond to a definite stage of development of their material productive forces. The sum total of these relations of production constitutes the economic structure of society, the real foundation, on which rises a legal and political super-structure and to which correspond definite forms of social consciousness. The mode of production of material life conditions the social, political, and intellectual life process in general. It is not the consciousness of men that determines their being, but, on the contrary, their social being that determines their consciousness.
(Marx 1970 (1859))

This passage contains most of the key concepts of the structural conflict approach, namely 'forces of production', 'relations of production', 'legal and political super-structure' and 'social consciousness'. Together, these concepts describe a model of the organization of society in which, from the top down, social consciousness corresponds to the legal and political superstructure which arises from the relations of production which correspond to the material productive forces. To analyse the structure of a society in this way is to describe its 'political economy'. According to Carver (1982), and in contrast to crudely deterministic versions of Marxism, the relations among these 'levels' are not causal but in part 'conceptual', that is, matters of logical entailment or definition, and in part those of 'structural correspondence'. This is the interpretation we adopt here.

The forces of production are the means by which goods are produced in society. These means include what economists describe as the 'factors of production': land, labour, capital, organizational skills and technology. The relations of production are those forms of association which people take up in order to make their living. These will differ according to the state of development of the forces of production. 'Social classes', for Marx, are the most significant relations of production. They are nowhere defined explicitly by Marx, but Giddens (1971: 37) asserts that it is 'relatively easy to infer from the many scattered references which Marx makes in the course of different works' that:

Classes are constituted by the relationship of groupings of individuals to the ownership of private property in the means of production. This yields a model of class relations which is basically dichotomous: all class societies are built around a primary line of division between two antagonistic classes, one dominant and the other subordinate. In Marx's usage, class of necessity involves a conflict relation.

(Giddens 1971: 37)

Thus, for example, these groupings may be related in the sense that one may own the bulk of land and capital whilst the other may possess only their labour power. In so far as the means owned or possessed by each grouping are jointly required for production then the two classes may be said to be interdependent. But in so far as the political domination of the one is built on the economic exploitation of the other then the relationship is necessarily one of 'conflict'.

The forces of production and the relations of production, taken together, comprise the economic 'substructure' or 'mode of production' in a given society. On this base is erected the legal and political superstructure. This consists of the whole range of social institutions – the state and other political organizations, the legal system, the education system, religion, the family, the elite and mass media, the means of cultural expression, including the arts, etc. Expressed in and through these institutions are the ideas, values and beliefs that comprise the social consciousness or 'ideology' of society at a given stage of its development. Ideology is said to legitimate the underlying mode of production. As Marx and Engels put it, in the *German Ideology* (1970 (1845/46): 64): 'the ruling ideas are nothing more than the ideal expression of the dominant material relationships, the dominant material relationships grasped as ideas.'

The ideas of the ruling class are in every epoch the ruling ideas, i.e. the class which is the ruling *material* force of society, is at the same time its ruling *intellectual* force. The class which has the means of material production at its disposal, has control at the same time over the means of mental production, so that thereby, generally speaking, the ideas of those who lack the means of mental production are subject to it.

(ibid, original emphasis)

With respect to the origins and development of one set of 'ideas', namely the criminal law, the analytic procedure is to uncover the connections between a particular law and the social, economic and political structures comprising the prevailing mode of production (Hall and Scraton 1981: 471). As we saw in Chapter 1, the nature of the connections may be analysed more instrumentally, bringing out how the state is using the law to serve the primarily coercive interests of the dominant class, or more structurally, emphasizing the state's role in reproducing the dominant forms of social relations. Increasingly in work embodying the structural emphasis the 'dominant forms of social relations' or 'structures of dominance' have come to embrace those founded on sex and race as well as those based on class. There is lively debate in the field about the analytic independence, salience and interconnectedness of patriarchal (sexist), neo-colonial (racist) and capitalist (class-based) social relations in contemporary 'capitalist' societies. A characteristic statement is that of Scraton:

> Critical criminology, then, is a progression from unidimensional discourse and analysis. Its main theoretical construction is the synthesis and application of a framework sensitive to the interconnections between social relations of production, reproduction and neocolonialism. Within this framework there is no hierarchy of oppressions and no clearly defined boundaries to the analysis of institutional process or social interaction.
>
> (Scraton 1990: 22)

Pushing this further one arrives at the 'complementary holism' of the South End Press collective/network in which the standard series of monist treatments of the different types of domination – classism by Marxism, sexism by feminism, racism by 'nationalism', political authoritarianism by anarchism – is abandoned in favour of an approach in which 'economic, political, kinship and community spheres . . . may be usefully characterized by a predominant activity and particular defining social relations and group structures – *each entwined with the others in a complementary holist fashion*' (Albert *et al.* 1986: 21, original emphasis). It sounds depressingly reminiscent of Parsons's functionalist conception of the 'social system' (Parsons 1951; Cuff *et al.* 1990: 41–49).

Within the constraints outlined in Chapter 1 we try to recognize some of these differences in the examples selected in this chapter. We should also note that this mode of analysis can be applied to the creation of law in feudal society as it can to capitalist or socialist society.

There is, then, a functionalist component in this mode of analysis. However, unlike the functionalism in the structural con-sensus approach, that in the structural conflict approach seeks to describe not how a particular institution contributes to the overall stability and persistence of society (as evaluated from an a-social and a-historical God-like position), but instead how institutions serve the interests of those with most to gain from current social arrangements, whether (in the case of the institutions comprising the legal system) via the direct instrumentality of the state in the interests of the ruling class, or more indirectly if nevertheless ultimately through the state's reproduction of the structures of the dominant social relations. In either case the structural conflict approach pays particular attention to the way in which the state secures ruling-class domination by using the criminal law as a means of controlling class conflict in other-than-class terms. We treat this question in more detail in discussing the various ex-amples below, particularly that of Comack's analysis of Canadian narcotics legislation.

STRUCTURAL CONFLICT THEORY AND THE SOCIAL CONSTRUCTIONIST APPROACH

In the social constructionist approach, as we saw in Chapter 2, the focus is on the variety of groups which are active in the creation of new laws. Society is conceived in pluralist or 'democratic' terms. Conflict in society is seen to occur along a variety of dimensions, including status, ethnic, organizational and political lines. Conflict is often a matter of competing moralities as analysts, in keeping with symbolic interactionist premises, attempt to describe arenas of social interaction in terms of members' activities and their corresponding definitions of the situation, that is, from the inside. For the structural conflict theorist, however, this focus on claims-making activities and definitions of the situation is said to entail a neglect of the all-important structural context of power differ-entials among groups in society. For example, Comack (1985: 71) declares that 'the labelling [or social constructionist] perspective . . . lacks any in-depth analysis of broad structural – i.e. political, economic, and class – variables'. Moreover, to the extent that control by some source of authority is addressed it is standardly conceptualized as social control rather than the state control identified by the structural conflict position.

Such a declaration as Comack's is perhaps unduly positivistic with its reference to 'variables', but it does point to the absence of structural analysis in the constructionist approach. The latter is often criticized for failing to pursue the kinds of structural analytic interests which are distinctive for the structural conflict theorist. We should add that this supposed 'failure' is a matter of contentious debate within sociological theory, turning on whether the theorist subscribes to a realist or interpretivist position. These positions and this debate will be considered more fully in Chapter 5. For now we may conclude with Carlen (1976: 98) that inherent in the Marxist critique of the constructionist/interactionist position is 'the normative assumption that the phenomenological dream of ontological pluralism and egalitarianism is, in a capitalist society, socially transcended by a material reality of social inequality and coercion.'

STRUCTURAL CONFLICT THEORY AND THE CREATION OF LAW: CASE STUDIES

The first two case studies below and that by Small in Chapter 2 are also reviewed in Brannigan's (1984) useful opening chapter on 'laws and the social construction of criminal behaviours'. However, unlike Brannigan's our account specifically attends to the theoretical frameworks that inform the original analyses and we mark the differences between the interactionist/constructionist perspective of Chapter 2 and the structural conflict perspective of this chapter.

Criminal law as class control: Chambliss on vagrancy

Chambliss's (1976a, 1964) work on the development of vagrancy laws is a classic structural-conflict analysis of the origins of criminal law. It relates law creation to the mode of production in society, showing how changes in the law were designed to serve the interests of the economically and politically powerful. It employs the instrumentalist variety of structural conflict analysis.

The first vagrancy statute was passed in 1349. Its aim was to support the interests of the landowners in the feudal or manorial system of production, in which a large supply of labourers were required to work the land for the lord of the manor or 'landlord'. The landlords were thus dependent on these labourers for their livelihood. In return for their labour the workers, or serfs, were allowed to work small strips of land for their own subsistence. Underlying the passage of the first vagrancy law was a substantial decline in the labour supply. This was caused firstly by the fourteenth-century practice of engaging in religious wars and crusades. Landlords were required to contribute money to these enterprises and they often had to sell their serfs their freedom to obtain the necessary funds. The serfs wanted their freedom because the growing towns offered the prospects of greater personal freedom and a higher standard of living. The second cause was the 50 per cent depletion of the population brought about by the Black Death of 1348. Both of these factors meant that the wages of 'free' labourers rose, not only making it more costly for the landlord to cultivate his land but also depressing the conditions of life of the 'unfree' labourers. In turn, because of this, the unfree labourers became increasingly inclined to absent themselves from the feudal estates. In total these conditions amounted to a threat to the very existence of the manorial system of production.

The vagrancy statute of 1349 was designed, then, to force labourers to accept employment at a specified low wage (pre-Black Death) in order to ensure an adequate labour supply at a price the landlord could afford to pay. The statute prohibited, firstly, the giving of help to those capable of but reluctant to work. It made it a crime to give alms or handouts to any beggars or other 'idle' persons. Secondly, it stipulated that it was illegal for anyone under 30 years of age who was without a trade or craft to refuse work. Those who refused, and those who left, employment without reasonable cause during their term of 'service' were liable to imprisonment.

According to Chambliss this vagrancy statute was devised in order to alleviate the economic plight of those who stood to benefit most from the feudal mode of production, that is, the landowning class. The rationale for these laws was purely and simply economic self-interest. As Brannigan puts it:

> The labour-intensive manorial system was put into jeopardy. The 1349 vagrancy law effectively minimized the ability of free men to move about to maximize their economic self-interests. The net effect of the laws was to impress into jobs all those who were available to work and to make it difficult for anyone to move about to exploit wage differentials and thereby to

threaten the manorial reliance on peasant labour. The law had an obvious economic motive despite being a vagrancy law.

(Brannigan 1984: 3)

This statute fell into disuse as the manorial system itself declined through the fifteenth century. As Chambliss points out, one result of this decline was that the curtailment of the geographic mobility of labourers became superfluous. However, the statute was not eliminated from the law. Instead, it became modified during the sixteenth century, and together with subsequent modifications remains in effect at the present time. Chambliss turns his attention to the structural conditions underlying the modifications made in the sixteenth century.

Chambliss identifies what he calls a 'shift in focal concern' for the vagrancy statutes in the sixteenth century. This shift is from a concern with labourers to a concern with criminal activities. In the statute of 1530 it was stated:

If any person, being whole and mighty in body, and able to labour, be taken in begging, or be vagrant and can give no reckoning how he lawfully gets his living; . . . and all other idle persons going about, some of them using divers and subtil crafty and unlawful games and plays, and some of them feigning themselves to have knowledge of . . . crafty sciences . . . shall be punished as provided.

(Chambliss 1976a: 72)

At this time the severity of the punishments for the various types of vagrancy was increased. One merely idle and without a good account of their means of livelihood shall be

had to the next market town, or other place where they (the constables) shall think most convenient, and there to be tied to the end of a cart naked, and to be beaten with whips throughout the same market town or other place, till his body be bloody by reason of such whipping.

(ibid: 73)

For those who use 'divers and subtil crafty and unlawful games and plays', etc., the punishment is ' . . . whipping at two days together in manner aforesaid'. For a second offence such persons would be ' . . . scourged two days, and the third day to be put upon the pillory from nine of the clock till eleven before noon of the same day and to have one of his ears cut off'. For a third offence the offender would ' . . . have like punishment with whipping standing on the pillory and to have his other ear cut off' (ibid).

Five years later the punishment of death is applied to the crime of vagrancy and a further change in terminology is evident in that the statute now makes those who repeat the crime of vagrancy 'felons'. These and subsequent changes in both offence descriptions ('lurking', 'loitering', 'wandering') and punishments (branding with a 'V' for vagabond) are explained by Chambliss in terms of changes in the social structure and, in particular, the emergence of new class interests. The sixteenth century has been called the 'age of mercantilism' when a new class of manufacturers and traders emerged whose interests needed to be protected against attacks from predators. As Chambliss puts it:

> Concomitant with the breakup of feudalism was an increased emphasis on commerce and trade . . . With commercialism came considerable traffic bearing valuable goods . . . England became highly dependent upon commerce for its economic surplus. Italians conducted a great deal of the commerce of England during this early period and were held in low repute by the populace. They were subject to attacks by citizens and, more important, were frequently robbed of their goods while transporting them . . . Such a situation not only called for the enforcement of existing laws but also called for the creation of new laws which would facilitate the control of persons preying upon merchants transporting goods.
>
> (Chambliss 1976a: 74)

This introduces Hall's (1952) study of the 'carrier's case' and the criminalization of theft, a matter we take up in Chapter 8.

Criminal law for colonial exploitation: Chambliss on the African Poll Tax Laws

Another example of law created because of the political and economic interests of a ruling class is the case of the African Poll Tax laws in colonial East Africa between 1890 and 1930. Thus, a major problem facing the European settlers in Uganda, Kenya and Tanganyika during this period was to produce tea, coffee and sisal from plantations for export and for profit. Such production required a large supply of cheap labour. The colonialists could have imported convicts to do the job, but this would have been very costly and by this time the practice of using prison labour as a productive resource in the colonies, as had been done previously during the eighteenth century, had ceased to be part of correctional thinking. Consequently, the colonialists turned to the native population and set about devising ways of 'persuading', or perhaps more accurately 'coercing', large numbers of natives to abandon their traditional life style of subsistence agriculture – cattle-raising and slash-and-burn agriculture – and instead to work on the plantations. Thus, the Poll Tax and registration laws required everyone of working age to pay a tax to support colonial rule. Clearly, the only source of money to pay such taxes was plantation work. Chambliss (1976a: 68) indicates that this arrangement was 'actively endorsed by colonial administrators'. In 1895 Sir Harry Johnston said:

> Given abundance of cheap labour, the financial security of the Protectorate is established . . . All that needs to be done is for the Administration to act as friends of both sides, and introduce the native labourer to the European capitalist. A gentle insistence that the native should contribute his fair share to the revenue of the country by paying his tax is all that is necessary on our part to ensure his taking a share in life's labour which no human being should avoid.
> (cited in Chambliss 1976a: 68)

Compliance with this extortionate and coercive arrangement was obtained through the threat of fines, imprisonment and corporal punishment for those who failed to pay their taxes. However, these measures turned out to be less than fully successful. Many native labourers simply ran away from the plantations. As a result labourers were required to register their fingerprints with the authorities so that those that ran away could be returned to their plantation employers. As in England several centuries before, vagrancy laws were enacted in order to prevent natives from leaving their reserves and taking up other employment. Finally, a policy of low wages was used to stop the labourers from acquiring sufficient money to pay off their poll taxes and leave the plantations.

**Criminalization to divide-and-rule: Comack on the origins of
Canada's drug laws**

In contrast to Chambliss's instrumentalist accounts Comack brings
a structuralist interpretation to the role of the state in criminalization. In the previous chapter we examined Shirley Small's social
constructionist account of the origins of Canada's narcotics
legislation. We are fortunate in having, in Elizabeth Comack's
(1985) study, a Marxist account of the very same legal events. This
happy coincidence affords a relatively rare opportunity for comparing and contrasting rival accounts of the 'same' phenomena.
Indeed, Comack begins by summarizing and criticizing Small's
approach in the terms introduced in the second section of the
chapter. Small's focus on the activities of moral, professional and
organizational entrepreneurs such as, respectively, Mackenzie
King, Colonel Sharman and the RCMP, prevents her, claims
Comack, from seeing the conflicting material interests at stake.
Small's formulation of the relevant context in terms of racial and
status conflict fails to take account of the underlying class conflict
and the connected problem of state control.

This failure, says Comack, becomes apparent when the question
is raised of why the criminalization occurred when it did, that is, in
the period 1908–1923. For the very same moral concerns, racial
tensions and status conflicts that Small appeals to were present in
the 1880s in British Columbia (BC) (the province at the centre of
these happenings), but the BC Government's repeated attempts to
introduce appropriate legislation did not succeed. Each bill the
provincial legislature passed was later declared unconstitutional by
virtue of trespassing on the federal government's jurisdiction over
matters of criminal legislation. And the federal government itself
did not introduce a bill, as we have seen, until 1908. Why was this
so?

The clue to the answer is afforded, ironically enough, by
Mackenzie King himself. King was the Deputy Minister of Labour
in the Laurier government. That the deputy minister of *this* department of the government was sent to BC indicates that the state
defined the problem represented by the Anti-Asiatic riots of 1907
in Vancouver as one of labour unrest. As Marxists are fond of
pointing out in other contexts, conflicts carried out in ostensibly
religious or racial terms – such as those in Northern Ireland and
South Africa (and Oka? see Chapter 8) – conceal, even as they

express, the deeper struggle of class conflict over ownership of the means of production. Thus, for example, '"the Troubles" remain a persistent reminder of the inherent contradiction of the British state in Northern Ireland, whose "attempts to reform sectarianism abstract it from class relations"' (O'Dowd *et al.* 1980; cited in Sim *et al.* 1987: 24). To appreciate why drug laws were seen as the appropriate means of responding to an apparently racial problem of conflict between Chinese and whites which was defined more fundamentally as a labour problem (!), one must turn to an examination of the political economy of the late nineteenth-century period of BC history. This requires that the analyst consider the four elements of the structural conflict model of society outlined in the first section of the chapter: the stage of development of the forces of production, the nature of the class relations of production, the role of the legal and political superstructure, especially the state, and the prevailing consciousness or ideology. (Embree provides a related analysis of the passage of the Harrison Narcotics Act of 1914 in the USA as reflecting a 'policy which grew from domestic, racist, anti-Chinese feelings and from the United States' colonialist policy in Southeast Asia, particularly in the Philippine Islands' (Embree 1977: 194)).

Briefly, this period in the development of the forces of production in BC is one recognized as the early stage of industrialization characterized by 'increased rationalization of the production process through mechanization and application of scientific management techniques' (Comack 1985: 73). In terms of the relations of production the industrialization is capitalist in form. A small minority of non-producers own as private property the principal means of production, especially the industrial capital (the mines, factories, machinery, etc.), while the mass of producers exchange their labour power (both skill and sheer labour) with the owners for a wage. Conflict between these two principal classes – the capitalists and the workers – thus describes at its simplest the social relations of that mode of production known as industrial capitalism.

To elaborate, for BC in the 1880s increased rationalization of the means of production was in part a device used by the capitalists to deskill workers and thus reduce whatever control the latter could exert over the production process. By developing a 'split labour market' – pitting skilled workers against a growing army of unskilled workers – important divisions are created within the working class; 'divide-and-conquer' is a well-tried method of class control. Immigration supplied a ready source of cheap, unskilled labour. For various historical and geographical reasons it was the Chinese (but also the Japanese and East Indians) that filled that bill in late nineteenth-century BC. They were widely employed in the canneries, mines and, of course, in the construction of the Canadian Pacific railroad. One partial explanation, then, for the racial hostility the Chinese were subjected to throughout this period is to be found in the resentment of skilled workers at a group which employers encouraged them to see as the cause of 'wage differentials and conflicts within the workplace' (Comack 1985: 75). The 'Chinese question', as one prominent theme of the prevailing ideology of the times, is to be understood, then, as 'an ideal expression of the dominant material relationships.'

That the Chinese question came to be dealt with through the criminalization of opium only in 1908 depended on the role the state played, as the chief actor in the legal and political super-structure, during this stage in the rise of industrial capitalism. Within structural conflict theory the state's function in capitalist society, under the structuralist interpretation, is seen to be the reproduction of capitalist social relations. This involves the three tasks of accumulation, coercion and legitimation we introduced in Chapter 1. Comack confines herself to a consideration of accumulation and legitimation.

'Accumulation' refers to the work of creating the conditions that foster profitable capital growth. This is standardly achieved through providing grants, loans, tax breaks and the like to the capitalist class. 'Legitimation' refers to the work of securing the consent of the working class to this (unequal and exploitative?) social arrangement. It standardly occurs within the context of a 'liberal democratic', not to say 'social democratic', framework. This is because such a framework provides the greater potential for persuading and coopting the working class and for mystification of the power relations of capitalism. Great emphasis is placed on the legitimation of state power in this framework. Legitimation is achieved through the 'powerful ideology-producing institutions' such as the educational system, the mass media and organized religion (Center for Research on Criminal Justice 1975: 16). Each of these contributes to the mystification of state power and its relation to capitalist interests. Such mystification is achieved by the presentation of state power as being independent of, and above, class conflict, as standing for the interests of all the population, rather than as a means of control for the ruling class. (Notice it is hard to avoid some degree of instrumentalism in the Marxist account.) Mystification is also achieved through the work of the social welfare institutions (social security, unemployment, welfare). These reinforce mystification by ameliorating the more exploitative aspects of capitalism such as poverty and unemployment. Clearly, the two tasks – accumulation and legitimation – stand in a relationship of tension since an overemphasis on either one can only be at the expense of the other.

It is Comack's contention that the period of the 1880s was one in which the state saw its principal task as that of nurturing accumulation: thus John A. Macdonald's 'National Policy' fostered and protected nascent Canadian industry while government policy promoted Chinese immigration as a source of cheap labour for such projects as building the Canadian Pacific Railroad. Until that was completed the state managed the legitimation problem presented by the Chinese question by the 'symbolic gestures' of establishing a Royal Commission (1885) and instituting one of its recommendations, namely a '$50 head tax on all Chinese entering Canada (except for officials, merchants, and students)' (Comack 1985: 69).

Although the head tax had increased by the early 1900s to $500, such devices would no longer suffice. While the perceived racial problem had assumed more significance the essential difference was the growth of industrial trade unions and their accompanying socialist ideology. Unlike the more conservative craft unions, whose skilled workers were hostile to the Chinese (because of the threat to wages posed by cheap labour) but willing to accept the capitalist wage contract, the larger industrial unions were prepared to enfranchise the Chinese labourers but were quite ready to kick capitalism into the sea. The state's problem was now one of legitimation. As Comack puts it:

> a serious political crisis of legitimacy dawned in early-twentieth-century British Columbia as the socialist movement grew in strength there. The re-establishment of working-class consent, which was imperative if capitalist industrialization was to proceed, depended greatly on the repression and discrediting of the socialist movement . . . [However, in terms of Marxist

theory], for the state to mediate class conflict successfully such 'threats' must be dealt with in other than class terms.

(Comack 1985: 80)

When the 'labour problem' came to a head with the formation in July 1907 of the Asiatic Exclusion League by members of the Vancouver Trades and Labour Council (a grouping of conservative craft unions) and the ensuing Anti-Asiatic riot, the state responded publicly in an all-too-familiar fashion by (1) trying to pin responsibility on 'foreign agitators' (Americans), (2) interpreting the conflict as a 'race problem' and (3) defining the situation, thanks to Mackenzie King, as a 'moral problem' arising from the opium trade carried on by the Chinese. Above all, the problem was not to be publicly perceived as one of class conflict, even as the measures being taken were designed to address it, albeit in disguise, at that level. Like Small and Green in Chapter 2, Comack sees the Opium Acts as creating a social problem out of drug use. But notice the sharp contrast in the analytic under-standing of this process. This is no 'unintended' consequence.

In essence the criminalization of opiate use amounted to the creation of a social problem by the state . . .
There appears to be a clear and inescapable connection between legislation aimed at the 'immoral' habit practised by the Chinese and the ideology of an 'alien element'. Opium-smoking became an easy symbol for the dangers and evils embodied in the fantasy of the 'Yellow Peril', and the opium legislation helped to affirm Oriental immigrants as a major cause of social problems. Consequently one could argue that the drug laws were not so much directed at the Chinese but rather helped to identify them – and by extension 'foreigners' and 'aliens' – as a source of the problems confronting B.C. society. In doing this the laws de-legitimized further the competing view of the socialist movement, which insisted on defining labour issues in *class*, not racial, terms. Moreover, the continuing identification of unrest with aliens was more or less a symbolic concession to the so-called 'legitimate' conservative unions, which were willing to co-operate with capital (as contrasted with the so-called 'illegitimate' socialist unions that were more hostile to capital). *In this fashion the drug laws drove another wedge – however small – into working-class unity.*
(Comack 1985: 83, emphasis added to the last sentence)

To recapitulate, in brief: by criminalizing (non-medicinal) opium use the state effected a change in the legal superstructure so as to shape social consciousness about the nature (moral) and source (racial) of problems affecting society, thereby to divide the working class, divert the socialist counter-ideology and so maintain capitalist social relations in the ultimate interests of the ruling class. Solving the legitimation problem permits accumulation once more to proceed.

Legislating the 'authoritarian state': recent developments in Britain

Claims remarkably similar to those of Comack on turn-of-the-century British Columbia have been made about criminalization in the UK of the 1980s.

> In part, what we have seen in the 1980s has been a successful 'divide and rule' strategy in which divisions between ['us' and 'them', the 'productive' and 'parasitic' . . . male and female (124)], black and white, north and south, rich and poor, employed and unemployed have been exacerbated and manipulated to generate *consent behind the state* amongst certain relatively privileged sections of the middle and working classes for control through conflict *against* other less privileged sections of the working class (the unemployed, blacks and Asians, and workers in struggle) as well as *déclassé* groups such as travellers, students, and peace protesters
> (Norrie and Adelman 1989: 117, emphasis in original)

What role has been played by the criminal law in 'driving a wedge into working class unity', and how is the 'authoritarian state' under 'Thatcher's law' (Gamble and Wells 1989) to be understood in structural conflict terms?

Norrie and Adelman (1989) list the key developments throughout the British criminal justice system in the 'drift toward a law and order society' (Hall 1980). In Chapters 7, 8 and 11 we consider these changes as they relate to the practices of the police, courts and prisons, respectively. Here we note the changes in criminal law. Firstly, the passing of the Police and Criminal Evidence Act 1984 has increased police discretion and 'has extended police powers of detention, stop and search, search of premises, and the creation of roadblocks according to very loosely defined criteria'

(Norrie and Adelman 1989: 115). Secondly, the Public Order Act 1986 has also increased police discretion and given 'unprecedented powers to the police to ban and impose conditions on marches and to restrict demonstrations and pickets' (ibid). Thirdly, 'under the "new, improved" Prevention of Terrorism (Temporary Provisions) Act 1984 the original legislation [has been] extended to include within its potential ambit the members and supporters of any organization in the world which uses "violence for political ends"' (ibid). Fourthly, 'the 300-year-old right to silence has been abolished in Northern Ireland and will soon be ended in England and Wales' (ibid).

Many of the changes brought about by these Acts reflect those already in operation in the USA. Our concern here is not so much with the detail of the control practices enabled by this legislation, as we shall discuss these in later chapters, but rather with their interpretation in structural conflict terms. There is a substantial interpretative literature, including debate, directed to specifying just what these changes signify. Analysts appear to agree that they represent part of the state's efforts both to coerce those opposed to current political and economic arrangements and to legitimate those very same arrangements by winning the consent of those who benefit from them through appealing to their interest in 'the rule of law and order'. Analysts differ over the relative importance of material and ideological factors, continuity and change, and consensus and conflict in explaining just why these steps have been taken during this period of the 1980s. In picking out some strands of these debates we wish to give a feel for the sort of theorizing which comprises them.

The view that emphasizes the distinctiveness of these measures explains them as the necessary complement to Thatcherite economic and social policy. The freeing up of market forces through the privatization of former state enterprises and the relative withdrawal of the state from the provision of a range of social services has increased social inequality with its attendant economic distress and social division. This, in turn, has generated opposition and resistance in the form of strikes, riots and demonstrations. These have been met with increased repression by the state in the form of laws giving the police, the courts and the prisons greater powers to enforce order and discipline. And the state has engaged in a 'hegemonic project' – employing the ideological rhetoric of '"the individual", "the family", "the nation", "law and order", "the enemy within"' (Norrie and Adelman 1989: 123) to win the consent of the electorate to these policies. In this view emphasis is given to the change from the preceding period, to the degree of conflict between capitalist and working classes, and to the role of ideology. As against this view Norrie and Adelman (1989) argue (1) that rather similar repressive steps characterized the period of Labour government in the 1970s preceding Thatcher's law, and indeed can be traced back to the nineteenth century, (2) that such laws have enjoyed rather greater consensual endorsement than the opposing view allows, that being because a section of the working class has, from 1850, subscribed to the capitalist wage contract and (3) that therefore 'material' factors assume rather more importance. That is, industrial capitalism has always produced divisions within the working class between a 'labour aristocracy' of skilled tradesmen who benefited from, and in part ran, capitalist social relations, and the mass of ordinary unprivileged workers who, moving in and out of employment, were more obviously exploited by those relations and more violently opposed them. This distinction is one made by the police and we address it in Chapter 7. It is the major feature of capitalist social relations that Norrie and Adelman claim grounds for the 'consensual authoritarianism' that they see as a persistent feature of the relations between the better-off, 'respectable' working class, its trades unions and political party (Labour) and the police and the state. The erosion of this consensus began, they argue, in the 1970s before Thatcher. The distinctiveness of Thatcher's law, according to them, resides in the radical, ruthless and ideologized way it was put at the service of the Thatcherite socioeconomic project, and used to criminalize those who suffered or opposed its consequences. 'Thatcherism seeks not to integrate the poor and underprivileged but to manage their protest' (Norrie and Adelman 1989: 123).

The appeal to 'crisis', the disconcerting finding that similar conditions nevertheless prevail as one moves back in time, and the phenomenon of working-class consent remain persistent problematic features of and for structural conflict theorizing. We will encounter them again when examining developments in policing in Chapter 7 in connection with American and Canadian as well as British experience.

Women and rape: Snider on changing Canadian law

On 4 January 1983 new sexual assault laws replacing and abolishing the existing rape statutes were proclaimed in Canada. Snider (1985) analyses the involvement of various interest groups in the creation of these new laws in a fashion initially quite consistent with social constructionist accounts. But, like Comack, she goes beyond the results of such an inquiry to show how the state shaped the outcome of the legislative process so as to extend its disciplinary control over the underclasses in the ultimately material interests of ruling-class hegemony.

Following a process of legal reform begun in the feminist movement and the Law Reform Commission's *Report on Sexual Offences* (1978) the Government of Canada introduced (after a failed attempt in 1979) Bill C-53 in 1981 to reform and amend criminal laws relating to sexuality in four areas. These were (1) sexual assault (as stated above), (2) public morality (buggery, bestiality, gross indecency, etc.), (3) offences against young people (child abduction and child pornography . . .) and (4) assault and vagrancy (prostitution). After first and second readings the bill went to committee on April 22, 1982. Following several months of hearings it emerged for a third reading and was passed as Bill C-127 on 4 August 1982, reduced in scope, changed in some areas and having a rather different impact from what was originally broached. The major changes may be summarized as follows:

1   The old rape statutes were indeed abolished and replaced with a new three-tier classification of sexual assault (simple, with a weapon, aggravated). Wives could now charge their husbands. The evidentiary requirements were changed: corroboration is not required for assaults; the doctrine of recent complaint was abolished; questions about the victim's sexual history with persons other than the defendant were generally forbidden; consent remained a defence only if unforced, and the availability of 'honest, mistaken belief' about consent was restricted as a defence.
2   The public morality offences, used chiefly against homosexuals, were left unchanged.
3   Laws regulating the sexual activity of teenagers, and offences involving 'seduction' were left essentially unchanged. Matters relating to the sexual exploitation of young people (child pornography) were turned over to what became the Badgley Royal Commission.

4 'The sections on procuring and prostitution were left virtually
unchanged . . . , although "prostitute" was defined and de-
gendered,' and the matter turned over to another (the Fraser)
Royal Commission (Snider 1985: 341–342).

In short, while the rape law was reformed, much of the rest of the
reforms proposed in Bill C-53 did not survive to C-127. It is Snider's
contention that while these changes appear to represent at least a
partial victory for the women's movement in having rape, especially, redefined as a crime of violence rather than sex, in fact the
real winner is the state whose interest in social control was reinforced even as the modality of that control was somewhat shifted.

To demonstrate this argument she first analyses the positions
and contributions of the various interest groups represented at the
hearings before the Standing Committee on Justice and Legal
Affairs. This is a step entirely in keeping with social constructionist
premises. Thus, we are led through the arguments of (1) the
women's groups, (2) the law enforcement community (chiefs of
police, Attorneys-General), (3) the Bar associations and (4) the
gay community. The position of the women's groups is 'liberalizing' in intent. It is designed to remove the discrimination against
women in the substance and administration of the 'rape' laws, by,
for example, bringing them into line with other assault offences
through, for example, removing the corroboration requirement
and permitting wives to charge husbands. It seeks to encourage
reporting and prosecuting of offences and convicting of offenders
by not increasing penalties, trading severity of punishment for
frequency of conviction. (It should be noted, however, that
Snider's interpretation of this particular goal of the women's
groups is contested by Los (1990: 172).) The gay community's
position is similarly liberalizing and abolitionist, and that of the
lawyers liberal if critical. What then of the outcome?

What makes Snider's account an example of structural conflict
theorizing is the second step in her argument in which she redes-
cribes the 'feminist victory' in the 'competition of interest groups'
as 'the extension of social control' through 'the hegemony of the
state'. To do this she analyses closely both the amendments introduced and the reasons given by the government itself through the
Department of Justice as represented by the then Minister of
Justice, Jean Chrétien, in the course of 6 weeks before the
Committee after the other witnesses had been heard.

The burden of the government amendments, Snider argues, is one of resisting liberalization and extending state control. She summarizes the case as follows:

> Looking closely at the successes of the women's groups – in allowing women to charge husbands, the division of the law into three tiers with specified punishments for each, the changes in the amount and type of evidence required to convict a defendant – one sees that all of these made the chances of successful conviction higher. They may make it easier for women victims to testify, but *they are changes which tighten up the criminal justice system, making the criminal law on sexual assault (on paper at any rate) more punitive and effective.* Reform has come to mean changing the laws so that they are *in theory* equally repressive for all. (*In fact*, criminal law targets the powerless just as it always has.) The very different concerns of women and of the state to tighten control coincided over this issue; this was not essentially a pluralist or feminist victory over patriarchy.
>
> (Snider 1985: 350, original emphasis)

She explains the other changes and lack of changes in the same way. Thus feminists wanted lighter penalties but instead they were increased. The reforms intended to lessen or remove state control over the consensual sexual activity of teenagers and of homosexuals failed.

At the level of ideology Snider indicates how Chretien, before the Committee, credited the sexual assault reforms to the women's groups and the absence of liberalizing reforms in the other areas to 'public opinion' and the 'lack of a consensus'. In fact, it turned out 'that the law enforcement agencies of the state had exercised the real power. It came out that private meetings had been held with senior law enforcement personnel before the Committee hearings even began' (ibid: 345). It is Los's view, however, that the state's interest in reforming the rape law derived from its anticipation of court challenges to it under the equal rights test of the Canadian Charter of Rights and Freedoms then (1982) being enacted as part of the Constitution Act (Los 1990: 163).

More broadly, despite the liberalizing rhetoric associated with the earlier (partial) reforms in the areas of divorce, homosexual relations and abortion 'the reality is', asserts Snider, 'that there has been a continuous *increase* in control through criminal law in Canada during the post-war period' (ibid: 349). As elsewhere,

universal, egalitarian, '[l]iberal and humanitarian ideas in this
sphere are inevitably processed and transformed by the crime
control culture and its allied institutions into policy initiatives
which have a very different impact than their proponents en-
visaged' (ibid: 352). Writing of Britain, Snider says:

> Certainly middle and upper class adults, whose abortions [now
> also in Canada], homosexual liaisons [partially in Canada],
> divorces, and marijuana habits [not in Canada!] no longer had
> the problems which attend illegal status, were the main
> beneficiaries. However, while the substitution of control by
> professionals means less repression for them, it may mean more
> repression for the less articulate youth, the working, and the
> underclasses . . . The elite groups' fear of losing control, of
> opening up, of 'licence', is connected to this need to retain
> disciplinary patterns of control over the working class (and the
> middle class, although their control is conceived differently),
> since these habits of abstinence and puritanism are still crucial
> to maintaining a controllable labour force and a manageable
> populace.
>
> (ibid: 348–349)

Finally, Snider predicts that the passage of Bill C-127 will not lead
to a decrease in sexual assault, and that with the exception of 'a
few atypical and highly publicized cases in which middle-class
feminist victims insist on prosecution' any increase in enforcement
will fall on 'young, poor sexual assaulters . . . [who] account for no
more than a minority of assaults . . . [since] [t]he majority of
assaults are intra-, not inter-class, performed by male relatives,
acquaintances, and dates' (ibid: 352; see Box 1983: 120–164). Why
Snider would think that administration and enforcement of these
laws would have this character we examine in Chapters 7 and 8.

While Snider doubtless holds patriarchy to be its own structure
of dominance, it appears from this study that she is prepared to
argue that the state is willing to sacrifice, at least symbolically, some
degree of patriarchy in order to retain disciplinary, that is coercive
and repressive, control over the underclasses in the ultimate
interest of fostering the 'working conditions' conducive to ongoing capitalist accumulation. For a somewhat different feminist
assessment readers may wish to consult Los (1990) and the discussion and references therein.

STRUCTURAL CONFLICT AND THE SCOPE OF CRIMINAL LAW

Whilst the social constructionist approach appears content to limit its inquiries to the activities and definitions which 'construct' existing criminal law and hence crime, structural conflict theorists are also committed to evaluating existing criminal law in terms of a wider social and political programme and to advocating its 'reconstruction', as we stated in Chapter 1. We have seen how this critical position informs structural conflict analyses of the origins and functions of criminal law. It can also be seen in critical criminology's claim that 'human rights rather than legally operative definitions' be 'used to earmark criminal behaviour' (Schwendinger and Schwendinger 1975: 136). The attention, therefore, of critical criminologists is directed to putatively harmful acts that have, to date, escaped the purview of criminal law. According to this view 'social injury' should be the criterion for defining 'crime'.

In a succinct and powerful statement Box (1983: 9–11) lists the injurious acts of commission and omission traditionally excluded from the criminal law. The criminal offence of murder does not include such forms of avoidable killing as, for example, 'deaths resulting from . . . employers' failure to maintain safe working conditions in factories and mines', or 'to conduct adequate research on new chemical compounds before . . . marketing,' or 'to recall and repair thousands of known defective vehicles because they calculate that the costs of meeting civil damages will be less'. The criminal offences of robbery and theft do not include such forms of property deprivation as, for example, result from 'manufacturers' malpractices or advertisers' misrepresentation', and from extra taxation for ordinary citizens because 'corporations . . . [use] tax havens', Defence Department officials take kickbacks for ordering 'more expensive weaponry systems or missiles in "excess" of those "needed"' and 'multinational drug companies charge . . . national health services prices . . . millions in excess of alternative supplies.' The criminal offence of rape has traditionally excluded such 'non-consensual sexual acts' as forced sexual intercourse between husband and wife (now criminalized in Canada and the United States), most of those 'achieved by fraud, deceit, or misrepresentation' or by men using 'economic, organizational, or social power rather than actual or threatened force to overcome an unwilling but subordinate, and therefore vulnerable female'. The criminal offence of assault excludes such forms as 'verbal assaults', those 'whose injuries become apparent years later,' '"compulsory" drug-therapy or electric-shock treatment', and 'chemotherapy prescribed to control "naughty" schoolboys'.

Finally, the criminal law expressly (and rightly) prohibits the 'retail' terrorism of 'usually exploited or oppressed' individuals and groups, but does not concern itself with the 'wholesale' state terrorism of governments as in the United States' (with Canadian support) bombing of civilians in the war in Indochina, or American, British and Canadian support for Indonesian (partial) genocide in East Timor, or that directed against the people of El Salvador, Guatemala, Palestine (the Occupied Territories) . . . 'The criminal law, in other words, condemns the importation of murderous terrorist acts usually against powerful individuals or strategic institutions, but goes all quiet when governments export or support avoidable acts of killing usually against the under-developed countries' poor.' The distinction between retail and wholesale terrorism, and related examples, are not Box's but are drawn from the seminal works of Chomsky (1987, 1988, 1991a), Chomsky and Herman (1979), Herman and Chomsky (1988) and Herman and O'Sullivan (1989). We believe, however, that he would not disapprove of their inclusion.

Chapter 4

Ethnomethodology's law

In this chapter we shall firstly describe the central concepts of the ethnomethodological view of criminal law, with particular reference to the indexical nature of rules, the dependence of rule meaning on common-sense knowledge, and the relationship of rules to membership. Secondly, we compare this view briefly with the preceding views of making law. Thirdly, we illustrate its use with reference to the relationship between rationality and morality in five instances of law application pertaining to the determination of sex, negligence, murder, suicide and involuntary manslaughter in a case of drinking-and-driving.

ETHNOMETHODOLOGY AND THE LAW

In Chapter 1 we set out four principles of ethnomethodological inquiry. These are (1) conceiving social action in terms of the concept of 'recipient design', (2) treating social facts as interactional accomplishments, and social order as a local production, (3) examining members' knowledge and language use as topics of, rather than just resources for, inquiry and (4) viewing members as practical, rule-using analysts rather than 'pre-programmed cultural dopes'. In this chapter we shall be considering from an ethnomethodological point of view the issue of law making, and our emphasis will be on the third and fourth principles. The first and second principles are more easily explicated in the chapters dealing with the courts and the police where interactional studies are more readily available. In this chapter, with the exception of Garfinkel's jurors study, we rely exclusively on texts relating legal arguments and legal judgments.

The central phenomenon of ethnomethodological interest in

the 'making of law' is the intelligibility of the constituent activities through which criminal law is made. In the first place criminal law is made through the claims-making activities described in Chapter 2, the work of legislative assemblies and their committees, law commissions, judges' interpretations and applications of statute and case law, and through the work of appeal courts, amongst others. But, as we shall go on to argue, for ethnomethodology law is 'made' whenever 'law' is invoked or otherwise used, that is, in the ordinary work of courtroom prosecutions and police apprehensions. The several strands of ethnomethodological inquiry may be brought to bear on this wide range of activities and settings.

From that strand of ethnomethodological inquiry known as conversation analysis we can focus our attention on the sociolinguistic organization of the occasions in which criminal law is made, that is, drafted, debated, spoken to, passed, judged. We therefore may consider, for example, the 'speech exchange system' operative in legislative assemblies such as the House of Commons, hearings before parliamentary committees (such as the Standing Committee on Justice and Legal Affairs referred to in Chapter 3), sessions of the Court of Appeal, and the like. Then, from the point of view of membership categorization analysis, we may consider the production and recognition of such activities as 'passing a law', and 'rendering a judgment' . . . both verbally and textually. The third strand, mundane reason analysis, which provides for an examination of the use and operation of presumptions of objectivity and intersubjectivity with respect to the nature of persons, agency, chance and responsibility, is also applicable here. The criminal law treats as unproblematic numerous 'conventional' activities, and uses taken-for-granted knowledge about the social world and social activities as a resource.

These contemporary strands have emerged from the foundational work of Garfinkel (1967). Drawing on the phenomenological social philosophy of Schutz, Garfinkel's early work consisted of a series of demonstrations of the thesis that social order is a moral and cognitive phenomenon constituted through members' methods of practical reasoning. These methods include the 'documentary method of interpretation' (see Chapter 10), the use of 'indexical expressions', of the 'retrospective-prospective sense of utterances', 'ad hocing', the use of 'et cetera', of 'unless', of 'let it pass' and so on. In Chapters 6 and 10 we shall be explicating the work of conversation analysis, membership categorization analysis and mundane reason analysis. In this chapter we shall be confining our attention to illustrating the concepts and methods discussed in Garfinkel's early work. We shall attend particularly to the points emerging from his demonstration that common understandings are practical, interpretive achievements rather than measurable, shared agreements on substantive matters. As we shall see this leads into a preliminary consideration of members' use of membership categorizations and of other taken-for-granted features of common-sense knowledge and mundane reason.

> Apparently no matter how specific the terms of common understandings may be . . . they attain the status of an agreement for persons only insofar as the stipulated conditions carry along an unspoken but understood *etcetera* clause. Specific stipulations are formulated under the rule of an agreement by being brought under the jurisdiction of the *etcetera* clause. This does not occur once and for all, but is essentially bound to both the inner and outer temporal course of activity and thereby to the progressive development of circumstances and their contingencies . . . Not only can contingencies arise, but persons know as of any Here and Now that contingencies can materialize or be invented at any time that it must be decided whether or not what the parties actually did satisfied the agreement . . . That the work of bringing present circumstances under the rule of previously agreed activity is sometimes contested should not be permitted to mask its pervasive and routine use as an ongoing and essential feature of 'actions in accord with common understanding'.
>
> This process, which I shall call a method of discovering agreements by eliciting or imposing a respect for the rule of practical circumstances, is a version of practical ethics.
>
> (Garfinkel 1967: 73–74, cited in Jayyusi 1984: 208,
> original emphasis)

This relationship between a common understanding or agreement or, more simply, rule and the considerations relevant to its application on any occasion of its use is itself immediately applicable to the law. For it is just the 'work of bringing present circumstances under the rule of previously agreed activity' that describes what the courts (and police and citizens) do and what they are for. And this shows immediately how, for ethnomethodology (EM), the law is, in a real sense, its application. That the courts decide what 'in the end' and 'for all practical purposes' really happened, and register convictions under the rule of law, does not, of course, rescue such decisions from Garfinkel's point. For 'new evidence' may be found, new trials held, convictions overturned, pardons granted and so on, indefinitely. Three notorious examples illustrate this process. Thus, after he had spent 11 years in prison in Nova Scotia Donald Marshall was adjudged to be not guilty of murder (Harris 1986). Similarly, after the group of Irish workers who were known as the Birmingham Six were released from prison on appeal they were said to have been 'innocent' all along. Most recently, the body of former US President Zachary Taylor was exhumed to determine if, after all, he had not died of natural causes but had been murdered by being poisoned. Finally, to cite a classic sociological study, some time after she had successfully persuaded clinic staff to perform a sex-change operation on the grounds that 'nature had made a mistake' and she had been female all her life, Agnes revealed to staff that 'she' had been taking female hormones since puberty in order to develop female secondary sex characteristics (Garfinkel 1967). We take up the 'Agnes study' in more detail below.

The law is made, then, each time it is invoked or otherwise used. This explains why ethnomethodologists would want to examine judges' judgments and sentencings, lawyers' examinations (of witnesses) and arguments, police chargings and arrestings and citizens' decisions to report perceived offences or not. And so it is that the EM studies reported here and in Chapters 6 and 10 all represent inquiry into the law. What we shall try to bring out in the examples to follow are three features related to Garfinkel's 'version of practical ethics', namely (1) the open-texture or indeterminacy of rules (such as criminal laws) and concepts (such as insanity), what Garfinkel would call the indexical features of accounts, (2) the dependence of rules and concepts for their meaning on the 'form of life' in which they are embedded, what Garfinkel would refer to as members' reliance on 'common-sense knowledge of social structures' and (3) the way in which rules and concepts are tied in to the very idea of membership in society.

From the point of view of sociological theory the moral order consists of the rule governed activities of everyday life. A society's members encounter and know the moral order as

perceivedly normal courses of action – familiar scenes of everyday affairs, the world of daily life known in common with others
and with others taken for granted.
  They refer to this world as the 'natural facts of life' which, for
members, are through and through moral facts of life.

(Garfinkel 1967: 35)

ETHNOMETHODOLOGY VERSUS THE OTHER SOCIOLOGICAL PERSPECTIVES

Since a truly adequate account of differences between EM and the
other sociological perspectives would involve a fairly lengthy
theoretical excursion of perhaps doubtful value for the overall
aims of the book, we shall content ourselves with briefly identifying
three main points of contrast, appending some references, and
relegating further comparative discussions to their appropriate
places in the text.

1 As opposed to the position, common to the two structuralist
   perspectives, that views actions as designed to serve the needs or
   interests of the larger social system, ethnomethodology insists
   on an 'internal' view of all social action; actions are designed for
   their recipients (Sharrock and Anderson 1986); therefore, such
   notions as 'social system', the 'wider social structure' and the
   'capitalist mode of production' are all locally produced versions
   of social order, and do not have some privileged existence
   independent of the situated, that is, local practices through
   which they are made evident.
2 In contrast to the social constructionist view, ethnomethodology is indifferent to the phenomenal field being addressed;
   thus whereas the constructionists treat activities such as claims-
   making as a resource for the solution of the sociologist's
   problem of accounting for the origins of criminal law, the
   ethnomethodologist examines such activities as topics and
   accomplishments in their own right (Woolgar and Pawluch
   1985).
3 In contrast to the 'finished' conception of criminal law (in all
   the preceding perspectives), ethnomethodology favours a view
   of criminal law as a continually contingent production of the *in
   situ* practices of participants in legal proceedings and settings.

ETHNOMETHODOLOGY AND THE LAW: FIVE EXAMPLES OF MANAGING THE INTERCONNECTEDNESS OF RATIONALITY AND MORALITY

We begin with a case that is drawn from the civil, not the criminal, law since it provides an opportunity to introduce Garfinkel's classic treatment of the topic.

Mr Justice Ormrod on sex in the light of Garfinkel on Agnes

The following is an extract from Mr Justice Ormrod's summing-up of the case of *Corbett v. Corbett (otherwise Ashley)* (in the English Law Reports of 1971).

It appears to be the first occasion on which a court in England has been called upon to decide the sex of an individual and, consequently, there is no authority which is directly in point . . . The fundamental purpose of law is the regulation of the relations between persons, and between persons and the state or community. For the limited purpose of this case, legal relations can be classified into those in which the sex of the individuals concerned is either irrelevant, relevant or an essential determinant of the nature of the relationship. Over a very large area the law is indifferent to sex . . . On the other hand sex is clearly an essential determinant of the relationship called marriage because it is and always has been recognized as the union of man and woman. It is the institution on which the family is built, and in which the capacity of natural heterosexual intercourse is an essential element . . .

Since marriage is essentially a relationship between man and woman, the validity of the marriage in this case depends, in my judgment, upon whether the respondent is or is not a woman . . . The question then becomes, what is meant by the word 'woman' in the context of a marriage, for I am not concerned to determine the 'legal sex' of the respondent at large. Having regard to the essentially heterosexual character of the relationship which is called marriage, the criteria must, in my judgment, be biological, for even the most extreme degree of transsexualism in a male or the most severe hormonal imbalance which can exist in a person with male chromosomes, male gonads and male genitalia cannot reproduce a person who is naturally capable of performing the essential role of a woman in marriage. In other words, the law should adopt in the first place, the first three of the doctors' criteria, i.e. the chromosomal, gonadal and genital tests, and if all three are congruent, determine the sex for the purpose of marriage accordingly, and ignore any operative intervention. The real difficulties, of course, will occur if these three criteria are not congruent. This question does not arise in the present case and I must not anticipate, but it would seem to me to follow from what I have said that the greater weight would probably be given to the genital criteria than to the other two. This problem and, in particular, the question of the effect of surgical operations in such case of physical inter-sex, must be left until it comes for decision. My conclusion, therefore, is that the respondent is not a woman for the purposes of marriage but is a biological male and has been so since birth. It follows that the so-called marriage of 10 September 1963 is void . . .

Marriage is a relationship which depends on sex and not on gender.

(cited in Douglas 1973: 115–117)

Though it is very tempting we will not attend here to the matter of marriage as it arises in the above, but confine our remarks to the topic of sex.

Firstly, note that Justice Ormrod is concerned to define not the concept of sex as it might apply universally, nor the legal concept of sex as it might apply in matters of social relations generally, but the legal concept only in so far as it has to do with marriage. That is, 'sex' here means 'sex-for-the-purpose-of-deciding-if-persons-are-legally-married'. That is, it is a legal-organizational concept. The generic point is one that has been well made in ethnographic studies of a variety of organizational settings by ethnomethodologists (and, to some extent, by symbolic interactionists). Thus, for example, Sudnow (1967) indicates that for the medical and administrative staff at the two hospitals he studied a patient would be described as 'dying' when it was expected that the patient would not be leaving (alive) from this stay at the hospital. The concept of 'dying', then, had its place in a patient's career of hospital contacts and in the organizational activities of staff. It was a signal, for example, for the morgue attendant to make preparations for another case. To return to legal matters, Sharrock extends an argument from Garfinkel's (1967) study of jurors' methods of

decision-making (see p. 79) to assert that the legal concept of guilt
amounts in the end to 'guilty as charged, on the strength of the
evidence adduced, to the satisfaction of the jury's under- standing
of what is ordinarily possible and reasonable' (Sharrock 1984:
104).

Secondly, the phrase 'what is ordinarily possible and reasonable' serves to introduce the point that for all that Justice
Ormrod's argument involves considerations that would appear to
indicate that a person's sex is a matter of decision, underlying his
argument is a set of culturally given assumptions to the effect that:
there really are only two sexes; these are given in nature; in the
'normal' case a person's sex is determined by inspection, not by
decision (Jayyusi 1984: 58); the absence or mixture of the distinguishing characteristics of each sex is 'abnormal' or a 'mistake',
and that in those circumstances a decision may have to be made on
the basis of appropriate biological tests, but that decision discovers
what a person's sex really is; and so on. In short, while the criteria
may vary for practical organizational purposes, sex is not a matter
of election, is not essentially arbitrary and there are not more than
two (plus 'freaks').

The point has been made in a lengthy, detailed and now classic
ethnomethodological study by Garfinkel (1967) of 'Passing and
the managed achievement of sex status in an "intersexed" person',
known as Agnes. The partial list of assumptions given above is
extended by Garfinkel in what he calls 'a preliminary list of
properties of "natural, normally sexed persons" as cultural objects'
(ibid: 122). Most important, perhaps, is that feature whereby 'for
the *bona fide* member "normal" means "in accordance with the
mores". Sexuality as a natural fact of life means therefore sexuality
as a natural and *moral* fact of life' (ibid: 124).

What is particularly interesting is that Agnes, a 19-year-old
young woman with fully developed male genitalia, subscribed to
this view with conviction.

*Agnes agreed with normals in her subscription to this definition of a real
world of sexed persons, and treated it, as do they, as a matter of objective,
institutionalized facts, i.e., moral facts . . . Agnes did not depart
from this point of view even though her sex was for her a matter
of wilful election between available alternatives. This knowledge
was accompanied by a burdensome necessity for justifying the
election. The election consisted of choosing to live as the*

normally sexed person that she had always been . . . In seeking
a change of birth certificate Agnes treated the change as the
correction of an original error committed by persons who were
ignorant of the 'true facts'.

(Garfinkel 1967: 122, 125–126, original emphasis)

Thirdly, it is just the ability to sustain the presupposition that
there are two natural sexes, etc. that provides part of the basis on
which membership in society is assigned. As Agnes found, it is of
the nature of this property of everyday life that, unlike a game in
accordance with rules where it is possible to decide when the game
is in play and when not, as of any given moment it was for the
future to decide whether she had, in fact, passed as a woman.
Unlike 'normals', this was not something she could ever take for
granted.

We turn now to a second classic ethnomethodological study,
one that relates to the making of law in an area that falls at the
boundary between criminal and civil domains, namely negligence
cases (Garfinkel 1974: 16).

Harold Garfinkel: jurors' decision-making in negligence cases

In the mid-1950s Garfinkel participated in an American study in
which jurors' deliberations were tape-recorded and jurors subsequently interviewed about the way they had made the decisions
constituting the verdicts. Garfinkel's report on the study may be
said to make four points: (1) jurors' decisions about what they
were going to take to be the 'facts' of the case, that is, about 'what
happened', were based overwhelmingly on common-sense models
of what is ordinarily possible – 'if the interpretation makes
good sense, then that's what happened' (Garfinkel 1967: 106);
(2) furthermore, decisions were responsive to what is practically
possible for twelve (or however many) people to agree on, that is
to the organizational exigencies of the jury process; (3) however,
while respecting common-sense and practical exigency jurors also
tried to respect simultaneously the 'official juror line' by which the
good juror 'treats the situation as an object of theoretic play' (ibid:
111) where his preferences, interests, commitments, assessments
of the import of his decision for the defendant, judgment about
what is fair and so on are deemed irrelevant; the ambiguity
introduced by trying to satisfy both this ideal and the rules of

decision-making in (1) and (2) produced troublesome incongruity for jurors; (4) in contrast to 'rational choice' models of decision-making in which 'persons know beforehand the conditions under which they will elect any one of a set of alternative courses of action', Garfinkel proposed that 'for decisions made in common-sense situations of choice whose features are largely taken for granted, i.e., in everyday situations, . . . the person defines retrospectively the decisions that have been made. *The outcome comes before the decision*' (ibid: 113–114, original emphasis).

All four of these points may be said to elaborate the second of the three topics we are treating as themes for this chapter. That is, the first and third themes, namely the open texture of rules and concepts and the relation of these to membership in society, are not explicitly raised in the study. But the second of the themes, the embeddedness of rules and concepts in the mores, is its principal subject. Thus the first point brings out the cultural component of common-sense knowledge; the second point speaks to the organizational component of its application; the third point raises the difficulties that arise when the attitude of everyday life is required to be suspended in favour of the special, theoretic attitude demanded by the law (as by science); and the fourth point treats of that curious temporal feature of decision-making in common-sense situations of choice whereby:

> It is only by coming upon a proposal that is accepted that one finds that one has reached the verdict – one was not to know, even as that proposal was put forward, that it was the one which would prove acceptable. One finds that it is the decision because it *has been* accepted: 'the outcome comes before the decision'.
>
> (Sharrock and Watson 1984: 441, original emphasis)

In short, what gets to be a crime (or a case of negligence here) is a matter of the cultural, organizational, attitudinal and temporal features of the practices comprising the application of the law.

Lena Jayyusi: rationality, practice and morality

Among the presuppositions of the criminal law are two that are fundamental. Crimes are acts that are wrong, and so we say that the criminal law is underlain by and embodies moral judgments. Were we to think that a particular (class of) act proscribed by the criminal law was right, we would still be making a moral assessment. The criminal law, then, presupposes the possibility of making moral decisions. But secondly, we might say, the criminal law (and morality) presuppose rationality. That is, for persons to be able to act so as to avoid breaking the criminal law they must be able to understand the concept of crime, know the law, evaluate their circumstances, judge their ends and weigh their means. In short, they must be able to act rationally. In the traditional language of the law for an act to be judged criminal it must satisfy the two criteria of the *actus reus* and the *mens rea*, which we may crudely translate as the 'act-thing' and the 'mind-thing'. One must do the act-thing and intend the mind-thing. Without the intention, the mind-thing, one's act is not criminal. But to form intentions is to be capable of rational thought and therefore rational actions. And so crime, the moral matter, can be predicated only of rational beings.

So far so good. But when we come to examine particular cases we see that morality and rationality become interestingly intertwined. It is, of course, for the courts to decide in particular cases whether the act-thing and the mind-thing are present. We are likely familiar with the use of the 'insanity defence', particularly against murder charges. Let us turn to the following piece of courtroom data and Jayyusi's consideration of the methods of reasoning involved in the very conceptualization of the law. The defence counsel is speaking:

> Suppose after that interview you had been told and believed that on two occasions in two different homes Stewart tried, actually tried, to put his little baby in a burning fire and was prevented only by physical intervention by at least one person, maybe two or three, and that on another occasion he gave every indication of wanting to throw his baby out the window and was again prevented only by physical force from doing so; suppose you believed he did those things, would you classify him as normal?
>
> (Jayyusi 1984: 182)

Jayyusi indicates how the judgment of insanity that the counsel is inviting here is one based on a moral assessment of the gravity of the posited actions. That is, the judgment of insanity – a matter of rationality – is being based on a moral standard. Trying to put his baby in a burning fire and wanting to throw his baby out of a window are actions deemed so morally bad as to bring into doubt the man's sanity.

On the other hand the claimed 'inhuman' character of an action may be just what makes its perpetrator guilty (and therefore presumed sane) and worthy of punishment. This is evidently what is being argued by the prosecutor in the following section of his closing statement to the jury in the trial for first-degree murder of a man charged with stabbing to death a woman during a sexual assault in a secluded part of a beach. (The accused was subsequently found guilty of second-degree murder (*Globe and Mail* 27 June 1991, p. A7).)

> Describing the crime as 'gruesome', an 'unmitigated act of inhumane brutality', and 'a bizarre and twisted, horrible outrage', [Crown Attorney Paul] Stunt maintained that there was no need to look for a motive as the perpetrator was 'not a person motivated by normal human emotion'.
>
> (*Globe and Mail* 25 June 1991, p. A8)

While, then, we may call a killer a criminal responsible for his actions and deserving of punishment, for other purposes we may call him mad and deserving of treatment. This has consequences:

> It is not simply drawing the boundaries of moral membership as when we call someone 'inhuman' or treat him as 'deviant'; we are going further – we are almost calling that person non-human; *we are drawing the boundaries of rational membership through the use of a standard of moral membership.* In other words, we are denying that person the status of membership at all.
>
> (Jayyusi 1984: 183, original emphasis)

It is also true that 'certain actions are treatable by members equivocally as evidence of either being "sick" or being "bad"' (ibid: 184).

> The point is that where an action is deemed morally so groundless, so unacceptable, that membership is denied the actor, through the ascription of irrationality, then paradoxically this ascription serves to excuse that actor from full responsibility for his action, from moral responsibility.
>
> (ibid: 184)

The decision to treat a given action as 'immoral' or as 'irrational' rests on 'evidence and criteria ultimately external to the action and its immediate context, for example tests and psychiatric examinations, etc.' (ibid: 185). Disagreement as to the applicability of the two descriptions is itself moral. Consider the cases of Jim Jones (of the Jonestown mass suicide) or Ian Brady (of the 'Moors Murders') or Marc Lepine (of the Montreal Massacre). 'Which of two such judgments made in any case is ultimately a practical matter' (ibid: 186).

Jayyusi then makes the following point:

> it seems as though the distinction between doing an activity for no specific reason outside that activity and doing it for a reason (purpose, motive, interest) *beyond* the activity itself is one that is regularly important for members in their categorization of persons . . . [Furthermore], [c]ertain reasons for action and certain actions by their very nature make relevant for members the ascription of insanity.
>
> (ibid: 187, original emphasis)

For example, to engage in murder, theft or (for some, though not for us) homosexual activity for its own sake counts as 'unnatural' or sick, a sign of insanity, whereas to do it for profit, while wrong, is seen to be rational, understandable and thereby criminal. The Montreal Massacre of 6 December, 1989 provides an interesting, if chilling, case in this context. Marc Lepine's systematic setting apart, shooting and killing of fourteen women (thirteen students and an office worker) in the classrooms and corridors of l'Ecole Polytechnique in Montreal was widely represented as the act of a madman. By thus removing Lepine from societal membership this interpretative step also removes him from the relevant social status 'man', his victims from being relevantly describable as 'women' and his action from the possibility of being described as 'a man murdering women because they are women/feminists' (he perceived his victims, incorrectly, to be feminists). That is, in rationality being denied to his action the hideous, gynephobic message it contains is simultaneously suppressed. Not surprisingly, when feminists attempted to 'save the phenomenon' by insisting on the misogynist reading of Lepine's action (as he himself did in his suicide note), they became the subject of complaint and vilification (and, in some cases, of victimization) (see now Malette and Chalouh 1991). While, as Garfinkel (1967: 106) says, 'if the interpretation makes good sense, then that's what happened', echoed by Sacks (1972a: 57), 'members take it that they may choose among proposed competing facts by deciding that the fact is present for which there is an adequate explanation, and the fact is not present for which there is not an adequate explanation', we have to turn to the structural conflict perspective (see Chapter 7) for an explanation of why it is that for some groups rather than others – and notably women – this constitutes a perpetual risk. What we wish to draw from this discussion that is particularly relevant to understanding EM's perspective on the criminal law are illustrations of the three points referred to at the end of the first section above.

1 No definition of any rule, such as a criminal law, or of a concept, such as insanity, can stipulate all the cases or circumstances that may be counted as falling under it. The meaning of the rule or concept is open-ended. What the rule or concept means, then, depends on how good an argument, say, can be made for the applicability of the rule or concept to the case in question. We see the defence counsel making such an argument for considering the action of 'trying to put his baby in a burning fire' as falling under the concept of insanity. Such a decision is not given in advance.

2 Such arguments and decisions themselves depend on, draw on and are embedded in what has traditionally been called in sociology 'the mores'. The 'mores' are the concepts, methods of reasoning, norms, practices and institutions that make up the fabric of everyday life. What Jayyusi's account brings out is the socially organized nature of our recourse to 'common-sense knowledge' and common practices. It is in Sacks's work on 'membership categorization analysis' that this organization is revealed. It turns out that in describing persons, their actions, their motives, reasons, obligations, knowledge and the like, we build our accounts in accord with substantive and formal features of a cultural grammar of possibilities. We take up Sacks's membership categorization devices (MCD) work, as already noted, in Chapter 6. Here, let us simply note that the defence counsel's argument in the baby-in-the-fire case trades on 'the special ties expected to exist between the standardized relational pair parent/child [to] make accountable the strength of the moral breach' (Jayyusi 1984: 182). That is, it is just the taken-for-granted, culturally given, expectable norms of behaviour for this pair of categories that, irrespective of any knowledge about any particular parent and child, can be used to found the moral assessment that underlies the legal

judgment about whether a crime was committed, or a symptom of illness exhibited, in the case in question.

3 It is just the criminal law's presupposition of the mores that makes it available as a device, as Jayyusi shows, for drawing the boundaries of membership in society for particular persons in particular cases. We here gain an ethnomethodological entrance to a classic sociological problem addressed by Durkheim in his famous chapter on 'Rules for distinguishing the normal and the pathological' in *The Rules of Sociological Method* (1982) (see Chapter 12). But we leave a discussion of it for another place and another time.

Hart and Wilkins on rules, defeasibility and suicide

A further illustration of these points is afforded by some of the work of the legal philosopher, H.L.A. Hart (1965; Hart and Honoré 1962), and the sociologist, James Wilkins (1970). We have seen how the understanding and application of the criminal law – and, therefore, the determination whether a given instance of action is a crime or not – is embedded in the cultural matrix of everyday life. We have seen that this matrix is socially organized, for example, in terms of what can count as rational or irrational behaviour, and how those predicates can be assigned. The insanity defence is one of a number of ways, formalized in the law, by which the application of a legal definition or rule to a particular instance of action can be *defeated*. That is, to the charge 'Smith hit her' it may be pleaded:

1 'Accidentally'
2 'Inadvertently'
3 'By mistake for someone else'
4 'In self-defence'
5 'Under grave provocation'
6 'But he was forced to by a bully'
7 'But he is mad, poor man'

(Hart 1965: 170)

As we saw in Chapter 2, in 1990 in Canada it became possible for a woman to be acquitted of a charge of murdering her husband, on the grounds of what is called the 'battered wife' defence, that is where she had been repeatedly beaten and feared for her life from a subsequent beating. This perhaps marks a change in the

conventional understanding of the norms of behaviour attached
to the husband–wife standardized relational pair, at least with
regard to what is actionable at law. How this will come to be used
in deciding particular cases remains to be seen. But again it exemplifies (1) how the extension of a concept, here, say,
'provocation', is open-ended, now having been enlarged, (2) how
it is embedded in the (changing) norms regulating interaction
between incumbents of a standardized relational pair and (3) how,
perhaps, it offers opportunities for redrawing the boundaries of
membership in terms of the interconnectedness of rationality and
morality.

Hart continues:

> Similarly, the legal student will not have learned the concept of
> contract until he knows the list of defences which can defeat an
> otherwise valid claim . . . The list . . . consists of such items as
> 'fraudulent misrepresentation', 'duress', 'lunacy', 'intoxi-
> cation', 'contract made for immoral purposes', 'war'.
>
> (Hart 1965: 155–156; cited in Eglin 1979: 361)

Similarly, a verdict of suicide may be defeated by automatism or
mental illness. For the latter case, which we shall briefly examine
here, it is Wilkins who appeals to Hart and Honoré:

> Cases of suicide by insane persons raise some difficult problems.
> An act intended to produce the consequence which it in fact
> produces usually negatives causal connexion but an act done
> without a full appreciation of the circumstances does not.
> Courts have some rope to play with here [sic!], and while many
> have held that an act of suicide negatives connexion unless it is
> the result of an uncontrollable impulse, or is accomplished in
> delirium or frenzy, others have allowed recovery if the suicide
> took place during a depression caused by insanity, mental
> instability, or acute anxiety neurosis, since the latter are now
> recognized as 'things which in fact would dethrone the power
> of volition of the injured man' [sic].
>
> (Hart and Honoré 1962: 145–146, cited in Wilkins 1970:
> 197–198)

Like Jayyusi, however, Wilkins shows via two examples how complex are the judgments involved in seeking to apply the 'unless'
clause of mental illness. Again we see the recourse to 'common-
sense knowledge of the social structures' in deciding whether

mental illness is present, and therefore whether suicide can be said to have been committed.

One case was officially judged not to be a suicide in which a woman stabbed herself and took an excess of drugs in her locked bathroom. That she stabbed herself repeatedly, had been under psychiatric care, was about to enter a psychiatric hospital, and that her family was present in the house as she killed herself were apparently the items of information which produced an official verdict of undetermined cause. It appears from the transcript that the decisive argument was to the point that she was mad.

(Wilkins 1970: 198)

The opinion of Wilkins's research staff, in this study conducted in Chicago, was that this was a suicide 'possibly as they also had in view her statement to the suicide prevention center that she planned to commit suicide' (ibid: 198). Notice that this judgment, no less than the official verdict, depends on the common-sense interpretation of an item of 'evidence', here the statement to the suicide prevention centre (SPC) about her plan, a statement that is now read, in the light of the death, as a statement of suicidal intent (rather than of an intended hoax, or cry-for-help-that-went-wrong, or the ramblings of an overtaxed mind).

The complexities in the judgment that one is sufficiently mad as not to be able to suicide are further suggested by comparing the preceding case to another one in which a mental hospital patient, who had attempted suicide with lye and claimed to have often tried to kill himself previously, killed himself by jumping from a hospital window and was recognized to be a suicide by both officials and the research staff.

(ibid)

Again we see how, for ethnomethodology, consideration of the criminal and quasi-criminal law – suicide and attempted suicide were criminal offences in Canada until 1973, in Britain until 1961, but to our knowledge have never been so in the United States – leads to an examination of its application in the administration of justice and law enforcement, and that its interpretation at all stages rests on that taken-for-granted 'common-sense knowledge of the social structures' or mores. Atkinson (1978) provides a telling ethno- methodological account of suicide, while Smith (1990:

Chapters 5, 6) excavates the common-sense ideological reasoning that informs how women particularly come to be seen as mad.

Joseph Gusfield: constructing the killer-drunk

While Gusfield's study of drinking-driving is not ethnomethodological but indeed a fine example of an account of the social construction of a public problem (as in Chapter 2), he cites a case and a legal judgment which may be used to make ethnomethodological points.

On November 8, 1919, Glenn Townsend took Agnes Thorne for a ride on Lover's Lane in Kalamazoo, Michigan, in the course of which his Cadillac Eight roadster left the road and struck a tree near the fence line. A side of the auto caved in, injuring Mrs. Thorne so that some time later she died in the hospital of blood poisoning resulting from the wounds. Townsend was uninjured. After the crash he crawled out of the car and produced a bottle from which he drank and offered drinks to spectators. He was so drunk that he did not realize what had happened to the car or to Agnes.

Townsend was charged with and convicted of involuntary manslaughter. On appeal to the Michigan Supreme Court, Townsend's attorney claimed that though the intoxication while driving was a criminal act in itself, it should not, without further evidence of recklessness, be converted into manslaughter following a fatal accident. The court thought otherwise:

> the purpose of the statute is to prevent accidents and preserve persons from injury, and the reason for it is that an intoxicated person has so befuddled and deranged and obscured his faculties of perception, judgment and recognition of obligation towards his fellows, as to be a menace in guiding an instrumentality so speedy and high-powered as a modern automobile. *Such a man* is barred from the highway because he has committed the wrong of getting drunk and thereby has rendered himself unfit and unsafe to propel and guide a vehicle capable of the speed of an express train and requiring an operator to be in possession of his faculties . . .
> It is gross and culpable negligence for a drunken man to guide and operate an automobile upon a public highway, and one doing so and occasioning injuries to another,

causing death, is guilty of manslaughter . . . it was criminal carelessness to do so. (*People v. Townsend*, 16 A.L.R. 905, 906 (1921); emphasis mine)

(Gusfield 1981: 111–112)

As Gusfield argues, the appeal court's judgment constructs and trades on an extra-legal entity, namely a particular kind of person, the 'killer-drunk', a folk category with particular assigned characteristics, both cognitive (impaired by the chemical effects of alcohol) and moral:

> Townsend is more than a casual violator of the traffic rules; he has 'obscured . . . obligation', 'rendered himself unfit and unsafe', perpetrated an act of 'gross and culpable negligence'. He is 'such a man', antisocial and dangerous, whether or not accident and injuries were incurred. He is a 'menace'.
>
> (Gusfield 1981: 112)

In case it is thought we are dealing here with an 'antique' concept, consider the following judgment as reported in the *Kitchener-Waterloo Record* (22 November 1990, p. A2):

DRUNK DRIVER GETS 4 YEARS IN PRISON

TORONTO (CP) – A first offender responsible for the death of a 14-year-old girl in a drunk-driving accident was sentenced to four years in prison today. The parents of Cheri-Lyn Roarco wept in court as prosecutor Hank Goody described the case as a 'terrible tragedy that left the family forever scarred'. Justice Donna Haley told 35-year-old Ramzan Alli: 'You chose to drink and get behind the wheel of a car. When you did that, you became a menace to every other person on the highway and their loved ones.' Alli, who was permanently crippled in the crash, pleaded guilty.

Notice the following steps in the construction of the category and its application to the person in question, Townsend. They are listed in accordance with the three thematic elements of this chapter.

1 Of the possible causes of Thorne's death – the condition of the automobile ('a side of the auto caved in'), the condition of the road, the state of traffic, the availability and speed of ambulance services, the quality of medical care at the hospital (she died of

blood poisoning), the prior condition of Thorne, whether Townsend drove recklessly, Townsend's drunkenness – the last alone is sufficient to warrant the invoking of the category, given that he was driving and she died. Furthermore, what is otherwise usable as a means for defeating the assignment of criminal responsibility, namely intoxication, is here constitutive of such (ir)responsibility. Without the driver having committed any traffic offence, to be in the state of drunkenness while driving is judged a criminal act in itself.

2 The force of the argument depends on the tacit appeal to 'what-everyone-knows-about-being-drunk-that-need-not-be-spelled-out-here'. But this appeal is to the cultural construct of 'drunken comportment' (MacAndrew and Edgerton 1969), as we argued in Chapter 2, not the behavioural one of physical compulsion.

3 Once the category is ascribed, the incumbent becomes eligible for description in the moral terms that are tied to the category, without further evidence. In contrast with the redeemable 'folk crimes' that traffic offences comprise, successful ascription of the category 'killer-drunk' is deeply implicative for the management of the incumbent's societal membership thereon.

In conclusion, we have noted how the meaning of legal rules and concepts is open-ended, is embedded in broad cultural conventions constituting common-sense knowledge of the social structures or mores, and is thereby for members tied in to consequential matters of societal membership. We have briefly examined such items of common-sense knowledge as the 'two natural sexes', methods for assessing guilt, behavioural norms for the category pair 'parent–child', the links among rationality, motivation and morality as they apply to murder and suicide, and the norms of drunken comportment in relation to driving. These minimal analyses, we hope, have served to suggest just what sort of sociological understanding of crime is afforded by an ethnomethodological examination of law.

Chapter 5

Policing as symbolic interaction

In this chapter we shall consider policing from the symbolic interactionist perspective. We review some of the central concepts in this approach, including the self, self-indication, role-taking, interpretation, defining the situation, judgment, self as object, self-image, the actor's point of view and labelling. We show how this approach, when applied to the study of policing, focuses on the police decision-making involved in selecting crime and criminals. We compare two models of this selection 'process': the 'crime-funnel' and 'crime-net' models of police (and judicial) decision-making, and offer a critique of them based on the distinction between 'realist' and 'interpretivist' conceptions of crime. We review selected studies of police decision-making conducted under the auspices of this approach: Piliavin and Briar, Chambliss, and Hunt. We examine the significance of these studies for our understanding of the meaning of official statistics on crime and criminals. We then introduce labelling theory and consider the role of the police in the amplification of crime.

THE SYMBOLIC INTERACTIONIST APPROACH TO CRIME

As we said in Chapter 1, symbolic interactionism as an approach has been expounded primarily in the works of George Herbert Mead (1934) and Herbert Blumer (1969; see now Plummer 1991). The key concept in the symbolic interactionist approach is that of the 'self'. The self is conceptualized in two ways. Firstly, there is the idea of the self as process. Secondly, there is the self as object. As process, the self refers to the distinctively human capacity for self-interaction. This means that the human being is able to interact with his or her self. This is achieved through a process in which the actor makes 'indications' to him or herself and then responds to these indications by making further self-indications. Self-indications are made whenever the actor notes or points something out to him or herself.

According to Athens (1980: 15), the process of self-indication has two 'essential features'. The first is that the humans make these indications to themselves as if they were making them to someone else, except that they are made in a 'shorthand or more abbreviated and rapid manner'. The second is that 'when making self-indications', actors are always role-taking or implicitly indicating to themselves 'from the standpoint of another person, a small discrete group of persons, or a generalized other' (ibid).

It is through the process of self-indication that actors construct interpretations of the situations in which they find themselves. There are two sides or 'phases' to the process of interpretation in the symbolic interactionist framework. The first is definition. This involves the actor defining the situation he or she faces. Central to this defining is the process of role-taking in which the actor takes the role or roles of the other people in the situation and indicates to him or herself from their standpoint the meaning of the gestures which they are making. The second phase in interpretation is judgment. It is through this phase that the actor decides the course of action to be taken in the situation, given his or her definition of it. Judgment is achieved through taking the role of a generalized other and indicating to him or herself from that standpoint how to act. The role of the generalized other is the perspective of an abstract other or group which the actor builds up over time from his or her interaction with other people. The role of the particular generalized other that the actor takes in judging a situation depends on his or her definition of the situation. Even after forming, as a result of this process, a 'plan of action', subsequent redefinitions of the situation may result in further judgments and revised plans of action.

The second aspect of the self is that of the self as object. This refers to the human capacity for having a picture of him or herself. This picture is called the self-image by symbolic interactionists. Self-images are developed through a process in which the actor looks at him or herself and then judges what is seen. Actors cannot see or judge themselves directly; they can do so only indirectly, by taking the standpoint of others towards themselves. These others may be selected persons, small discrete groups or generalized others. They are central to a person's sense of 'who they are'.

The concept of self underlies Blumer's three premises of symbolic interactionism which we identified in Chapter 1. There we expressed them in relation to the study of crime and listed the particular topics of inquiry they made relevant. Thus, to recap, the premises are that human beings act towards things in terms of the meanings the things have for them, that the meanings arise out of social interaction, and that they depend on a process of interpretation. Action, meaning and interpretation all depend upon the human capacity for self-interaction, that is, on the possession of a self. When applied to the study of crime the three premises translate as follows: whether a given (class of) act is criminal or not depends on the meaning attributed to it (that is, it is a matter of definition); the selection of a particular act (or instance of action) as criminal is an interactional matter; and it is also a matter of interpretation. Of the topics of inquiry thereby made relevant we examined the definition or construction of acts-as-criminal, that is the making of criminal laws, in Chapter 2. In this chapter our attention is focused first on the selection of particular acts (or instances of action) as criminal, that is, in the first place, on the decision-making of the police. To appreciate what this entails we shall begin by elaborating our account of the main concepts of the symbolic interactionist perspective, and show just what it is about police-work-as-the-selection-of-crime they allow us to see.

The symbolic interactionist concept of the self and the frame-work of ideas derived from it has been applied to the study of crime in several different ways. In particular, the idea of the self as process has provided for studies of the selection of crime, and the idea of the self as object has been applied by that variety of symbolic interactionism known as labelling theory to the study of the impact of selecting and treating people as criminal on their self-images and conduct. We shall examine labelling theory in the next-to-last section (p. 108) (and again in Chapter 11). At this juncture our concern is with symbolic interactionism and the selection of crime with particular reference to the police.

SYMBOLIC INTERACTIONISM AND THE POLICE: SELECTING CRIME AND CRIMINALS

The symbolic interactionist approach provides the view that crime is a matter of definition rather than an inherent property of any particular act or person. Crime is a relative rather than an absolute phenomenon. From a symbolic interactionist perspective, crime is a constructed or interpreted reality rather than a pre-existing, objective reality. Accordingly, symbolic interactionists have examined the processes of selection through which the label 'criminal' is applied to both behaviour and persons. This is not to say that other varieties of criminology have not been interested in the processing of crime by the agencies of law enforcement. They have, but with the exception of ethnomethodology, it is only symbolic interactionism which has adopted a fully fledged constructionist conception of crime. Others have instead worked with a 'realist' rather than an 'interpretivist' model of crime. Brannigan (1984), for example, in summarizing the sociological work on the selection process, develops a distinction between the crime funnel and the crime net as ways of understanding how acts and persons are identified as criminal. Unfortunately, this distinction fails to bring out sufficiently the radically constructionist character of the symbolic interactionist view. The crime-funnel model posits the existence of 'criminal behaviour' in society but only some of it comes to the attention of victims, complainants and police. Only some of the crime thus attended to is acted upon: victims don't always inform the police and the police do not always record complaints as crimes. Of the total number of recorded crimes, only a smaller percentage result in charges, even less in convictions. The result, according to this model, then, is that there is a progressive 'editing out' of 'crimes' as offences are processed through the 'funnel' of the criminal justice system. Compared to the 'real amount of crime' out there in society, the amount actually recorded by the police and dealt with by the courts is much smaller, though we have no way of knowing how much smaller it is because we don't know how much crime there 'really is'. Criminologists call this real amount of crime which exists independently of law enforcement recognition the 'dark figure of crime'.

The crime-net model is also a realist model of crime. It is favoured by the proponents of the structural conflict perspective. Its aim is to bring out features of the criminal justice process which are left unexamined in the crime-funnel approach. In particular, the crime-net model is used to draw attention to the highly discretionary and selective character of policing in particular, and law enforcement in general. Like the crime-funnel model, the crime net posits the existence of a vast amount of 'real crime' in society which exists independently of its recognition by officials or laypersons. Metaphorically, this crime is likened to an ocean of fish.

Cod, haddock, sharks, swordfish abound. There are 'big' fish and 'little' fish. The police are then likened to fisherpersons who, with their 'crime nets' go fishing for the fish–criminals. In doing so, they have to make decisions as to where to fish and what types of fish they wish to catch. Studies have shown that they tend to concentrate their efforts on the 'little' fish (that is, only certain types of crime, typically lower-class ordinary crimes of the power-less), leaving the 'big' fish (upper-class crimes of the powerful) to swim free.

Though these two models are useful in bringing out different aspects of the work of law enforcement, it is important to bear in mind their similarities of approach. Thus, both posit the existence of 'real crime' which is independent of the work of the police and courts. It is for this reason that both are 'realist' models of crime. In contrast, the symbolic interactionist approach, together with the ethnomethodological perspective, prefers to take an 'inter-pretivist' or constructionist view: there is *no* crime apart from that which is actually identified as such.

We shall return to this distinction between the realist and inter-pretivist models in Chapter 10 when we discuss the work of some symbolic interactionists, notably Becker, who confuse the realist and interpretivist models of crime. For the present, we wish to emphasize that the symbolic interactionist view of crime provides for the examination of policing as involving the interpretation of acts and persons as criminal. It is through these interpretations that some acts and some persons are selected to be our crimes and criminals. This view provides, then, for the examination of how crime is identified and who is selected for the role of criminal. These tasks fall to the police as one 'crime-defining agency'.

Symbolic interactionist interest in the process of selecting crime follows from its view of the police as actors just like any other social beings. That is, they are viewed as possessing selves with which they act in, and interact with, their environment. The self is conceived as a process through which humans point things out to themselves, thereby constituting the 'outer world' as a meaningful one at the same time as appropriating that world as their own. The resources used in this process of making meaning include 'concepts', 'frames of reference' and 'definitions of the situation'. In short, what a person 'sees' in the world depends on their 'point of view'. Thus, what counts as an act(ion) is behaviour under some mean-ing conferred on, or attributed to, it by the actor. To understand the actions of the police the sociologist must 'take the role of the other' in order to see how police perceive their circumstances and accordingly construct their actions. Similarly, the police engage in a similar process of role-taking in attributing meaning to the behaviour of those they define as criminal.

Symbolic interactionist studies of policing have therefore paid particular attention to the processes of social interaction and interpretative schemata through which certain acts and persons are 'selected' or identified as criminal.

SELECTED STUDIES OF POLICE DECISION-MAKING

Studies of police decision-making are heavily weighted in favour of the uniformed branch. They standardly consist of detailed examinations of the routine work of the beat or patrol officer. Although there is a small number of studies of the plain-clothes branch, that is of detectives (for example, Ericson 1981; Hobbs 1988; Sanders 1977; Skolnick 1975 (1966)), we remain with the 'street cop' in the examples that follow.

Piliavin and Briar: police encounters with juveniles

Piliavin and Briar (1964) studied police decision-making in settings where they spotted 'wanted' youths or they observed youths behaving suspiciously, often at or near the scene of a reported offence. It emerged that the outcome of the juvenile–police encounter was determined only in part by the knowledge that an offence had occurred or that a particular youth had committed an offence. This finding led Piliavin and Briar to look at the influence of non-offence-related criteria in police decision-making. They found that the central task for the police in each encounter was to make a selection from a range of 'dispositions', from outright release, release and submission of a 'field interrogation report' and an official remand at the 'soft' end, to citation to juvenile court and arrest and confinement in Juvenile Hall at the 'harder' end. It also emerged that the full range of these dispositions was used with respect to every category of offence, even though it was department policy to arrest and confine offenders where offences involved theft, sex, battery, possession of weapons, prowling, peeping, intoxication and disturbance of the peace. The reason for this 'failure' to follow departmental policy was said by the police themselves to be because dispositions were also meant to be based on such considerations as age, attitude and prior criminal record. Dispositions were supposed to be in the 'best interests' of the juvenile. Police actions, then, had to be justified not just in terms of offence-related criteria, they also had to reflect the character of the juvenile in question.

Assessing the character of apprehended youths presented fewer problems in the case of serious crimes such as robbery, homicide, aggravated assault, grand theft, auto theft, rape and arson. Youths who committed these offences were seen as 'confirmed delinquents'. However, in the case of minor offences, the violation *per se* took on an insignificant role. Some minor offenders were seen as serious delinquents, but others were seen as 'good' boys whose offences were atypical. The officers had little information to go on so they obtained cues from their interaction with the juvenile. They looked for cues such as the youths' affiliations, their age, case, grooming, dress and demeanour. Older juveniles, members of known delinquent gangs, blacks, those with 'greasy' hair, black jackets, soiled denims or jeans and boys who were not respectful received the more severe dispositions. Of these cues, the most important was demeanour. This referred to the degree of co-operation displayed by the juvenile. Thus, juveniles who were contrite, respectful and fearful of sanctions were regarded as 'salvageable'. In contrast, those who were fractious, obdurate and nonchalant in the face of authority were regarded as 'would-be tough guys' or 'punks' and were, as a result, given the most severe dispositions such as arrest and confinement.

Like other studies of this genre, Piliavin and Briar show that the police display a 'bias' or prejudice in the exercise of their discretion. Blacks and those conforming to the delinquent stereotype were frequently stopped and more seriously dealt with than their white and apparently 'non-delinquent' counterparts. This is explained through the concept of police culture or knowledge. The police believed that blacks and youths displaying stereotypical delinquent cues were more likely to exhibit a recalcitrant demeanour (the sign of a confirmed delinquent) and they assumed that blacks and 'toughs' committed more crime. It was because of these beliefs that the police were more likely to exercise surveillance in areas inhabited by such youths and to accost them more frequently.

These beliefs and the practices based upon them, as Piliavin and Briar point out, produced a self-fulfilling prophecy. More frequent encounters with the police and disproportionate surveillance created hostility among the youths subject to them and it also reduced the significance of the encounter for these juveniles (it became routine). This hostility and nonchalance then led to the very responses which were for the police indicators of serious delinquency. They also vindicated the police officers' prejudices and thereby provided in a viciously circular manner for closer surveillance.

William Chambliss: the 'Saints' and the 'Roughnecks'

The findings of Chambliss complement those of Piliavin and Briar. He compares two groups of High School students, the 'Saints' and the 'Roughnecks'. The 'Saints' were children of 'good, stable, white upper-middle-class families, active in school affairs, good pre-college students' (Chambliss 1976b: 148). Yet they engaged in delinquent behaviour such as truancy, drinking, wild driving, petty theft and vandalism. Nevertheless, in the two years during which Chambliss observed them none of them was officially arrested for an offence at all. The situation was very different with the 'Roughnecks'. They were lower-class white boys who engaged in fighting, theft, and drinking. In contrast to the Saints, 'the Roughnecks were constantly in trouble with police and community even though their rate of delinquency was about equal with that of the Saints' (ibid). Chambliss examines the reasons for this disparity and its result.

There were three main 'variables' (Chambliss's expression) which helped to explain the disparity in police and community reaction: visibility, demeanour and bias. Thus the Roughnecks were much more visible than the Saints. Because of the economic standing of their families, the Saints had access to cars and could keep out of sight from the community. The Roughnecks, without transportation, had to hang out in the centre of town since their homes were scattered through the community and any non-central meeting place put an undue hardship on some of the members. By gathering in the crowded area of town, everyone, including their teachers and the police, became aware of the Roughnecks, an awareness which they exacerbated through their rude remarks to passers-by and their occasional fights. The Saints, however, were either in a cafe on one edge of town or in the pool hall on the other. They were thus typically inside somewhere when they were truanting, and when they went on their escapades outside, they usually went to a neighbouring big city where they were also relatively invisible.

As far as the school was concerned, the Saints feigned compliance with school norms in order to 'escape' (for example, making 'legitimate' excuses to leave) and once off the school premises could rapidly disappear in their cars. The Roughnecks, being without cars, faced almost certain detection.

There were also differences in demeanour between the two groups. The Saints were apologetic and penitent in the event of a confrontation with an accusing police officer. In contrast, the Roughnecks' attitude was one of hostility, disdain or 'insincere' respect.

The third variable was bias. Thus, the delinquencies of the Saints were perceived by the community, the police and school officials as less serious than those of the Roughnecks. As Chambliss puts it:

> In the eyes of the police and school officials, a boy who drinks in an alley and stands intoxicated on the street corner is committing a more serious offence than a boy who drinks to inebriation in a nightclub or a tavern and drives around afterwards in a car. Similarly, a boy who steals a wallet from a store will be viewed as having committed a more serious offence than a boy who steals a lantern from a construction site.
>
> Perceptual bias also operates with respect to the demeanour of the boys in the two groups when they are confronted by adults. It is not simply that adults dislike the posture affected by boys of the Roughneck ilk; more important is the conviction that the posture adopted by the Roughnecks is an indication of their devotion to deviance as a way of life. The posture becomes a cue, just as the type of offence is a cue, to the degree to which the known transgressions are indicators of the youths' potential for other problems.
>
> Chambliss (1976b: 158)

Visibility, demeanour and bias, then, are the variables which Chambliss uses to account for the day-to-day operations of the police with respect to law enforcement against the Roughnecks and benign neglect and ignorance with respect to the Saints. However, Chambliss does not leave the matter here. He combines these insights produced through his observations with the kind of

structural theorizing favoured by proponents of the structural
conflict approach. Thus, he argues:

> Visibility, demeanour and bias are surface variables . . . Why do
> these surface variables operate as they do? Why do the police
> choose to disregard the saints' delinquencies while breathing
> down the backs of the Roughnecks?
> The answer lies in the class structure of American society and
> the control of legal institutions by those at the top of the class
> structure. Obviously, no representative of the upper class drew
> up the operational chart for the police which led them to look
> in the ghettos and on streetcorners – which led them to see the
> demeanour of lower-class youth as troublesome and that of
> upper-middle-class youth as tolerable. Rather, the procedures
> simply developed from experience – experience with irate and
> influential upper-middle-class parents insisting that their son's
> vandalism was simply a prank and his drunkenness only a
> momentary 'sowing of wild oats' – experience with cooperative
> or indifferent, powerless, lower-class parents who acquiesced to
> the law's definition of their son's behaviour.
>
> (ibid)

Jennifer Hunt: the police use of 'normal force'

A central concern of symbolic interactionism, going back to
Sutherland (1949) and, before him, Mills (1940), is with the
rationalization of action, and its relation to crime. Excuses, justifications, vocabularies of motive, techniques of neutralization,
rationalization, in short 'accounts' are viewed as pivotal in
translation of an abstract 'willingness' into actual behaviour. In
order words, the actor must have 'good reason' to act in the way he
does, projected courses of action must be excusable or justifiable
if they are to become more than projections. Accounts for action
are then embodied in the cultural perspective of the person or
group, the task of the sociologist being to try to appreciate this and
then to use it as a resource in explaining the action under
consideration.

This approach to the study of action has been used extensively
in criminology and the sociology of deviance in order to show how
crime follows from the permissive character of rationalization. We
shall go into more detail on this topic when we consider the

symbolic interactionist perspective on the administration of justice in the courts in Chapter 9. For the present, we will consider an example of this approach in relation to the use of force amongst the police. According to Bittner (1980), the capacity to use force stands at the core of the police mandate. Hunt looks at the police use of force from a symbolic interactionist perspective. She says that 'sociologists working within the symbolic interactionist tradition have displayed particular interest in the police officer's own assessment of what constitutes necessary force' (Hunt 1987: 132). Hunt examines how police 'classify and evaluate acts of force as either legal, normal, or excessive' (ibid). 'Legal force' is the 'coercion necessary to subdue, control and restrain a suspect in order to take him into custody'. Normal force, on the other hand, although technically labelled excessive, involves coercive acts that specific 'cops' on specific occasions formulate as necessary, appropriate, reasonable or understandable.

As in other symbolic interactionist studies, the method for exploring this topic was participant observation. By participating in, and observing, the actions of the police, Hunt developed an appreciative understanding of their point of view. She discovered that the police contrast what occurs 'on the street' and what is 'taught at the academy'. At the latter, force is taught by reference to legality, officers being issued with 'regulation instruments' and being trained 'to use them to subdue, control, and restrain a suspect'. Deadly force may be used if the officer is threatened with 'great bodily harm'. However, the formal, academy view is that the baton, jack, or gun cannot be used 'unnecessarily to torture, maim, or kill a suspect'. In the 'informal world' of street policing, however, 'normal' as well as 'legal' force is recognized. Rookies 'learn to adjust their arsenals to conform to street standards', being 'encouraged to buy the more powerful weapons worn by veteran colleagues as these colleagues point out the inadequacy of a wooden baton or compare their convoy jacks to vibrators' (ibid: 133). It seems that soon after joining the informal world of policing

most rookies have dispensed with the wooden baton and convoy jack and substituted them with the more powerful plastic nightstick and flat headed slapjack. Some officers also substitute a large heavy duty flashlight for the nightstick . . . [since] . . . . If used correctly, the flashlight can inflict more damage than the baton and is less likely to break when applied to the head or other parts of the body.

(ibid)

Another difference between formal tuition and informal experience and instruction relates to actual street use of these weapons. At the academy, police are taught not to hit people on the head or neck for fear of causing their death. By way of contrast, they are taught, on the street, to hit wherever 'it causes the most damage in order to incapacitate the suspect before they themselves are harmed' (ibid). The respect of colleagues is earned not through observance of 'legal niceties' in using force, but by being 'aggressive' and using whatever force is necessary for a given situation.

Becoming a 'real street cop' involves learning to use normal force. Women rookies are said to encounter special problems in this process because, unlike their male counterparts who 'are assumed to be competent dispensers of force unless proven otherwise', they 'are believed to be physically weak, naturally passive, and emotionally vulnerable' (ibid). Consequently, opportunities to display their physical abilities in order to deal with such male bias and obtain full acceptance have to be created and exploited. This involves acting 'more aggressively' and displaying 'more machismo than male rookies' (ibid: 134).

The police account for their use of 'normal force' in two analytically distinguishable ways: the situational and the abstract. In situational accounts force is represented as responsive to situational specifics requiring a need to restore control and order and power. Abstract accounts 'justify force as a morally appropriate response to certain categories of crime and criminals who symbolize a threat to the moral order' (ibid: 136).

A central theme in the situational accounts is that of physical threat or harm to the police on the part of suspects: where the police are physically threatened or harmed then 'technically excessive' force is acceptable and desirable, that is 'normal'. Hunt offers an example of this in the form of a case where

an officer was punched in the face by a prisoner he had just apprehended for allegedly attempting to shoot a friend. The incident occurred in the stationhouse and several policemen observed the exchange. Immediately, one officer hit the prisoner in the jaw and the rest immediately joined the brawl.

(ibid)

This collective response was seen as 'normal'. A second theme of the situational accounts is that of the 'symbolic assault on the officer's authority and self'. From the perspective of the police those persons who verbally and symbolically challenge them are 'assholes' (Van Maanen 1978: 224) and therefore justify 'a forceful response to maintain control' (Hunt 1987: 136). Included in this category would be cases where a suspect violates an officer's property such as his or her police car or hat. Hunt reports the example of the suspect who was apprehended, cuffed and 'thrown' in the back of the police vehicle but who then had the audacity to run away with the police officer's property, that is the cuffs. The response is described as follows:

all of a sudden Susan [the police officer] looks up and sees her cuffs running away. She (Jane [– the other police officer]) said Susan turned into an animal. Susan runs up the steps grabs the girl by the legs. Drags her down the five steps. Puts her in the car. Kicks her in the car. Jane goes in the car and calls her every name she can think of and waves her stick in her face.

(ibid)

Female police officers often encounter special difficulties with respect to these symbolic threats to their authority. Some suspects, typically male, refuse to accord female officers the same respect and symbolic control they accord male officers; they are viewed as provoking confrontations by sexualizing the police–suspect encounter. Under these circumstances women officers justify force to rectify what are defined as 'insults' and to re-establish control.

In contrast to these 'instrumental' accounts which normalize force as a means for regaining control that has been symbolically or physically threatened the 'abstract' accounts justify force 'as an appropriate response to particularly heinous offenders' (ibid: 138). Such persons include 'cop haters who have gained notoriety as persistent police antagonizers', 'cop killers or any person who has attempted seriously to harm a police officer', 'sexual deviants who prey on children and "moral women"', 'child abusers', 'junkies and other "scum" who inhabit the street' (ibid). In contrast, those whom the police define as 'clean' criminals, including high-level members of the mafia, white-collar criminals, and professional burglars are rarely subjected to force. Nor are violent and non-violent predators of 'adult males, prostitutes, and other categories of persons who belong on the street'. These victimizers of the 'morally unworthy', like the 'psychos and the demented' who are 'so mentally deranged that' they are not responsible for their acts, are less likely to experience 'abstract, punitive force' (ibid).

These justifications in terms of abstract categorizations of persons invoke, from the police point of view, 'a higher moral purpose that legitimates the violation of commonly recognized standards' (ibid). It is an example of what Emerson (1969: 149) calls a 'principled justification' where 'one depicts the act as an attempt to realize some absolute moral or social value that has precedence over the value violated by the act' (cited in Hunt 1987: 138). Hunt offers as an example of this the following case:

> a nun was raped by a 17-year-old male adolescent. When the police apprehended the suspect, he was severely beaten and his penis put in an electrical outlet to teach him a lesson. The story of the event was told to me by a police officer who, despite the fact that he rarely supported the use of extralegal force, depicted this treatment as legitimate. Indeed, when I asked if he would have participated had he been present, he responded, 'I'm Catholic. I would have participated'.
>
> (ibid)

The permissive character of accounts with respect to the exercise of 'normal force' notwithstanding, police culture also provides a set of informal controls for exceptional and inappropriate police conduct. 'Technically excessive' force may be both circumstantially and abstractly justifiable but that does not mean that 'anything goes' (though it may sometimes mean precisely that). Rather, police culture contains definitions as to what constitutes 'excessive' force as far as the police themselves are concerned. Thus, firstly, 'Police recognize and honour some rough equations between the behaviour of the suspect and the harmfulness of the force to which it is subject. There are limits . . . to the degree of force that is acceptable in particular circumstances' (ibid). Cultural disapproval pertains to cases where 'symbolic assailants' (Skolnick 1975 (1966): 45) are 'mistakenly' subjected to 'more force than [they] "deserve"' (Hunt 1987: 138) (for example, killing a 'rude drunk'), where officers 'lose control' (for example, doing serious harm to a suspect whom the police officer regards as morally reprehensible, such as a child abuser) and where the officer engages in 'unnecessary' force such as fighting with 'crazy people' who make aggressive approaches to the police.

POLICE WORK AND THE MEANING OF OFFICIAL
STATISTICS

[T]he government are very keen on amassing statistics – they collect them, add them, raise them to the nth power, take the cube root and prepare wonderful diagrams. But what you must never forget is that every one of those figures comes in the first instance from the . . . [village watchman], who just puts down what he pleases.

(Stamp 1929: 258)

Josiah Stamp, who was not a symbolic interactionist, nor indeed a sociologist, captures here in a particularly colourful way a point that no serious practitioner of criminology would deny, whatever their sociological perspective. Indeed, criminal justice workers themselves, notably the police, are some of the strongest critics of the utility of official crime statistics as measures of the 'real' volume of crime, as teachers of criminology who have them as students can testify. When reference is made in the news media or elsewhere to 'crime statistics' what is meant is what police record as 'offences known to the police'. While the criminal justice system also counts convictions and the dispositions of offenders by sentence (fine, probation, prison, etc.) we will confine ourselves to the count known as 'offences known to the police' in what follows.

The errors to which crime statistics are prone are evident from the work we have discussed in the previous sections of this chapter. Thus:

1 Victims may not know they have been victimized. An employer or employee may be defrauded by the other and never discover it. Citizens may be 'disappeared' by the security forces of their country without those concerned about them ever knowing for sure.
2 Victims may never report alleged offences to the police for understandable reasons.
3 When reports are made the police may never record them as such. Officials in Canada and the United Kingdom have in recent years publicly acknowledged that police have standardly 'unfounded' about a third of reported rapes (*Globe and Mail* 4 October 1982, front page; Eglin 1987: 191). Bell (1960) revealed a practice employed by New York detectives of holding back complaints and reported.burglaries so as to reduce the

number of unsolved crimes. If a felon was apprehended, they were then more or less coerced into confessing to some number of this backlog of offences thereby allowing the police to clear their books (Duncan and Eglin 1979: 13).

4 In observing the 'sanctity of work shifts' and the 'division of department labour' police officers will ignore (i) perceived offences that occur as they are 'going in' at the end of a shift and (ii) offences that do not concern them, such as thefts they encounter while doing narcotics work (Turner 1969).

5 The selection of the category under which to record some reported or detected offence will vary with the administrative recording procedures of the jurisdiction in question (Silverman 1980).

6 Charging practices are also responsive to policy guidelines. The 1980s have seen a general increase in the number of charges of assault (causing bodily harm) laid by police in cases of wife beating, as departments have started to treat these occurrences as crimes (Burris and Jaffe 1986).

The vicissitudes of such guidelines are indicated, however, by a case being reported in the Canadian press as we write (*Kitchener-Waterloo Record* 7, 8, 9 May 1991). An emergency (911) operator received a call from a woman in the early hours of a Saturday morning which was aborted when she screamed and hung up. The operator, located in the police communications room, told the police dispatcher it sounded like a 'domestic' and gave the address. Operating in terms of their received wisdom about 'domestics' the police did not send a car at once, but tried to call the party back. Some 20 minutes later the woman called again to report she had been sexually assaulted (raped) by an intruder; the police sent a car.

Several days later Canadian Press reported (*Kitchener-Waterloo Record* 15 May 1991, p. B14) the case of Francine Turcotte-Berard who, according to Laval Police Chief Jean Marc-Aurèle, 'arrived at the police station at 3 p.m. last Tuesday and told the officer on duty she was afraid her former lover would hurt her'.

She talked to a police officer at the station for about 30 minutes. 'But she refused to give either her name or that of the man,' he said. 'Before she left the station, the officer told her to call 911 in the case of even the slightest sign of an emergency and he also gave her the means to protect herself. The officer even told

her he didn't think it was a good idea that she return to her
home . . . ' Berard did return to her home . . . At around 8 that
night she was shot in the head by a man who had taken her
hostage just minutes before.
(An ethnomethodological analysis of a related case is to be
found in Whalen *et al.* (1988))

Battered women . . . were usually not perceived as being in
dangerous situations. Women cried and shook with fear as they
told officers their husbands or lovers were going to hurt them.
But repeatedly officers responded with a 'call if anything
happens,' rather than giving them the immediate protection
they sought. Everything appeared to officers to be 'under
control' because they could see no visible signs of danger.
(Ferraro 1989: 69)

Ferraro (1989: 61) reports that in her ethnographic study of a
large US metropolitan police department where officers were
mandated to arrest batterers, 'officers made arrests in only 18
percent of assaults involving intimate partners'. On the basis of
considerable research evaluating 'progressive' policy changes by
the Metropolitan Police of London in 1987 relating to the police
response to domestics, Edwards (1990: 157) concludes that 'the
implementation of this policy has been variable depending on
individual divisions' and stations' within divisions willingness to
embrace the policy and translate it into practice, especially by front
line officers'.

The situation is further specified by the police practice of con-
ceptualizing offences in racial terms: 'If the family were white, the
police would take the offense more seriously. A stabbing by a white
woman of her husband suggests a potential homicide to police,
while a similar Black cutting can be written off as a "North
Westville battery"' (Skolnick 1975 (1966): 172). (A structural conflict explanation of the differential evaluation of persons in terms
of class, gender and race by the criminal justice system is set out in
Chapter 8.)

To talk, however, of the 'errors' to which official crime statistics
are subject is to miss the full import of the symbolic interactionist
critique. It is not just that for reasons such as the above police may
fail to detect the presumed 'real' amount of crime that is 'out
there'. That would be to subscribe to the 'realist' position discussed earlier in the chapter. Rather it is through their use of such

cultural beliefs and their orientation to such organizational imperatives as outlined above that police come to perceive and thereby to 'create' the offences they do end up dealing with. This is the force of the 'interpretivist' position. When followed through to its logical conclusion – and symbolic interactionists are not always consistent on this (see Eglin 1987: 207; Hargreaves *et al* 1975; Pollner 1974b) – it means that official crime statistics could not possibly be faulty. For they are no more and no less than what they are – 'a result of three-way *interaction* between an offender, victim or citizens [witnesses], and official agents' (Wheeler 1967: 319, emphasis added). They are above all – once the reporting activities of citizens have been taken into account – the record of the decision-making of the criminal justice personnel whose actions they represent. At bottom they reflect the volume and nature of police work (Stoddart 1982).

POLICING AND THE AMPLIFICATION OF CRIME: THE CONTRIBUTION OF LABELLING THEORY

In this book the concept of 'amplification' refers to the process of social interaction through which crime is made worse or 'amplified' by law enforcement. We shall be using the concept in two main ways. Firstly, we shall be examining how social control can amplify crime in the sense of increasing its apparent frequency and seriousness. Secondly, under the rubric of labelling theory we shall consider how social control can contribute to the onset of criminal identity and the building of deviant careers.

Social control and the amplification of crime

The concept of amplification was first used in the study of crime by Wilkins (1964). He used the concept to describe a social process whereby the consequences or 'feedback' of an action taken, say, to solve a problem, can in fact increase the problem. One of the earliest studies to consider this notion in the field of crime and deviance was that of Cohen (1972 (1980)) who in a now classic investigation of deviant youth subcultures in the 1960s showed how the endeavours of social control and the attendant publicity surrounding them not only exacerbated but transformed the problem to which they were directed. Thus, the 'mods' and the 'rockers' were, in the early stages of their development, two largely independent youth lifestyles. Though the proponents of these lifestyles dressed differently, had different musical tastes, different leisure activities and were symbolized by different modes of transport (the bike and the scooter), the early relationship was one of distance and disdain rather than overt conflict. Some small-scale fighting between the groups and the resulting vandalism at an English seaside resort in 1964 changed all that. The newspapers covered the story and characterized the events as 'gang warfare'. It became a 'hot' story to be pursued relentlessly by the media over the next couple of years. A 'moral panic' was set in motion in which the public and the guardians of its morality expressed and in a sense became obsessed with the imagined threat that these 'opposing' groups posed to social order. The result was that the differences between these two groups were increasingly attended to by the members themselves such that the character of membership changed. A *sine qua non* of membership became opposition to the other group. Consequently, greater violence between the groups occurred. The police expected it and at holiday time in the seaside resorts thousands of them were drafted in to 'prevent it'. Thousands of mods or rockers turned up expecting it too. The result was a self-fulfilling prophecy all round.

Similarly, Young (1971b) and Scull (1972) found the concept of amplification useful in understanding developments in the social control of illegal drugtaking in the late 1960s and early 1970s. To best understand these it is useful to consider a distinction made by Schur in his earlier work, *Narcotic Addiction in Britain and America* (1962). There he contrasts the 'British System' of narcotic control with that prevalent in North America. In the former case addiction to narcotics such as heroin and morphine was officially perceived largely as a 'health' problem; addicts to these drugs were registered with a physician who prescribed a maintenance weekly dose of the drug to which they were addicted. Two results of this system, says Schur, were a very small addict population, since addicts were not motivated to sell part of their supplies to obtain money to buy more drugs, and the non-existence of addiction-generated crime because addicts did not have to steal or prostitute themselves to obtain money to buy their drugs on the black market. The situation in North America was very different. There, addicts could only obtain their supplies on the black market. The results were large numbers of addicts and a massive, drug-related crime problem.

Things have not changed much in North America but several
events occurred which transformed the situation in the 'British
System' and which illustrate the utility of the concept of amplification in illuminating the connections between crime and social
control. Thus, in the mid-1960s the British authorities decided to
alter their method of drug distribution. They were ostensibly
alarmed by the prescribing practices of some physicians in private
practice who were seen to be taking advantage of the system and
not only prescribing more than maintenance dosage levels but also
prescribing to 'visiting' North Americans keen to avail themselves
of drugs in the liberal British climate of control. Henceforth
addicts were required to register not with their local physician but
at one of a few national clinics where they would be prescribed a
heroin substitute, methadone, as part of a programme of drug
withdrawal. The result was that almost overnight a black market for
the preferred 'real thing', that is, heroin and morphine, was
created and in just a few years' time Britain would be brought into
line in terms of the features of its drug-control system and the
connections between drugs and crime. By the early 1970s Britain,
too, had large numbers of addicts, a 'healthy' organized-crime
network dealing in drugs and a large drug-related crime problem.
    In the mid-1960s also there was a crackdown against the users of
soft drugs like marihuana and LSD. Users of these drugs regarded
themselves as members of a different social world of drug use from
that of the 'hard' drug addicts. However, a moral panic about drug
use at this time led the police to harass drug users indiscriminately.
The resulting large numbers of arrests fuelled the panic and led to
a tougher crackdown. What had been a largely peripheral activity
now became a symbol of the kind of person the soft drug user was,
someone who belonged to a group whose interests were opposed
to those of conventional society. They shifted from being a 'subculture' to being a 'counter-culture'. More than this, the earlier
ideological barriers against hard drugs began to break down and
the community of interest *vis-à-vis* the police and courts became
ever more evident. By the early 1970s the 'drug problem' had been
amplified in two senses: firstly, soft drug users had been
increasingly alienated from conventional society and their
commitment to an 'alternative' lifestyle deepened, and secondly,
increasingly large numbers of previously soft drug users had
developed a willingness to try hard drugs. The result was that many
did, in fact, go on to become addicted.

Labelling theory, amplification and the social process of becoming deviant

There is now a wealth of literature under the title of 'labelling theory'. We cannot review it all here (see Plummer 1979, 1991). The most prominent labelling statements are those by Lemert (1948, 1951, 1964, 1967 (1972), 1974, 1976), Kitsuse (1962), Becker (1963, 1973) and Matza (1969). Erikson's (1962) account is problematic in so far as it is wedded to a structural consensus position derived from Durkheim; we discuss it in Chapter 12. The basic proposition of labelling theory is that 'social control leads to deviance [including crime]' (Lemert 1967: v; cited in Box (1981: 19)). This occurs, it is argued, because the person labelled as criminal internalizes that label and comes to see him or herself as essentially criminal, and because social control creates for the person so labelled certain problems whose solution is the commission of further criminal acts.

In keeping with our discussion of symbolic interactionism in Chapter 1 we should point out that labelling theory is a retrospective construction of what is a melange of related positions. Partly for this reason Plummer (1979) prefers the title, 'the labelling perspective'. Thus the expression 'leads to' in the basic proposition advanced above has been construed by practitioners and critics both (1) interpretively – that is, as making the 'constitutive' claim that 'the social control reaction or labelling *constitutes* a given behaviour as deviant/criminal' – and (2) deterministically – that is, as making the 'causal' claim that 'the social control reaction or labelling *causes* deviant behaviour'. It is not our purpose to resolve this dilemma here. For now we simply adopt the first position, postponing further discussion until Chapter 10. It remains true, however, that in the matter that immediately concerns us, namely the acquiring of a deviant identity, analysts do not always make explicit just what position they are taking on the nature of the connection between labelling and identity acquisition.

Even though labelling theory is symbolic interactionism applied to the problem of deviant identity and behaviour, it is probably best to locate its origins in the early work of Lemert (1948, 1951) who is only 'reservedly' a symbolic interactionist (Plummer 1979: 87). He was responsible for a conceptual distinction between two kinds of deviation: primary and secondary deviation. These were not only qualitatively distinct, they also originated in different ways. Primary deviation refers to occasional or initial deviation which is normalized, that is explained away as part of what Lemert calls 'normal variation'. We all commit the odd deviant act now and again for a wide variety of social, psychological, biological and no doubt other reasons but we do not think of ourselves as essentially deviant; the fact that we may have done something wrong, perhaps even illegal, is not, for us, the most central feature of our identity or our lives in general. The secondary deviants, on the other hand, not only centre their lives around the facts of their deviance, they also consider themselves to be a deviant kind of person. Their deviance *is* the most central or organizing feature of their identity. Furthermore, what labelling theory directs our attention to is the role played by the labelling carried out by agencies of social control in the onset of the identity change which is definitive of the secondary deviant. Social control creates problems such as community rejection, stigmatization, discrimination, economic difficulties and police surveillance; the solution for these problems may be found in the commission of further deviant acts. It is in that sense that the deviance becomes 'secondary', that is, a deviant response to social reactions to earlier deviant behaviour.

Perhaps the most sophisticated statement of the labelling process and its role in the process of becoming deviant is to be found in the work of Matza (1969). He describes four 'stages' in the process of social interaction between the deviant and the agencies of social control, the first two of which are relevant here.

The process of becoming deviant begins with the problem of 'ban and transparency'. This is the first stage and refers to the fact that those who engage in behaviour prohibited or 'banned' by the state encounter problems of keeping their behaviour secret. They will face the problem of concealment and the related anxiety that others will 'see through' their attempts to 'cover up' their misdemeanours. Matza argues that this may be sufficient to give the deviant 'identity doubts' in the sense that if they 'are only playing at being normal, then who or what are they really?' This is a first step on a path leading to identity change.

The second stage is referred to as 'apprehension and labelling'. It is at this point that the offender is arrested and treated in accordance with the routines and conventions which social controllers employ for dealing with 'criminals'. Not only is the offender 'registered' as an alleged criminal, they are typically derogated and treated as representatives of that category of offender for which their offence qualifies them for membership. Most importantly, it is at this stage that the person loses that 'blissful' identity of being one who, amongst other things, happened to have committed an offence (for example, a theft). For all practical organizational purposes that person, whatever else he or she may be, is first and foremost a 'thief'. If the person had any identity doubts at the ban and transparency stage, they would most certainly be exacerbated at this one.

For some, the social process of becoming deviant may stop at this point, but for others it may not. For those that continue there will be ever heavier matters of social identity to consider and greater problems of social control to contend with. As the offender 'progresses' deeper into the world of social control the chances that he or she will undergo identity-transformation increase, not least because of the problems created by social reaction to their criminal offences. The next stages in the process are incarceration and post-prison stigmatization. We shall return to these matters in Chapter 11.

POLICING THE MYTHS OF CRIME

We saw earlier how symbolic interactionists have shown that the police operate with their own theories of crime and criminals. They use these theories in making decisions about the deployment of resources, whether to take citizens' complaints seriously, and the dispositions of alleged offenders. When these theories are compared with the findings of naturalistic research, that is, re-search which seeks to remain faithful to the nature of 'crime' as it appears to, and is organized by, 'criminals' themselves, marked discrepancies become evident. Much of the time the police appear to be operating with convenient myths about crime which bear little resemblance to the reality of 'crime' as it is experienced by its practitioners. This seems to be at least partly a reflection of admin-istrative policy which itself may reflect the political accommo-dation of police organizations to the demands of their paymasters. We do not mean to suggest that seasoned police officers do not possess rich knowledge of their domains. Rather we mean that policy concerning where and against whom to enforce the law implies certain images of crime which diverge from the 'social reality' of crime as experienced by 'criminals' themselves. This is evident in a number of cases including those of theft (ordinary theft as opposed to the 'theft' built into the structure of property relations in capitalist society), police crime ('bad apple theory' and the 'dirty harry problem') and crimes of interpersonal violence (the image of violent crime as occurring in public between strangers rather than in private between those known to each other – particularly applicable in the cases of violence against women (Chapter 2). Here, however, we elect to examine the police myths pertaining to the 'drug problem'. This is an area where there has been a degree of overlap between symbolic interactionist and structural conflict studies. We remain with the findings of more interactionist work, but recommend at the end of this section a structural conflict study which brings out the ideological functions of police myths about crime.

In Chapter 2 we distinguished two models of drug effects, namely the cultural model and the medical or pharmacological model. According to the latter, chemical stimuli are assumed to produce standard behavioural responses. In the former model, however, responses to chemical stimuli are shaped by the intermediating influence of culture. Present-day policy on alcohol and drug abuse is grounded in the tenets of the pharmacological model, and as such is reproduced in the everyday practices of police. There it is combined with two further mythical notions about the social world of drug use (cf. Blackwell and Erickson 1988: 131–138). The first of these is the distinction between the pusher or trafficker and the user. The second is the myth of drug progression.

The distinction between the drug user and the drug trafficker is at the core of present-day policies both in Europe and in North America. It underpins both the American and Canadian 'war on drugs'. The claim made in this distinction is that the drug supplier is an entirely different category of person from the drug user, often identified as a 'victim' while the pusher or trafficker is the real 'evil doer'. Except for the topmost levels of trafficking where money and the expensive lifestyle it affords is the prime motivation for drug dealing, this distinction is very misleading. Thus, one of the most well-established findings of naturalistic sociological research on drug use is that users tend to be supplied by their friends who are also users of that same drug. The rather distant relationship of consumer and supplier, common in the social world of legal trade and business, tends to be the exception rather than the rule in the social world of drug use. The motivation for supplying others is typically to cut the costs of, and perhaps make a profit from, one's own drugtaking.

Part of the pusher–user myth is the claim that pushers persuade others to become drugtakers. This again may be very misleading. As Becker (1953), Matza (1969) and others have shown, persons willingly enter into drug use through a process of affiliation in which they actively, as Box (1981) puts it, weigh the costs and rewards from their contemplated course of action. Metaphors of contagion, enslavement and shame are inappropriate for describing a process in which anyone may become a drug user but no one has to. In any case, such is the demand for illegal drugs that it is unnecessary for drug pushers to seek out innocent victims.

If these myths have been shown to be false by serious social scientific research it may be asked why they persist. One answer is that it is not necessary for social control policy in general and police practice in particular to be based on social scientific accuracy and fidelity to the nature of social reality. What is important is that those responsible for law enforcement in this society be seen to be doing a 'good job' at protecting the rest of us from the criminals. In pursuing that mythical creature the drug pusher the police can be seen to be 'doing something' about the 'problem' and so we may have renewed confidence in their pro- tective role in society. Even though, in the long run, the policy will be ineffective it does, for the present, serve an important social function.

A second myth perpetrated by the social control of drugs in society is the 'progression' hypothesis. This is the claim that the use of one drug leads inexorably to the use of other drugs. The direction of this progression is from the 'soft' drugs like marihuana to the harder drugs like cocaine and heroin. Drugs are treated as 'all of a piece', all part of 'one world of drug use'. This is a gross oversimplification of the social reality of drugtaking. Thus, it has consistently been shown by naturalistic researchers that there is a wide variety of worlds of drug use and that there exist definite barriers between them. These barriers may take the form of 'ideological supports' for a particular kind of drug and 'ideo-logical opposition' to others. In the 1960s and 1970s, for example, users of soft drugs such as marihuana or psychedelic drugs such as LSD or mescaline were typically not only disinterested but also opposed to the use of 'addictive' drugs like heroin and morphine.

The conflation of drug users into one big social world and the failure to recognize the distinctions which users themselves make has had several rather significant consequences. These have been discussed by symbolic interactionists under the rubric of the concept of 'amplification' which we examined earlier. To appreciate the larger ideological functions of police myths about crime readers should turn to the structural conflict analysis provided by Hall *et al.* (1978).

Chapter 6

The ethnomethodology of policing

In this chapter we shall consider, firstly, from an ethnomethodological perspective, the relation between identifications of crime and members' methods of membership categorization. Secondly, we shall review ethnomethodological studies of the use, by the police, of social knowledge and interpretive procedures in accomplishing the variety of tasks constituting the work of policing: Pollner on identifying crime, Sacks on identifying suspects, Bittner on making arrests in the context of peace-keeping and Watson on police interrogations.

MEMBERSHIP CATEGORIZATION AND THE IDENTIFICATION OF CRIME

Symbolic interactionists have shown that crime is a matter of definition (by the law), interpretation (by the courts) and selection (by the police). In the last chapter we considered the symbolic interactionist perspective in relation to policing. We showed how this approach has generated a body of work, a major focus of which has been on police decision-making as it is involved in identifying crime. In this chapter we continue to focus on the identification of crime but from an ethnomethodological point of view.

From both the symbolic-interactionist and the ethnomethodological perspectives, crime is regarded as a matter of definition or interpretation. The resources for defining or interpreting crime have been variously conceptualized in such studies. They include 'common-sense knowledge', 'particularized knowledge', 'typifications', 'interpretive procedures', 'mundane reason' and 'definitions of the situation', amongst others. There are, as we have suggested, important differences between symbolic interactionist and ethnomethodological approaches. Symbolic interactionists have tended to produce 'decontextualized' accounts of these processes, whilst ethnomethodologists have preferred to examine the particulars of their localized, *in-situ* production, and symbolic interactionists tend to treat as resources items which ethnomethodologists prefer to examine as topics. However, both of these types of inquiry have relied upon common sense, practical knowledge, in finding instances of 'definitions' and 'interpretations' for study. So, before describing some ethnomethodological studies of police work we wish to draw attention to an ironic feature both symbolic interactionism and ethnomethodology share in relation to this topic. The irony is apparent in that even though these studies have investigated how the police define and interpret crime, they have neglected a fundamental interpretive issue, namely how interpretations or definitions of crime are identified in the first place. This issue is important for two reasons: (1) it is a 'methodological' problem for the sociological researcher in the sense that if he or she is to investigate 'interpretations of crime' then some practical solution to the problem of locating instances of this phenomenon for study must be achieved; (2) it is also a problem for the 'definers of crime'. The crime-definers must be able to produce and recognize crime-defining activities if they are to coordinate their work. For both researcher and participant in the crime definition enterprise the problem is how to produce interpretations recognizably or, in Garfinkel's (1967) sense, 'accountably', that is 'observably–reportably'.

In the first part of this chapter, then, we shall be describing some methods for producing and recognizing identifications of, or more specifically, references to crime. The significance of these methods is that the intelligibility of identifications of crime and therefore of criminology as a discipline depend upon them. Unless persons are able to produce recognizable references to crime and unless those who interact with them can recognize them as references to crime, then intelligible talk about, and action in relation to, crime would be impossible. Jayyusi (1984: 3), pointing to the domain of the sociology of deviance as comprising 'the morally displayed and premised descriptions of persons by other persons (either "lay" persons or "officials")', has made a similar point:

> Indeed, the very sociological term 'deviant' is a normative description of members produced by, and incorporated or

presupposed within, the corpus of sociological work. 'Labelling theory' attempts to address the process of labelling someone 'deviant'. However, the categorization 'deviant' obscures the very diverse procedures, implications and consequences behind the production, use, display and practical intelligibility of various categorizations subsumed by that sociological rubric: murderer, marijuana user, prostitute, alcoholic, child molester, etc.

(Jayyusi 1984: 3)

We therefore show how studies of the identification of crime involve members' methods of membership categorization for recognizing identifications of, or references to, crime. Thus, if the sociologist is to study crime as it is identified then she/he will have to make use of methods for making identifications intelligible, that is accountable phenomena. These methods involve the use of members' knowledge of acts, actors and their contexts, organized, in ethnomethodological terms, as membership categorization devices, membership categories and category predicates. Thus, 'arresting', 'judging', 'punishing', 'stealing', etc., are only intelligible in the light and use of 'what everybody knows' about 'crime'. The intelligibility of these activities depends upon this knowledge which, we argue, can be analysed as an organization of members' methods of membership categorization.

A convenient source of data which we shall use in order to examine the production and recognition of intelligible references to crime consists of newspaper headlines about crime. Newspapers routinely contain numerous reports on the latest crimes to be reported and dealt with by the police and the courts. We (and readers generally) have no trouble in understanding them as reports about crime and the consequent activities of the law enforcers.

However, our suggestion here is that the apparent ease with which we recognize them as such reports rests upon our unnoticed use of certain sense-making methods or interpretive procedures. Such methods are the focus of ethnomethodology. We shall be concentrating our attention on the following headline:

MOTHER CHARGED IN DEATH OF CHILD

The conceptual framework for membership categorization analysis of this headline is derived from the work of Harvey Sacks

(1967, 1972a, 1974), Watson (1976, 1978, 1983) and others on 'membership categorization' (Eglin and Hester 1992, forthcoming). From this work we shall be using four main concepts: membership category, membership categorization device, rule of application and category predicate.

Membership categories

Membership categories are classifications or social types which are used to describe persons. This is perhaps an unnecessary limitation on the scope of the concept. It would seem possible and reasonable to speak of both 'personal' and 'non-personal' membership categories. Examples of personal membership categories include 'mother', 'father', 'son', 'daughter', 'hippie', 'hell's angel', 'athlete', 'scholar', 'geriatric', 'lunatic', 'bore', etc. Examples of non-personal membership categories are 'baseball bat', 'geranium', 'draught guinness', 'BMW', 'rocking chair' and 'apple tree'.

Membership categorization devices or 'category collections'

Membership categories, both personal and non-personal, are linked together to form 'natural collections' or 'membership categorization devices' which Sacks described as

> any collection of membership categories, containing at least a category, which may be applied to some population containing at least a member, so as to provide, by the use of some rules of application, for the pairing of at least a population member and a categorization device member. A device is then a collection plus rules of application.
>
> (Sacks 1974: 218)

The idea that membership categories form 'collections' refers to the fact that certain membership categories can be heard and are common-sensically assumed to 'go naturally together'. An example of a membership categorization device is 'family', a device which, on the one hand, collects or subsumes membership categories such as 'father', 'mother', 'son', 'daughter', 'uncle', 'aunt', etc., but on the other hand excludes categories such as 'footballer', 'police officer' and 'fascist', for example, in the sense that they do not naturally, that is common-sensically, 'go together'.

Of course, what may be a category within a device may, at another *level*, be a device in its own right in the sense that it, in turn, may subsume a further collection of categories. The category 'child', for example, may not only be a member of the device 'family' or 'stage of life' (Sacks 1974) but may also, in its own right, be a device which collects such categories as 'boy', 'girl', or depending on context, 'good child', 'bad child', 'clever child', 'stupid child', etc. Similarly, the device 'family' may, in its turn, become a category in a 'larger' device such as 'human groups' or 'domestic arrangements'. There is, then, a branching texture pertaining to the organization of membership categories such that a particular category may be alternately device or category depending on the context of use.

There are also categories which go together in what Sacks calls 'standardized relational pairs', some of which are also elements in membership categorization devices. For example, 'husband–wife' is such a pair and also belongs in the 'family' membership categorization device. Other pairs are related to different devices. For example, 'doctor–patient' bears a (problematic) relationship to the device which Sacks calls 'K' (for knowledge) comprising the two categories 'professionals' and 'laypersons'.

Rules of application: the economy and consistency rules

The 'rules of application' in relation to membership categories are the 'economy rule' and the 'consistency rule'. The economy rule provides for the adequacy of using a single membership category to describe a member of some population. Sacks (1974: 219) puts it this way: 'a single category from any membership categorization device can be referentially adequate'. This does not mean that more than one category cannot be used, it simply means that in making reference to persons, and to be recognized as having made such reference, a single category will suffice. The second rule of application, the consistency rule, holds: 'if some population of persons is being categorized, and if a category from some device's collection has been used to categorize a first member of the population, then that category or other categories from the same collection may be used to categorize further members of the population' (Sacks 1974: 219). This means, for example, that if a first person has been categorized as a 'goalkeeper', then further persons in the population being described may be referred to by that category or other categories of a collection of which they and 'goalkeeper' are co-members. In the context of the collection 'soccer players', for example, the other categories which are relevant, given the use of 'goalkeeper', are 'centre forward', 'midfield player', 'full back', etc.

Sacks also identified a 'corollary', or 'hearer's maxim' formulation, of the consistency rule. The hearer's maxim holds the following: 'if two or more categories are used to categorize two or more members of some population, and those categories can be heard as categories from the same collection, then: hear them that way' (Sacks 1974: 219–20). The now famous example in Sacks's work is the child's story beginning, 'the baby cried, the mommy picked it up'. Here, using the hearer's maxim or, more technically, the 'consistency-rule corollary', the two categories 'baby' and 'mommy' which are used to categorize the two persons may be, and are routinely and common-sensically, heard as both belonging to the collection 'family' (and, by virtue of the duplicative organization property, as belonging to the *same* family).

Category predicates

The final aspect of Sacks's conceptual framework which is used here is that of 'category-boundedness' or 'category predication'. Sacks speaks in particular about 'category-bound activities'. These are activities which are expectably and properly done by persons who are the incumbents of particular categories when those categories are drawn from certain collections or devices. Subsequent researchers have extended Sacks's work in this area. Jayyusi (1984), Payne (1976), Sharrock (1974), Hester (1992) and Watson (1978, 1983), for example, have all observed that category-bound activities are just one class of predicates which 'can conventionally be imputed on the basis of a given membership category' (Watson 1978: 106). Other predicates include rights, expectations, obligations, knowledge, attributes and competences.

The 'steps' in membership categorization analysis

These concepts are deployed by ethnomethodologists in investigating the intelligibility of talk and action. There is a simple three-step procedure in membership categorization analysis. Firstly, identify some description. This may be contained in some piece of conversation or, as is the case here, a newspaper headline. Secondly, record, that is write down, the ordinary or common sense which you, as the identifier of the description or reader of the headline, make of the description or headline. What does it mean to you? Thirdly, examine your interpretation of the description or headline by asking what methods of membership categorization did you employ.

Analysing 'mother charged in death of child'

Turning then to the headline, 'Mother charged in death of child', and following the procedural steps listed above, we may note that our 'common sense' reading of this report is that a mother has been charged by the police as having killed her child. This is our interpretation which we shall now subject to membership categorization analysis.

Clearly, not everything in our reading is 'contained' in the text of the headline so the headline is not all that we have to work with in reaching our reading. Beyond the headline itself lies our common-sense knowledge of society; we bring this knowledge to bear upon the headline and are, as it were, able to 'go beyond the information given' and 'fill in' the 'missing' information. Our question then concerns the character of this knowledge and its use in arriving at our interpretations of descriptions as descriptions of 'crime'. We can observe at least three things: firstly, that the headline does not say in so many words that the mother is the mother of the child in question and yet we hear her as such; secondly, the headline does not say that the mother was charged by the police but we assume that she was so charged; thirdly, it is not explicitly stated that the mother 'killed' her child, yet that is what seems obvious. How then do we arrive at these interpretations?

Using the consistency rule

We can begin by noting that this headline contains explicit reference to two membership categories: 'mother' and 'child'. These are recognized as being related in that the mother is *the* mother of the child; it is *her* child. This reading is made possible by the consistency rule corollary or 'hearer's maxim', outlined above. That is to say, if two categories, used to describe some population, can be heard as belonging to the same membership categorization device or collection then hear them that way. The headline could have been referring to 'any' mother and 'any' child. A 'mother' could have just happened to have killed someone else's child but our interpretive predilections do not make this a sensible option. We take it for granted, at least unless or until other considerations lead us to doubt it, that the 'obvious' relationship between these two membership categories or persons is *the* relationship.

The orientation to category predicates

A second observation is that the headline does not say that the mother was charged by the 'police' but we hear it that way. This is because of our orientation to category predicates. For us, 'charging' is an activity which is bound to or is predicated of such membership categories. When we read of charging there are, theoretically at least, several possibilities. The mother might have been charged in a number of senses: (1) she was asked to pay a certain price for the death of a (her) child; (2) she was being obliged to kill a (her) child; (3) she was being put under the supervision of another person in connection with a (her) child's death; (4) she was subject to someone's or something's violent rush forwards in connection with a death of a (her) child; (5) she enjoyed some thrill or pleasurable feeling at the death of a (her) child. We do not, it seems, interpret the meaning of 'charged' in this headline in any of these ways. We assume it means 'charged by the police' because charging is something properly and expectably done by the police. The orientation to category predicates permits the inference that the reference to 'charged' is a description of an activity done by the police to an offender and not, say, a reference to the activities of an animal renowned for such behaviour or to one of the other meanings of charged mentioned above. This is because there is an inferential relationship between membership categories and their predicates. It is possible to infer a category from a predicate. Thus, to describe someone as having obeyed may permit the inference that they are a 'servant' or a 'slave', even a 'worker'; to describe someone as 'getting a divorce' permits the inference that they are incumbents of the membership category 'married person'; to say of someone that they 'issued a prescription' implies that they belong to membership category 'doctor'. In the context of our headline we can infer a membership category, namely 'police', from the mention of the activity 'charge' because 'charging' is something this category of persons typically does; it is an activity which is bound to or predicated of this membership category, so that mention of the activity provides for the common-sense inference that this is charging done by the police in relation to some alleged offence. Furthermore, it may be observed that 'police' and 'charge', as membership category and predicate, 'mutually elaborate each other' in that not only are we able to infer 'police' from 'charged' but we can also achieve a sense of 'charged' from 'police'.

The orientation to 'standardized relational pairs', co-selection and the mutual elaboration of categories and predicates

The word 'charged' is not the only resource in this headline which, via the orientation to category predicates, is available for reckoning that the police are a relevant membership category and hence that this is a report about crime. It is possible to achieve a sense of 'charged' as 'charged by the police' by considering our common-sense presuppositions of the other words in the headline. This, we suggest, reveals the operation of some further 'methods of practical reasoning' for making the headline an intelligible description of the activities of the police in relation to a crime.

Firstly, we suggest that in the interpretation of any description we make use of the principle of 'co-selection':

> One general method or procedure available to members is to hear words as collections or co-selections. That is to say, members can hear any word as a co-selection with the words which precede and follow it. The parts of an utterance can be heard as mutually constitutive in that how any part is heard can depend upon, among other things, how other parts are heard. It is the speaking and hearing of words as co-selections which helps to constitute situations to be observably what they are.
>
> (Payne 1976: 35)

Speakers and hearers, then, assume that words are consistently co-selected. This means that it is taken for granted that words are not chosen randomly or incoherently but instead are selected because they cohere and are consistent with each other. They are designed to 'go together' as selections which inform or mutually elaborate the meaning of each other. In terms of the consistency

rule the co-selected items composing the description are heard to
go together, if they can be heard that way.

In accomplishing a sense of the word 'charged' as being
'charged by the police', the method of co-selection 'works' not
only in conjunction with the 'orientation to category predicates'
which we have already described above but also with a method
called the 'orientation to "standardized relational pairs"' (Sacks
1972a: 37). Payne describes this method in the following way: 'In
our culture, certain categories are routinely recognized as paired
categories, and the pairing is recognized to incorporate standardized relationships of rights, obligations and expectations' (Payne
1976: 36). These standardized relational pairs include not only the
intimate pairings of 'husband–wife', 'parent–child', 'girlfriend–
boyfriend', etc., but also those relevant in certain 'institutional'
settings, such as doctor–patient, lawyer–client, master–slave,
teacher–pupil, shopkeeper–customer, victim–offender, judge–
defendant and police officer–offender or criminal. Each member
of these pairings implies the other so that mention of the one
makes relevant the other. If, in some stretch of talk, reference is
made to one member of the pair and if mention is made of
another person who could be heard as the incumbent of a category
paired with the first then, in line with the consistency rule, 'hear it
that way'.

Just as membership categories are relationally paired so also are
their predicates. Examples of this include the buying and selling in
the customer–shopkeeper relationship and the teaching and
learning in the teacher–student pairing. Furthermore, predicates
may 'stand for' their relationally paired membership categories
such that through a substitution procedure a category may be
implied by or inferred from mention of the predicate of a category
with which it is paired or vice versa. Thus, to say of someone that
they have been 'arrested' permits the inference that this has been
performed by a 'law enforcer' and that they, therefore, belong to
the category 'offender'.

Category-bound activities of this sort, then, may be said to be
done by incumbents of a particular category to the incumbents of
categories with which they are 'relationally paired'. In particular,
in the case of the membership category 'police', 'charging' is
relationally paired with 'offending', an activity bound to the membership category 'offender'. If there is reference to such a paired
category then our sense of 'charging' as an activity performed by

the police can be confirmed. Though there is no direct reference to an 'offender' it is possible to hear the mother as such by virtue of the 'death'. Thus, killing is an offence for which 'charging' is a properly and expectably paired next action. Charging and killing are activities bound to the membership categories, police officers and offenders, respectively. Charging, furthermore, is done *because* of the offence; the one action led to the other. The offence (killing) is a motivational predicate of the police officer's charge.

Clearly, if the production and recognition of a reference to, or identification of, 'crime' in the context of a newspaper headline is a matter of interpretive procedures and the use of members' knowledge, then so also will the production and recognition of references to, and action towards, crime in the context of law enforcement. The intelligibility of such actions as 'reporting a crime', 'identifying a suspect', 'arresting', 'releasing', 'charging', etc., will depend upon similar courses of practical reasoning involving membership categories, membership categorization devices and category predicates. Conversely, categories, devices, rules of application and predicates will be used in recognizing that 'crime' is not taking place or that witnessed activities are not being carried out by incumbents of the category 'police'. Thus, as a case in point, Sacks describes a scene where:

> a car pulls up and stops. It doesn't seem to stop anywhere special, just pulls up and stops on a street. The door opens and a girl of about 18 charges out, runs across a lawn and stops, and starts shrieking. In the front seat are an older man and woman. The guy jumps out of the car, charges across the lawn, comes up to the girl and gives her a smack right in the face. At which point some of the passing cars slam on their brakes, and some people start getting out of their cars.
> The man and the girl stand there, face to face, screaming at each other, and then he just grabs her and drags her back to the car. And people look at each other, shrug, and say, 'Oh well,' get back in their cars and go on their way.
>
> (Sacks 1989: 344)

The initial categorization of these events as involving a 'crime' turned on the use of the category 'kidnapper'. However, when it became 'apparent' that this woman and man were members of the device 'family' the scene became re-categorized as a 'family quarrel' rather than a crime or kidnapping.

With the exception of Sacks's seminal suggestions, however, it has to be recognized that most ethnomethodologists who have examined 'crime as a matter of interpretation and practical reasoning' have not examined the intelligibility of the activities comprising 'identifying crime' or 'doing references to crime' or 'describing deviance'. They have instead directed their attention to such matters as how the police themselves 'identify', 'describe' and 'refer to' crime as if these activities were unproblematic.

Having clarified the procedural character of the intelligibility of 'identifications of', 'references to' and 'descriptions of' 'crime', we are now in a position to consider some examples of ethnomethodological studies which have examined how the police identify crime.

ETHNOMETHODOLOGY AND THE IDENTIFICATION OF CRIME

With respect to police 'identifications of crime' and their 'interpretive procedures' we shall consider the work of Pollner, Sacks, Bittner and Watson.

Pollner: the police as mundane reasoners

Our exposition of the role of mundane reasoning in the criminalization process will be developed fully in Chapter 10. At this juncture we shall confine ourselves to introducing its central proposition, namely that mundane reason refers to the use of the assumption that 'crime' exists as a 'real' and 'objective' feature of the social world, one that is *not* a matter of 'subjective' interpretation. As Pollner puts it:

> The mundane model conceptualizes the deviance of an act as existing independently of a community's response. It implicitly posits that certain acts are (or ought to be) responded to in particular ways because they are 'deviant', that is, their 'deviance' is defined by criteria other than the fact that you or I happen to regard or experience the act as deviant.
>
> (Pollner 1987: 91)

Such a 'mundane' conception of crime is evident in the following remarks of a senior police officer:

A judge's decision to throw out charges laid during the Uniroyal Goodrich strike last year could have serious implications for future labor disputes in Waterloo Region, Deputy Police Chief Fred Mazurek said Friday. Mazurek said in an interview he is concerned that 'one of the worst strikes in our history' hasn't been perceived with the seriousness it warrants. He said it's probably that people prone to unlawful conduct at a strike might now get the idea that they can get away with it.

(*Kitchener-Waterloo Record* 13 October 1990, p. B1)

In this extract, then, what is of interest is how the police chief makes use of a distinction between the 'serious' and 'unlawful' character of the conduct of some strikers and the judicial response to that conduct. The police chief is suggesting, indeed assuming, that these features of the conduct exist even though the judge did not conceive of them in these terms. Clearly, then, from the police chief's point of view, for something to be 'unlawful' it is not crucial that a judge finds it so; rather its unlawfulness exists independently of judicial response. It is thus against some pre-existing judgment of seriousness and unlawfulness that a judge's actions may themselves be judged as inadequate. Judges, in this view, do not constitute crime in their judicial work, rather they merely respond to its already existing criminal character. This is mundane reasoning *par excellence*: it presumes some independent factual domain of criminality against which human perceptions can either correctly or incorrectly correspond.

This mundane model is evident again in the chief's reference to persons getting the idea that they can 'get away with it'. If crime were simply a matter of definition (constituted in social reaction) then until some agent of law enforcement showed up and 'laid down the law' then nobody would be getting away with anything. They would simply be engaging in activity which might conceivably, potentially, be defined as crime. But then anything can. However, within a world in which actions already have meanings (even though they have not had them attributed to them) people can be described as getting away with them. Even though they have not been caught, they are really guilty. This is the essence of mundane thought: guilt exists independently of the legal process through which it is decided.

It would, of course, be exceedingly difficult for the police, the lawyers and the judges to do their jobs with anything other than a mundane model of crime. It is perhaps a functional necessity that they act in what some might call 'bad faith'; they might otherwise only be pursuing the figments of their own imagination. What Pollner is suggesting is that perhaps this is precisely what they are doing anyway, even though through their assumptions about 'real' crime they have obscured their 'reality constructing' work from themselves.

Sacks: the police assessment of moral character

Given the assumption that crime exists independently of the methods for its recognition the practical problem for those charged with its identification then becomes how to detect it. Sacks's concern is with the methods used by the police on patrol 'for inferring from appearances such a probability of criminality as warrants the treatment of search and arrest' (Sacks 1972b: 281). In other words, Sacks is interested in how the police figure that persons are 'suspicious' and therefore warrant police action. In the interests of efficiency, the police require some method that will allow them to 'maximize the likelihood that those who will turn out to be criminals and who pass in view are selected, while minimizing the likelihood that those who would not turn out to be criminals and who pass in view are selected' (ibid: 282–283). From appearances, the police must predict successful searches and arrests.

There are, according to Sacks, two main components to their method of operation in this matter. The first is the organization of their field of operation as a 'territory of normal appearances'. The second is the 'incongruity procedure'. The concept of the 'territory of normal appearances' refers to the acquisition through experience of a set of expectations and a body of knowledge as to how any particular locale within the police officer's territory or 'beat' appears at particular times of the day or night. With reference, for example, to 2 a.m. in a certain downtown street the police officer would expect certain types of people to pass in view, perhaps, depending on the precise neighbourhood, delivery persons, taxi drivers, all-night clubbers, winos, prostitutes, business persons on their way home from their offices, street vendors, etc. Such persons would be engaging in the activities typical of them in this location. Likewise the police officer develops knowledge and expectations as to what is *not* typical of the area. Much of this knowledge, pertaining to both typical presences and absences is taken for granted, perceptually ingrained as an integral feature of the day's work.

Asked to describe a particular territory at a particular time and the police officer would have difficulty in articulating everything that he or she 'knows' about it but if something was 'out of place', unusual or incongruous then it would be thrown into perceptual relief. This is what Sacks means by the concept of the 'incongruity procedure'. It is a practice through which the atypical for a given territory stands out against the background of what is normal and typical. Poor people in rich neighbourhoods at times of the day that are 'inappropriate', rich people in poor neighbourhoods under similar conditions, persons equipped with 'unusual' objects, persons whose age does not correspond to what is typical for an activity or territory and, of course, persons who treat the presence of the police as something other than unremarkable and normal (though it must be remembered that the 'seasoned' criminal may be quite adept at 'passing' for normal, hence posing a major perceptual difficulty for the police). Whatever the precise details the procedure is similar, the police being attuned to their territory in a mode of typicality such that the atypical or incongruous is observable and, possibly, grounds for suspicion, surveillance and even stopping, searching and questioning. As we will see in the next chapter such an interactional event can itself generate typical and routine responses on the part of the police officer. We should note, too, that ethnomethodologists have paid attention to members' use of location as an interactional device across a number of settings. For a review see Eglin (1980).

Bittner: the police on skid row

Given their use of some generalized methods for identifying potential criminality, with what attitude do police approach their task? In particular, given that the great bulk of police work is taken up not with law enforcement *per se* but with peace keeping, 'how do the police decide what is their business in cases where they do not arrest, and how do those considerations affect the invoking of the law in those cases?' This is the question that Bittner (1967a) addresses in his classic ethnomethodological study of the mandate and practices of peace-keeping in policing on skid row.

> To be sure, there is vague consensus that when policemen [sic]
> direct, aid, inform, pacify, warn, discipline, roust, and do what-
> ever else they do without making arrests, they do this with some
> reference to the circumstances of the occasion and, thus, some-
> how contribute to the maintenance of the peace and order.
> Peace keeping appears to be a solution to an unknown problem
> arrived at by unknown means.
>
> (Bittner 1967a: 701)

The study is one in ethnomethodological ethnography, an area in
which there is some methodological and conceptual similarity with
symbolic interactionist studies (though we postpone a discussion
of it until Chapters 9 and 10). Thus, Bittner spent 11 weeks of his
12 months of field work observing police work in skid rows. Moreover, he confined his attention to the problem of peace-keeping as
seen by the participants, that is the police officers, themselves. He
described the problem in terms of the 'demand conditions' (see
Chapter 9) of their work circumstances as perceived by the police
and the solution in terms of the interactional practices adopted by
the police in response to those conditions. Further results of this
study, to do specifically with 'police discretion in emergency apprehension of mentally ill persons', are reported in Bittner (1967b).

The principal demand condition of police work on skid row is
posed by the type of people who inhabit it. Police regard skid row
as the natural habitat of incompetents and those disinclined to be
normal. Life-as-usual is perceived as radically 'occasional', where
trust is irrelevant, the past unimportant, the future incoherent.
Indeed, address, relationships and activities *are* not meaningfully
related over time so that 'life on skid row lacks a socially structured
background of accountability' (Bittner 1967a: 706). Violence is
seen as a constant possibility.

Given this view of the social constitution of life on skid row,
police formulate their task 'basically as the protection of putative
predators from one another' (ibid: 707). But because 'the reali-
zation of self-interest does not produce order' (ibid) they pursue
an overall goal of external containment. To do this effectively the
individual officer employs, according to Bittner, three essential
practices, the second and third of which are most relevant to our
concerns.

Since, 'if he does not know a man personally there is very little
that he can assume about him' (ibid), then a first practice of

peace-keeping is for an officer to acquire a rich body of particularized knowledge about the persons and places on his beat,
knowledge which provides the basis for an aggressively personal
approach to residents. In exchange for interrogation rights and
obedience – refusing to play by insisting on rights is one way to get
arrested – residents enjoy expressive freedom and a variety of
services officers render to them. This is not done, Bittner says, out
of a spirit of altruism, but because 'the hungry, the sick and the
troubled are a potential source of problems' (ibid: 708). Such
services range from providing help to get lodgings and welfare to
keeping an eye out for missing dentures.

Secondly, police adopt the practice of proceeding against
persons on the basis of perceived risk rather than culpability. For
officers:

> compliance with the law is merely the outward appearance of an
> intervention that is actually based on altogether different con-
> siderations. Thus, it could be said that patrolmen do not really
> enforce the law, even when they do invoke it [and 'In the
> majority of minor arrest cases . . . the criteria the law specifies
> are met'], but merely use it as a resource to solve certain
> pressing practical problems in keeping the peace.
>
> (Bittner 1967a: 710)

A similar orientation characterizes the practices of courtroom
attorneys as we shall see in Chapter 10. Just as attorneys face the
task of arriving at an offence with which to strike a plea bargain so

> the problem patrolmen confront is not which drunks, beggars,
> or disturbers of the peace should be arrested and which can be
> let go as exceptions to the rule. Rather, the problem is whether,
> when someone 'needs' to be arrested, he should be charged
> with drunkenness, begging, or disturbing the peace.
>
> (ibid)

For the minor matters which comprise the bulk of their work the
overriding police preference is for *not* arresting where control can be
effected in other ways. This does not hold for serious offences such as
cheque-passing; however, as other studies indicate, '[e]ven in a major
city like Toronto . . . district detectives and patrol officers averag[e]
15.5 criminal charges per *year*' (Hagan 1991: 151).

The third practice of peace-keeping consists of using coercion
to manage situations rather than persons. Put differently, it

amounts to an orientation on the part of police officers to seek to reduce aggregate trouble and prevent its proliferation rather than evaluating individual cases by merit. This helps to make understandable arrest decisions that otherwise appear *ad hoc.* Against the background of this general orientation situational factors become decisive. The action taken, including arrest, depends on visibility, face (see Chambliss in Chapter 5), location (as above), the importance of a quick decision and not having to return later in the shift, the removability of the troublesome party (whether culpable or not) and the availability of the police van. Since there is always more trouble than can be handled the law is regarded as less important than practical control. This is a view shared by residents themselves, who not infrequently ask to be arrested.

Bittner concludes by saying that for police on skid row 'playing by ear' is the hallmark of good craftmanship in peace-keeping. It is not something that can be systematically generalized nor organizationally constrained. They call it 'getting along with people' but as we have seen it depends on developing a rich body of knowledge about the beat and a set of skills that are critical even as they are taken-for-granted.

Watson: eliciting confessions in murder interrogations

Following arrest comes interrogation. In this last section of this chapter we consider the work of Watson (1990) on the elicitation of confessions in murder investigations. Watson's data consist of two videocassette recordings of police interrogations of murder suspects, Lewis Strawson and Stuart Riley, in a large North American city. Strawson is accused of having killed and dismembered a young woman and Riley is suspected of three murders. Both of them confess and Watson seeks to examine aspects of the 'methods' through which these outcomes are achieved interactionally. Watson's work is especially interesting because it combines each of the three main ethnomethodological themes we described earlier: membership categorization analysis, mundane reason analysis and conversation analysis. We shall consider briefly the contribution of each of these to an understanding of interrogations, paying particular attention, as Watson does, to conversation analysis. A student of Watson, Maria Wowk (1984), has made a related analysis of these materials in pursuit of 'the processes by which blame is allocated around constructions about "victims" which trade on "what we all know" about different kinds of women and their part in precipitating behaviours by men' (Wise and Stanley 1987: 226). Obviously, the main aim of interrogation from the point of view of the police is to obtain a confession. To this end a central task is getting the suspect not only to talk, but to continue to talk until a confession is obtained. By drawing on the modes of ethnomethodological inquiry mentioned above Watson is able to show in detail that 'getting the suspect to talk' and 'persuading' the suspect to confess are methodical and 'socially organized'.

Questions and answers: utterance positioning as an interactional resource

A key concept in conversation analysis is 'speech exchange system' (Sacks *et al.* 1974). Speech exchange systems are organizations of turn-taking in social interaction which are tied to different tasks and contexts. Some are formal in that many of their features are pre-specified in advance of the occasion (for example, marriages ceremonies, debates, trials) whilst others have their features decided on a 'turn-by-turn' basis (for example, ordinary conversation). Watson suggests that interrogation is a distinctive speech exchange system which contains many of the features of ordinary conversation. In particular, he argues that the inductive and persuasive character of the interrogation is dependent on and embedded in organizational features of ordinary conversation. That is to say, Watson argues that some elements of what is sometimes taken to be police officer control (including capacity to persuade and pressure) by virtue of objective power turn out to be at the disposal of any conversationist. This is illustrated in several ways.

In their work on speech exchange systems, conversation analysts have paid considerable attention to what they describe as 'adjacency pairs' of utterances (Sacks *et al.* 1974; Schegloff 1968; Atkinson and Drew 1979). These are utterances such as 'question-and-answer', 'summons–answer', 'greetings–return greetings', 'request–compliance (or denial)', 'invitation-acceptance (or rejection)'. Such pairs of utterances are said to 'go naturally together', so that the production of a 'first part' of an adjacency pair makes relevant the production of the 'second part' in the next turn. Non-production of the relevant second pair part is, for

conversationists, 'noticeably absent', a fact which conversation
analysts take as evidence of a 'members' orientation' to this
method for the co-production of orderly conversation.

A first feature of interrogation as a speech exchange system is
the alignment of the police officer and the suspect into the
positions of recipient and informant, respectively. This is achieved
through what Watson (1990: 278) calls a 'considerable measure of
pre-allocation of turns and turn-types'. Of particular importance
here are the turns constructed as questions and answers.
Questions help to keep the suspect talking. This occurs because
questions comprise first pair parts of adjacency pairs and as such
they maximize 'the chances of the suspect producing at least one
more utterance as an immediate next conversational action' (ibid:
279). The production of questions, and indeed other 'first pair
parts', is a useful interactional resource in keeping the suspect
talking.

Also important in achieving the alignment of the suspect as
informant and the police officer as recipient is the use of 'continuers' or acknowledgements. These are minimal utterances such
as 'mm hm' and 'aha' which display what Jefferson calls 'passive
recipiency', which is an utterance designed to indicate that its
producer does not wish to take a turn him or herself but rather
wants the current speaker to continue talking. Such a device is
widely used not only in ordinary conversation but, for example, in
therapy and interviews. In this context it serves, like the use of
questions, to 'keep the suspect talking' (see also Sanders 1976).

Preference organization and knowledge claims

Conversation analysts have developed our understanding of the
preceding issues by showing that where there are alternative,
second pair parts available to members, as there are with respect
to invitations, requests, accusations and various other first pair
parts, then speakers are oriented to a 'preference organization'
(Bilmes 1988; Atkinson and Heritage 1984: Part II (papers by
Pomerantz, Davidson, and Drew); Heritage 1984: 265-280; Sacks
and Schegloff 1979; Schegloff et al. 1977). This means that certain
second pair parts are 'preferred', whilst others are 'dispreferred'.
Preferred and dispreferred items differ with respect to their 'turn
shapes'. Thus, dispreferred items tend to be produced in conjunction with such features as the partial production of preferred

responses, delays, transition markers. Preferred responses on the other hand tend to be done immediately and directly following the first pair part. For example, the 'preferred' response to an invitation is acceptance. When a person wishes to accept an invitation he or she typically does so straight away with utterances such as 'Yes, I'd like to,' etc. In contrast, the dispreferred 'second' to an invitation, namely the rejection, is typically constructed with such additional components as partial acceptance tokens, hesitation, transition markers, accounts and the like, as in 'Well, that's very nice of you, errm, but I'm afraid I cannot, I have to visit my doctor.'

In this connection, Watson focuses on how 'knowledge is invoked and mobilized in the course of the interrogation'. This involves 'avowals, ascriptions, elicitations and displays of specific items of knowledge and the conversational vehicles and formats in which these are incorporated, embedded, and organized relative to each other' (Watson 1990: 265). In particular, he suggests that knowledge claims (for example, 'we know that . . . ') work to 'upgrade' claims and as such can be 'persuasive' (cf. belief claims). This is traced out in terms of preference organization 'in that knowledge claims, as opposed to belief claims . . . can . . . intensify a preference for confirmation rather than for disconfirmation of the claims being made by the officer. Such confirmation can . . . be highly implicative for a confession' (ibid: 266). Knowledge claims are said to redouble the relevance of confirmation, hence elevating the claims, accounts, etc., in a 'hierarchy of preference'. This is to say that the police officer's 'account', by being presented in this way, 'becomes preferred rather than dispreferred or of equivalent or equivocal status *vis-à-vis* other hypothetically conceivable accounts' (ibid). Bland denials, furthermore, of claims made via 'we were wondering . . . ' or 'we think you . . . ' are likely 'enough to terminate the sequence with, at most, a simple "reception" or acknowledgement from the officer in the third utterance of the sequence' (ibid: 267). However, in the face of knowledge claims a simple denial may 'not be enough to override the policeman's "comeback" in third turn' (ibid).

Story format and confession

A number of conversation analysts have shown how 'stories' or 'storytelling' in various contexts are socially organized in a distinctive 266)ive way (Cuff and Francis 1978; Jefferson 1978). The 'problem' for a storyteller is that stories (and jokes) typically take longer to produce than the 'average' turn at talk in an ordinary conversation where co-conversationists operate on the assumption that turn transition may occur at any 'turn transition relevance place' (for example, at the end of the current speaker's sentence). However, if a speaker has a story to tell which consists of a number of sentences, each of whose completion might be treatable as a juncture where another speaker may select themselves to speak, then some method for inhibiting this eventuality must be available to the speakers. If not, then the story might never get told as a unit of talk, becoming instead disconnected and fragmentary. Accordingly, storytelling involves a distinctive format in which (1) the teller and recipient produce a 'story preface' in which permission to tell the story is requested and granted, or where an invitation to tell a story is issued and accepted, (2) the 'story proper' is then told, typically via a narrative structure, followed by (3) a story response on the part of the recipient(s).

As Watson observes, the fact that for stories it is typical that 'the teller holds the floor so far as rights to tell the story are concerned' would seem to suggest 'certain incompatibilities between the interrogation and story formats' (Watson 1990: 278). Given that speaker transition is usually suspended or modified for the duration of the story, is there not an inconsistency between inviting the suspect to tell a story (and hence have the floor to tell it to completion) and that which is conventionally constitutive of interrogation, namely asking questions? In this regard Watson makes a distinction between the volunteered story and the invited story. Confessions are achieved in part via the format of the invited story. Like volunteered stories they take more than one utterance to do, and they provide for an alignment of the suspect and police officer into the positions of teller and recipient, respectively, but unlike them invited stories allow the recipient of the story to take turns, and often quite long turns, throughout the course of the story. The invited story format for interrogations not only allocates to the suspect the turn type 'telling a story', it also permits the recipient to ask questions and thereby collaboratively contribute to the build-up of the story.

Questions, continuers, preference organization and story invitations contribute to the production of confessions by achieving an alignment of the co-participants in which the suspect is continually selected as informant/confessor/story teller. These are, thereby, highly 'felicitous' devices for 'keeping the suspect talking'. They are also useful in controlling what the suspect talks about. By recurrently occupying first turn, so to speak, the police officer not only obliges the suspect to speak in next turn but also has some controls over what the suspect talks about. The police officer, within the limits of topical coherence imposed by the unfolding story, can introduce new materials for incorporation into the developing 'confession'.

Persuasion and membership categorization

Watson's work on interrogations also involves membership categorization analysis. Thus, he shows that persuasive pressure is also generated by the presentation of the telling of the prospective story as being a manifestation of (the extent of) the suspect's honour, such that telling the story might be seen as 'doing the honourable thing'. The activity 'doing the honourable thing' is predicated of the category 'man or woman of honour'. The police officer is counting on the fact that the suspect will regard himself as an incumbent of the membership category implied by this categorization. Category imputations, too, then, may be persuasive devices in interrogations.

Knowledge claims, social facts and mundane reason

Finally, we note that another aspect of interrogations and, in particular, the persuasive character of the police officer's interactional activity, recalls our earlier discussion of mundane reason. This is that the presentation of claims as '*knowledge* rather than supposition' works 'to "establish" the facticity of his version or reconstruction' (Watson 1990: 266; cf. Smith 1978; Hester 1991). It also helps to 'authorize' the account. Authorization procedures include: that the suspect is 'nailed to the wall'; that the evidence has been assiduously collected; that the evidence is genuine; that the police are not bluffing; that the witnesses are not lying; that their statements coincide with independently collected evidence; that the police officer's account is disinterested, cohort-independent; that the witnesses have not falsely accused the suspect; that they are not part of the police officer's 'team'. All of these features 'serve to forestall any counter-accusations by the suspect, based on the discrediting of the origins of the policeman's information' (Watson 1990: 268). They help bolster the police officer's claims as correct and factual. The use of that contrast structure in which 'the truth' is opposed to 'a con', 'a lie' or 'a bluff' works to upgrade and authorize the account; these 'procedures work in parallel with authorizations to elevate the account to the level of "facticity" or to bolster the account against straightforward challenges' (ibid: 269). Presentation of claims as independent of any single perceiver and as disinterested gives them a Durkheimian externality and a constraining quality. These features help to put pressure on the suspect and make it more difficult for him or her to deny the interrogator's accusations.

Chapter 7

The political economy of policing

> Empirical observation must in each separate instance bring out
> empirically, and without any mystification and speculation, the
> connection of the social and political structure with production.
> (*The German Ideology*, Marx and Engels 1970 (1845/46): 46)

In Chapter 3 we introduced the principal concepts of the
structural conflict perspective as derived from Marx. From this
perspective, sociological analysis of the origins and functions of
criminal law is undertaken in terms of the political economy of the
society in question, where that entails showing the relationship
between the forces and relations of production and the material
and ideological operation of the superstructural institutions in
question. For contemporary Western societies that involves
exhibiting the connections between the current state of capitalist
(and also, for example, neo-colonialist and patriarchal) social
relations and the state's efforts through coercion and/or accumulation and/or legitimation to reproduce those relations via the
criminal law in question. The same ideas and approach may be
used to account for characteristic features of the nature and operation of the police.

From a substantial body of work by radical and critical criminologists on police, we have selected the following cases to
exemplify the analytic fruits of this perspective: the slave police in
the American *ante-bellum* South, communal policing under
feudalism in England, the emergence of private policing in the
transition from feudalism to capitalism in England and particular
features of modern policing in the capitalist societies of Canada,
the USA and the UK. These features comprise a cluster of practices
associated with what is being called the 'authoritarian state' in

contemporary capitalist societies. We refer to (1) the increasingly coercive and technological nature of police work, in combination with (2) an emphasis on community policing and (3) a focus on particular 'problem populations', often with resort to illegal methods (we will consider such activities of the RCMP, the FBI and the Special Branch).

POLICING THE SLAVE ECONOMY

According to the Centre for Research on Criminal Justice the policing of the American slave economy began with the Southern slave patrols in the late 1700s.

Black slavery was the dominant mode of production in the ante-bellum South, and the largest 2–3 per cent of the planters ruled the legislatures of each of the Southern states. These legislatures established slave codes, starting with South Carolina's 1712 copy of the Barbados statute. The slave codes which provided for the brutal slave patrols, both protected the planters' property rights in human beings and held the slaves, despite their chattel status, legally responsible for misdemeanours and felonies.

The plantation slave patrols, often consisting of three armed men on horseback covering a 'beat' of 15 square miles, were charged with maintaining discipline, catching runaway slaves and preventing slave insurrection. In pursuing this duty, they routinely invaded slave quarters and whipped and terrorized Blacks caught without passes after curfew. They also helped enforce the laws against slave literacy, trade and gambling.

Although the law called on all White males to perform patrol service, the large planters usually paid fines or hired substitutes, leaving patrolling to the landless or small landholding Whites. These Whites hated the planters, who controlled the best land and access to markets, almost as much as the slaves, but whatever the object of their anger, the slaves were its most frequent target. The slaves in turn resisted the patrollers with warning systems and ambushes.

Policing, then, in its earliest years, developed as a planter class strategy of race and class control, designed both to keep the Black slaves in subjugation and to exacerbate the contradictions between Black slaves and poor Whites. The patrols did not

operate with bureaucratic routine and tended to lapse between outbreaks of slave revolt. They lasted, however, until the Civil War. In many respects, the post-Reconstruction Black laws reestablished the police practices of the slave codes, while nominally changing 'slave patrols' to 'police departments'.
(Center for Research on Criminal Justice 1975: 20)

In Marxist terms slavery is a particular 'mode of production'. In this mode of production the principal 'forces of production' are land and labour applied mainly to agricultural production; in the American South the principal crop was cotton, typically grown on plantations. The crucial 'relation of production' was that between (1) the plantation owners who owned both the land and the labour, namely African or Afro-American slaves and (2) the slaves themselves. The plantation owners both depended upon and exploited the slaves, much as the feudal landlords were dependent upon and exploitative of their serfs, as we shall see. The political superstructure was in turn dominated by the landowners and their representatives in the legislatures of state governments. Accordingly, the criminal and civil laws established by these bodies were designed to preserve and enhance the slave mode of production. In this system, then, the slave patrols were an instrument of class domination and discipline. When the slaves resisted their exploitation the slave police were used to crush their resistance in the name of the slave codes, the rule of law which embodied and reproduced the social relations pertaining to the slave economy.

COMMUNAL POLICING IN FEUDAL ENGLAND

Communal policing involves the community policing itself. It was the form of policing prevalent in feudal society in England, though non-feudal forms of it, together with other types, were used discontinuously (Lundman 1980) centuries later in the early settlements in both Canada and the USA. In the much discussed case of England (for example, Critchley 1967; Griffiths et al 1980: 43–47; Lundman 1980; Spitzer 1979; Spitzer and Scull 1977), communal policing developed from the practices that prevailed in the reign of Alfred the Great in the ninth century. These arrangements were based on the concept of the mutual responsibility which each person owed to their neighbours. Critchley describes the arrangements in the following way: .

from the reign of King Alfred, the primary responsibility for
maintaining the King's peace fell upon each locality under a
well-understood principle of social obligation, or collective
security . . . Every male person, unless excused through high
social position or property, was enrolled for police purposes in
a group of about ten families known as a tything, and headed by
a tythingman. If any member of the group committed a crime,
the others had to produce him for trial; if they failed to do so
they could be fined or called upon to make compensation. In
addition, all members of the tything had to find a security who
would appear to answer any charge preferred against them. In
essence, therefore, the system relied upon the principle that all
members of a community accepted an obligation for the good
behaviour of each other.

(Critchley 1967: 2)

It was this set of simple social arrangements which the Normans, at
the start of the feudal or manorial era in eleventh-century
England, took over, 'modified, and systematized under the description "frankpledge" . . . [This] has been defined as "a system of
compulsory collective bail fixed for individuals, not after their
arrest for crime, but as a safeguard in anticipation of it"' (Morris
n.d. cited in Critchley 1967: 3).

A further form of communal policing was introduced by the
Statute of Winchester of 1285. It provided for the formation of
'night watches' in each village which were to support local 'constables' – the feudal version of the tythingman – in their duties and
to arrest those who were disruptive and who violated the law. It also
included the 'hue and cry', a procedure to deal with persons who
resisted arrest by the watchman or constable. Those citizens who
did not respond to the hue and cry were subject to fines and other
penalties. Pollock and Maitland describe the hue and cry as
follows:

When a felony is committed, the hue and cry . . . should be
raised . . . The neighbours should turn out with the bows,
arrows, knives, that they are bound to keep and besides much
shouting, there will be horn-blowing; the 'hue' will be 'horned'
from vill to vill. Now if a man is overtaken by hue and cry while
he has still about him the signs of his crime, he will have short
shrift. Should he make any resistance, he will be cut down. But
even if he submits to capture, his fate is already decided . . . He

will be brought before some court (like enough it is a court hurriedly summoned for the purpose) and without being allowed to say one word in self-defence, he will be promptly hanged, beheaded, or precipitated from a cliff, and the owner of the stolen goods will perhaps act as an amateur executioner.

(Pollock and Maitland 1968: 578–579)

Critchley sums up the principles embodied in the Statute of Winchester:

First, it was a duty of everyone to maintain the King's peace, and it was open to any citizen to arrest an offender. Second, the unpaid, part-time constable had a special duty to do so, and in the towns he was assisted in this duty by his inferior officer, the watchman. Third, if the offender was not caught red-handed, hue and cry was to be raised. Fourth, everyone was obliged to keep arms with which to follow the cry when required. Finally, the constable had a duty to present the offender at the court leet. The Statute made no mention of frankpledge, and it can be assumed that compulsory enrolment of the population in tythings as surety for each other had by this date become obsolete. The preventive aspect of policing was secured by the watch by night and the ward by day, the repressive [aspect] by hue and cry, and the punitive [aspect] by presentment. There is no reason to suppose that, in the stable conditions of England in the Middle Ages, these arrangements were other than effective. At bottom, they enlisted the whole community in what today would be called the fight against crime, and penalised laxity by the imposition of a collective fine.

(Critchley 1967: 7)

By 1400 in England each parish or shire elected a constable on a yearly basis and each adult, male citizen had to accept election to this office for which he received no pay. Those who refused were subject to fines or to other penalties, though as we shall see, these punitive arrangements became subject to circumvention.

Understanding in Marxist terms the role of communal policing in feudal society involves seeing its connections with the political economy of this form of society. This political economy is distinguished by three characteristics: firstly, 'a domestic mode of agricultural production based on the family'; secondly, 'a politico-economic structure of the manorial estate [in which a class system of lords and peasants is based upon cultivation of the land in small-scale rural communities]'; and thirdly, 'a rigid social hierarchy involving legal and customary rights and obligations between lord and peasant, the institution of serfdom' (Francis 1987: 26, 6). Furthermore, as Francis indicates:

> The lord does not stand in relation to the land as its owner, in the way in which the capitalist owns his factories or mines. Land is not a market commodity, since feudalism is not a market society. The lord cannot dispose of his possessions at will. He also is tied to them, for they constitute an inherited seigniory which conveys title and position in society upon himself and his family.
>
> In feudal society, additionally, there is no equivalent to capitalist notions of profit and efficiency. Production is not governed by rational calculations of output maximization but by rules of custom and practice. In the towns, the craft guilds exist to enforce customary methods and standards. The master craftsman organizes his workshop as an extension of his family. His journeymen and apprentices form an extension of his household. Payment in money is secondary to the rewards in kind they receive.
>
> (Francis 1987: 6)

In the context of the feudal mode of production communal policing can be seen in both 'instrumental' and 'structural' terms. In the absence of the kind of surplus of liquid capital derived from commerce (that was to come later), communal policing may be seen both as a solution to the technical problem of controlling the underclass, and as embodying the very social relations it was designed to sustain. The first point has been made by Weber:

> The method of imposing a collective responsibility for the performance of public duties is, therefore, a response to the administrative problems of a regime that does not possess a coercive apparatus extensive enough to enforce the personal liability of the political subjects but instead assigns the power of enforcement to compulsory liturgical associations. Such associations are part of the mixture of traditionalism and arbitrariness that characterizes patrimonial regimes.
>
> (Bendix 1962: 340)

By 'compulsory liturgical associations' is meant just those frankpledge arrangements of obligatory membership in tythings discussed earlier. At the same time this system of collective responsibility was one in which the same kind of customary ties by which serfs and lords were bound in economic and political relations was reproduced.

PRIVATE POLICING IN THE TRANSITION FROM FEUDALISM TO CAPITALISM

Midway between the feudal system of communal policing (unpaid, obligatory, rotating, with minimal specialization, viz. the constable) and the modern capitalist form of policing (paid, employed, permanent, bureaucratic, specialized) stand the practices of private policing. This is policing carried out by specially appointed, elected or, indeed, employed persons. However, such 'specialists', unlike their modern counterparts, were not employed by or accountable to central government but served local interests; they also lacked continuity. Thus, they might take the form of special constables, watchmen, law-enforcement officials in the employment of a particular court (for example, the Bow Street runners were police officers employed to work for the magistrates of Bow Street Court in London in the eighteenth century), or police employed by merchants or manufacturers (for example, the Thames River Police were employed to protect the privately owned warehouses along the Thames in London in the eighteenth century). Furthermore, private policing flourished as private citizens were induced by material gain to collaborate in the suppression of crime. These material incentives included exemptions from the 'burden' of public office, pardons for accomplices, government rewards, rewards and gratuities from 'private individuals, insurance companies, prosecution societies, property owners associations, and groups of residents' (Spitzer and Scull 1977: 270). People were encouraged to become informers, the incentive being the prospect of pardons and shares in any goods seized by the authorities.

In keeping with the injunction of Marx and Engels that heads this chapter, we turn to the links between these emergent forms of private policing and the transition from feudal to (industrial) capitalist political economy. At the level of the forces of production, capital (in the form of money and of manufacturing equipment) was coming to replace land as the principal element. Corresponding changes were occurring in the relations of production as property was becoming increasingly privatized both in the towns and on the land. Land-'owners' were beginning to enclose their 'landed property', setting 'free' their bonded serfs to become agricultural labourers or to move to the towns to become the forerunners of the industrial proletariat. In the towns the feudal monopolies were eroding as markets expanded with the growth of trade and commerce and the urban bourgeoisie grew in importance.

At the level of the political superstructure these changes began to produce a growing demand for police services from the urban bourgeoisie even as the feudal arrangements for supplying such were breaking down. There were, that is, contradictory forces at work here. On the one hand, there was a decline in the communal aspects of the constable role as many men refused to perform their duties as constable. This avoidance led to the growth of deputization as the unwilling paid others (often trivial amounts) to take their turn. The effectiveness of constables became somewhat attenuated. However, the establishment of this practice then provided a field of opportunity for enterprising individuals who appreciated the pecuniary potential in the position of constable. Initially established as a pillar of the communal system of policing 'constables were able to demand rewards and portions of recovered goods in exchange for their services, and . . . private individuals and organizations began to contract those with experience in law enforcement for specific protective and investigative duties' (Spitzer and Scull 1977: 270). Just as the development of commercial society spelled the demise of feudalism so commercial society offered a new solution to the technical problem of social control: private policing.

Before moving on to discuss the development and functions of modern policing, we note that private policing is enjoying something of a comeback as corporations, retailers and others make use of security firms and other forms in the protection of their material wealth (Shearing 1982); that there are strong ties between the private security industry and the security establishment of the state (Bunyan 1976; Herman and O'Sullivan 1989); and that it has also been observed that, in light of the 'globocop' role of the United States in the Gulf Massacre (with backup from the UK, Canada and others, and paid for by the clients), policing has taken on a mercenary role on the international stage (Chomsky 1991b: 63).

CAPITALISM AND MODERN POLICING

Modern policing is distinctive in so far as it consists of policing by full-time employees of centrally accountable, bureaucratic organizations. The first modern police organization was established by the Metropolitan Police Act in 1829 in London, England. It was followed shortly thereafter by similar organizations in the US and in Canada. These police officers were employed full-time to enforce the law, they were uniformed and they had to meet special entrance requirements (height, character, etc.). They worked not for particular interests but, ostensibly, for the 'public' good.

The key question is why the modern form of policing emerged at the beginning of the nineteenth century and not earlier. In both Britain and North America there had, apparently, previously been considerable controversy about the establishment of modern police (Lundman 1980: 23). The successful argument, until the 1820s, was that 'the threat to personal liberty outweighed the civilizing potential of the police' (Lundman 1980: 23). What, then, was responsible for the change of attitude? The answer to this question, for the structural conflict theorists, is that the modern police institution, in fact, corresponds with the coming of industrial capitalism as the dominant mode of production in the Western world. The police were 'modernized' at this historical juncture because it was in the interests of the capitalist class (instrumentalist thesis) or capitalism-as-a-system (structuralist thesis) for them to be so.

The 'instrumentalist' account begins with the observation that the early part of the nineteenth century saw the Industrial Revolution accelerate. It witnessed the growth of the industrial capitalist class. The process of industrialization, furthermore, saw large numbers of labourers impoverished and unemployed because of the development of the factory system and population growth. In order to survive under these conditions many of the impoverished industrial proletariat turned to 'crime'. There re-emerged a fear of the 'dangerous classes', a term used to describe those who posed a threat to 'law and order' and, of course, to those who stood most to gain from the newly emergent capitalist society. Given these circumstances the potential abuse of police powers on the part of a nationally or centrally organized police force seemed a risk worth taking. In short, then, it was class interest which accounts for the emergence of modern policing. The effectiveness of the mobilization of that interest and the demonization of the 'mob' it provoked can be gauged from the following historical data:

> From my (no doubt) incomplete and imperfect record of the twenty-odd major riots and disturbances taking place in Britain between the Edinburgh Porteous Riots of 1736 and the great Chartist demonstration of April 1848 in London, I have totted up the following score: the crowds killed a dozen at most; while, on the other side, the courts hanged 118 and 630 were shot dead by troops.
>
> (Rude 1970: 27–28; cited in Bunyan 1976: 299–300)

In more 'structuralist' terms the development of modern policing and hence the demise of private policing are superstructural expressions of underlying structural rearrangements in the political economy of society. Public or modern policing is a feature of the 'rationalization of crime control' (Spitzer and Scull 1977). In terms of both national and international competition in the economic market place this 'rationalization' was a structural requirement for the developing system of industrial capitalism and, as such, it served the interests of those who had most to gain from this: the manufacturers, the traders and the commercial farmers, in short the bourgeoisie. Locally based systems of private policing were uncoordinated and unpredictable; there was widespread disorder and riot; they were a feeble means for promoting the kind of stable, predictable and orderly economic environment which would allow the unfettered growth of capitalism. A pervasive public order would have been exceedingly difficult to achieve through private policing. By its very nature, private policing tended to be local and responsive to individual, rather than to collective or public interests. It was just too great a task.

Furthermore, it was not in the interests of any particular capitalist to undertake private policing since the cost involved would put him at a competitive disadvantage. Public or modern policing, on the other hand, with its shift of policing responsibilities and powers from the local to the central (national, state, municipal, etc.) level was seen as promoting the kind of efficiency, coordination and predictability which was necessary for the smooth running and expansion of industrial capitalism. Where riots had previously been somewhat tolerated they were now seen by the industrial capitalists as 'incipient rebellion' and produced panic on the stock markets. Public stability was required for the comfort and confidence of the bourgeoisie: 'a stable public order was a precondition of rational calculation on the part of industrial capitalists, and in the absence of such calculability the development of all sectors of the market system – investment, production, trade – was held within strict limits' (Spitzer and Scull 1977). It was conceived then that modern policing would have a soothing effect on the financial markets, facilitate orderly commerce and maximize the accumulation of wealth.

This epoch, then, witnessed structural conflict not only between the bourgeoisie and the proletariat but also between the bourgeoisie and the landed gentry. The demise of private policing and the promotion of modern policing are expressions of that conflict. Private policing was thus in the interests of the landed gentry because it preserved power and influence at the local level. However, it was not in the interest of the increasingly powerful bourgeoisie. It inhibits the development of industrial capitalism. Public or modern policing, on the other hand, not only promotes the development of orderly markets, it thereby serves the interests of the bourgeoisie and, by shifting power and responsibility from the local level to the centre, to the state, it undermines the locally based power of the landed gentry.

This rationalization process, then, served well the interests of the commercial and manufacturing bourgeoisie, just as it contributed to the decline in the influence of the old rural aristocracy. Against the resistance of the landed class, the bourgeoisie moved for a more national approach to policing. More than this, though, it served the needs of capitalism itself.

It is beyond the scope of this discussion to consider the reception of the modern police institution by the population at large at this time or to trace the development of police–population relations and, in particular, police–class relations. However, before turning our attention to the role of the police in contemporary capitalist society, we should like to note that the reception of the police by the British public is a matter of debate among three positions. Thus, there is firstly the 'accepted wisdom that the consent of the public lies at the heart of the (British) policing tradition' (Gordon 1987: 122), from which point of view the police could apparently 'count on the active support and consent of the British public'. Secondly, there is the view that 'the imposition of the modern police was widely opposed, often violently, as the police came as "unwelcome spectators into the very nexus of the urban neighbourhood life"'. Thirdly, there is the view that working-class opposition, including violence, to the police came only from one section of that stratum, namely the poor, ordinary, unprivileged, 'non-aristocratic' workers (Norrie and Adelman 1989: 119). As these authors point out, resistance amongst the 'respectable' working class and the 'labour aristocracy' was conspicuously absent, thereby providing support for the claim that there was both conflict and consensus in working-class–police relations. This view is corroborated in a Canadian study by Shearing who found that the police he observed differentiated between the people they did things *for*, whom they called the 'public' and regarded paternalistically as helpless, stupid, demanding and exploitative, and the people they did things *to*, whom they regarded as the 'enemy' and called 'third or fourth class citizens', 'the people from the slum areas' or simply the 'scum' (Shearing 1983: 382).

POLICING IN CONTEMPORARY CAPITALIST SOCIETY

In general, structural conflict theorists interpret state control and, in particular, policing in terms of their relation to the requirements of capitalism. Recent Marxist analyses have varied in the emphasis they have given to 'instrumentalist' and 'structuralist' interpretations of these requirements. Thus the Center for Research on Criminal Justice has examined the police under the auspices of the instrumentalist notion that they comprise 'one part – along with the military and the penal system – of the apparatus of state force and violence, which directly serves the interests of the capitalist class' (Center for Research on Criminal Justice 1975: 15). In partial contrast, Scraton advances the more structuralist thesis that:

> the police . . . operate primarily to defend and service existing social relations (of patriarchy, of advanced capitalism, of neo-colonialism) and established property rights and to manage conflict by force when it cannot be contained through the formalized political and ideological procedures of negotiation.
> (Scraton 1987a: 181)

In either case, within capitalist society the state is considered in terms of the three functions of accumulation, coercion and legitimation which we introduced in Chapters 1 and 3. We cannot describe in all its detail the vast range of police practices which fulfil the coercive function and, indirectly, contribute to accumulation and legitimation. Accordingly, we select several features of contemporary policing and then analyse them in terms of these concepts. These features are (1) organizational and technological aspects of the increased use of force, including the creation of special response organizations and the use of 'excessive force', (2) the development of community (not to be confused with communal) policing and (3) the deployment of a variety of 'illegal' police practices in the targeting and control of groups described variously as 'subversive', 'dangerous' and 'the enemy within'.

More force: organizational and technological innovations

A major focus of attention for critical criminologists and sociologists of law has been on what Hall (1980) calls the 'drift to the law and order society'. That is, recent developments in the character of policing in both Britain and North America have been the subject of Marxist analysis wherein a connection is drawn between increasingly authoritarian measures of policing on the one hand and *laissez faire* economic policies on the other.

In the case of the United Kingdom it is pointed out by Gordon (1987: 121), for example, that 'the shape of British policing has changed dramatically, if not fundamentally,' since the late 1960s and early 1970s. Several changes are identified including the development of 'fire-brigade policing', the emergence of a quasi-military 'third force' concealed inside the ordinary police, the increasingly routinized use of guns, CS gas and the machinery of riot control and the expansion of surveillance, both in terms of technology and targeted population. The 'consolidation' of these changes accelerated after the 'urban rebellions' of 1980, 1981 and 1985 and were especially clear in the policing of the miners' strike of 1984 and 1985. In addition, as we discussed in Chapter 3, critical theorists have also pointed to the expansion of formal police powers through the passage of the Police and Criminal Evidence Act of 1984 and the Public Order Act of 1987.

For the United States the Center for Research on Criminal Justice has identified several features of the development of the police since the 1960s which anticipated those identified by Gordon (1987) and Scraton (1987a). These include an expansion of the number of police, increased government spending on the police, organizational centralization and sophistication of police operations, the application of war and space-programme technologies, professionalization of the police, and a 'variety of new "tough" specialized units – special anti-riot and tactical patrol forces, "special weapons" teams, and highly sophisticated intelligence units' (Center for Research on Criminal Justice 1975: 11). Examples of strong-arm and 'excessively' forceful methods used by the police are legion. They include the use of plastic bullets in crowd control in Northern Ireland, of mounted police to charge and trample strikers and pickets at Orgreave during the 1984–85 coal dispute in England, similar tactics being employed against anti-poll tax demonstrators in London in 1990, the killing of Blair Peach 'by an unknown member of the Special Control Group at an anti-fascist demonstration in April 1979' (Sim *et al.* 1987: 32), and the deployment of CS gas in the 'massive confrontation between police and the people on the Broadwater Farm Estate as riot-clad officers faced barricades and petrol bombs' (Scraton 1987a: 167).

The massive use of sophisticated force is also graphically described by Davis and Ruddick (1988) in their account of the various operations of the Los Angeles Police Department from the 1970s onwards.

Neighbourly cops: the police in the community

Another striking development in policing in the USA, Canada and the UK has been the growth of new strategies of community penetration and 'citizen participation' that have sought to integrate people into the process of policing and to secure the legitimacy of the police system itself. 'Community policing', as it has become known, includes the reinstatement of foot patrols, juvenile and community liaison programmes, neighbourhood watch schemes and the 'multi-agency' or 'corporate' approach to policing developed by Sir Kenneth Newman (Commissioner of the Metropolitan (London) Police). Community policing is a 'softer' approach to containment than that embodied in the more directly repressive measures made possible by the technological sophistication of the police and the extension of their powers. Community policing may be interpreted as a recognition that 'such open control may be counter-productive' and other means are necessary to 'break down community resistance, to engineer consent and support for the police, and to reinforce social discipline' (Gordon 1987: 141). Taken together, these developments represent an attempt by the police to forge a two-pronged policing strategy: reactive policing, with all the technological gadgetry to make it more efficient and ruthless, and proactive policing, to foster community consent and provide the police with intelligence and information.

Although community policing programmes have developed in America, Britain and Canada, space precludes a full discussion of these developments. We shall, instead, confine our remarks to the case of Britain which, in our view, happens to be typical with respect to this particular police strategy. Thus, the beginnings of community policing in the UK are to be found in the 'community relations' and 'community liaison' schemes for the black community and for youth, respectively. Community relations work began in the 1950s when it was recognized by both governments and the police that there was a lack of consent for, and resistance to, the police amongst blacks in Britain. Of course, this was not exactly surprising since as Gordon rightly points out, the first immigrants from the Caribbean and Indian subcontinent had experienced the British police as a colonial, white establishment force. Their experience in Britain itself did little to alter the view that had been formed in the colonies.

From the 1950s to the 1980s successive police administrations have implemented community relations programmes with the black community. The aim has been to foster consent and support for the police, 'to manage the black population and to mediate its opposition and distrust' (Gordon 1987: 123). Not that they had much success, which is not very surprising either since the police continued to use the 'same colonial policing policy'. Furthermore, the development of 'special' community relations organizations both within the police and outside of them served only to confirm the black community's separation from 'mainstream' British culture and ended up absolving 'the police in general of any notion that they were accountable to the black community'. Community relations neither altered the racist character of everyday policing nor brought about a reorientation amongst the black community towards the police.

Although police work with youth and juveniles began before the Second World War, the first special liaison scheme was set up in Liverpool in 1949. It aim was one of 'pre-emption', namely to learn of potential delinquents at an early stage in their deviant careers so as to prevent them from developing further their criminal proclivities. In 1952 the first Juvenile Liaison Department was established also in Liverpool, a development which, with Home Office encouragement, was adopted elsewhere. Since then youth liaison schemes have seen the police becoming increasingly involved with other youth-oriented agencies and programmes, such as social services departments, schools and youth clubs. As with the community relations scheme, the aim of youth liaison was to foster consent for the police and to obtain information about youth.

More recently, community policing has involved the reinstatement of foot patrols or beat policing, especially in the inner cities. One reason for this development was the evident unpopularity of mobile patrols and reactive policing. These were increasingly viewed as counter-productive: the public only encountered the police in contexts of confrontation or conflict and the police were failing to obtain the information necessary for what they regarded as the efficient performance of their duties. Returning officers to the beat was a method of dealing with both problems: it improved both the police image and intelligence gathering. The following 'job specification' of an 'area constable' is instructive in this regard:

1 secure the services of at least one observer in every street, not a paid professional informant, but someone who knows the inhabitants and is inquisitive enough to find out what is going on and who is willing to pass on such information gained;
2 get to know the habits and all other information about criminals in his/her area;
3 cultivate shopkeepers, tradesmen (sic) and garage proprietors who are a good source of information;
4 keep observation in parks, playing fields, schools and other places where children congregate.

(Gordon 1987: 134)

The beat officer, then, is expected to gather information and intelligence, tasks which have assumed greater significance with the development of the role of the 'police collator'. This involves the collation and dissemination of the information gathered by the beat, and other officers, throughout the police services.

High-ranking advocates of community policing such as the

ex-chief constable of Devon and Cornwall, John Alderson, have also increasingly put forward the concept of 'multi-agency policing'. Two steps in this direction were taken initially in Devon and Cornwall, and have since been reflected in similar developments elsewhere in the UK. The first, in 1982, was the Crime Prevention Support Group which examined 'problem areas' in order to identify crime and other community problems, to introduce new ideas of crime prevention, direct police resources and harness active public participation and support for good citizenship and community awareness (Gordon 1987: 132). The second was the Community Policy Consultative Group which involved the media, magistrates, churches, television and local authority services in discussion about how to most effectively reduce crime, serve community needs and develop multi-agency strategy (ibid).

Support for these ideas was subsequently expressed in the recommendations of the Scarman Report on the urban rebellions of 1981. To be sure, Scarman was not against 'iron fist' police methods but he thought it was sensible to deploy the 'velvet glove' as well. His suggestion was for the establishment of 'consultative committees' on which both police and public representatives would cooperate in order to prevent crime. According to Gordon (1987: 136) one key feature of these committees is their cooptation of the community into policing. They represent a further step in the direction of a systematic 'multi-agency' approach to policing.

Finally, we note a further constituent feature of community policing, namely the advent of the 'neighbourhood watch schemes' which have spread, initially from America and Canada, to all parts of Britain. Their basic aim was crime prevention through, for example, the police marking of property and the posting of signs indicating the existence of the 'neighbourhood watch area'. In addition, argues Gordon (1987: 139), they have been organized 'to mobilize support for the police among the middle class and respectable working class and to gather low-level intelligence'.

Secrecy and selectivity: policing politically problematic populations

Another side of the maintenance of law and order involves the tasks of surveillance and control of a variety of 'special groups', namely workers, aboriginal people, gays, feminists, dissidents, students, people of colour, peace activists, leftists and the like, whose legal party and extra-party political activities, demonstrations and strikes have traditionally been perceived as problematic for and by the state. According to Spitzer's (1975) Marxian theory of deviance there are two types of problem populations in the eyes of the ruling class, namely what he calls 'social junk' and 'social dynamite'. The aged, physically handicapped ('differently abled'), mentally ill and mentally retarded comprise the 'social junk'; their control is delegated to the therapeutic and welfare state. The welfare poor, gays, alcoholics and problem children move between the two categories, depending on a variety of aspects of the relationship between those populations and the control system. For example, it has been suggested that the notorious 1981 Toronto bathhouse raids by the Metropolitan Toronto police *Intelligence* Squad, in which 150 police officers charged 290 men with various morality offences, charges which proved unfounded in 87 per cent of the cases, were timed to occur just before the squad's budget review and just after the calling of a provincial election (Brannigan 1984: 99; see also Smith 1988). That is, the gay population was politically and organizationally useful as a scapegoat.

The 'social dynamite' are the rest of the groups listed above, notably workers, strikers, union activists and their political representatives, and, increasingly in Canada, aboriginal groups, visible minority groups and women's groups. Many, if not all of these groups, though not all equally, have standardly been dealt with not only by the regular police but also by the 'political police', for example the RCMP Security Service in Canada, the FBI in the United States and the Special Branch in the United Kingdom. Much of the work of these bodies in surveillance and control is carried out 'secretly', and usually does not come to be known publicly until its practitioners' own law-breaking is discovered. It has been said by Margaret Atwood (1972: 171; cited in Hagan 1991: 226) that 'Canada must be the only country in the world where a policeman is used as a national symbol'. The image of the 'mountie' has been for Indians and Metis an enduring symbol of 'internal' colonial authority since 1873. The mounties, officially known as the Royal Canadian Mounted Police (originally the North West Mounted Police), were created 'as a paramilitary force often used to control workers and native peoples' (Caputo *et al.* 1989: 9, citing Brown and Brown 1973 (1978)) with a view to facilitating the acquisition and securing of sovereignty over land

and the exploitation of its resources as the state was pushed westward following confederation in 1867.

In their *An Unauthorized History of the RCMP* Lorne and Caroline Brown (1973, 1978: vii) provide a 'partial list of secret police undercover operations over the past few years' (see also Dion 1982; Mann and Lee 1979). The list includes such criminal activities as breaking into, bugging and stealing files and documents from the offices of a press agency, a legal political party and a trades-union federation, spying on cabinet ministers, senior civil servants, MPs, legal political parties, trades unions, native organizations and 'a host of economic and political groups on the left of the political spectrum', '[b]urning down a barn, stealing dynamite from a construction site and destroying stolen files', illegally opening mail and so on.

They continue, 'It appears this may be only the tip of the iceberg' (ibid: vii). In the rest of their 'unauthorized history' the Browns document the use of the RCMP (and its predecessors the RNWMP and NWMP) to put down Indian resistance, break strikes, control workers' protests, spy on students, draft dodgers and farmers and so on. Such was the scale of the crimes of the RCMP Security Service that it was the subject of two Royal Commissions in the late 1970s, one result of which was to remove the domestic spying function from the RCMP and give it to a new body, the Canadian Security and Intelligence Service (CSIS) formed in 1984. There have since been reports that the RCMP responded by secretly recreating the equivalent of CSIS within itself under the name of the National Security and Intelligence Service (NSIS) and competing for turf with CSIS (*Globe and Mail* 4 July 1989, p. A1). And CSIS has itself come under criticism for its continued harassment of the peace movement in Canada (see Stark 1991), something its director says it has now abandoned (Morden 1989). The efforts of the RCMP to save Canada from the predations of foreign agitators (read 'communists') are well recounted in Whitaker's (1987) history of Canadian immigration.

A description of comparable events in the United States is afforded by the following remarks on Watergate and Counterintelligence Programme (COINTELPRO) (Perkus 1975) by Noam Chomsky:

> during the Watergate farce, largely a damage control operation by Congress and the media, there was much outrage over the

break-in at the Democratic Party headquarters, but not much
over the more serious crimes of the Nixon and earlier administrations, exposed at exactly the same time, including the use of
the national political police to undermine the Socialist Workers
Party by repeated burglaries and other illegal acts from the early
1960s – not to speak of other FBI operations designed to foment
violence in the ghettoes, undermine the civil rights movement
and other forms of popular action, etc. The Democratic Party
represents domestic power, the Socialist Workers Party – a legal
political party – does not; hence the predictable difference in
response to the major scandal concerning the SWP and the
minor thuggery involving the Democrats. Nixon's 'enemies list'
was a scandal, but not the FBI involvement in the assassination
of Fred Hampton by the Chicago police, exposed at the same
time; it is scandalous to call powerful people bad names in
private, but not to assassinate a Black Panther organizer.

(Chomsky 1988: 69–70; 1989: 189; 1975)

As with the Browns' history of the RCMP, Chomsky traces such
practices back at least as far as 'Palmer's raids' of January 1920
when, in response to US President Woodrow Wilson's fabricated
'Red Scare', 'thousands of alleged radicals were rounded up in
many parts of the country', hundreds being subsequently
deported (Chomsky 1989: 185–186). Also as in Canada the FBI has
been instrumental in putting down the resistance of native Indians
and their organizations. Recent claims charge the FBI with
sponsoring 'death squads' employed against the American Indian
Movement in the early 1970s at the Pine Ridge Sioux Reservation,
home of the Oglala Lakota people, 'in what is now the State of
South Dakota' (Churchill 1991: 103; also Churchill and Van der
Wall 1988).

In his *The History and Practice of the Political Police in Britain*
Bunyan (1976) documents a similar story for the United Kingdom.
He traces 'the development of the agencies of the state whose
function is to counter and contain political movements,'
considering 'the Special Branch, MI5, and the military . . . as part
of an independent matrix' (1976: ix). We shall briefly examine his
account of the Special Branch. Founded in the 1880s it 'has been
actively engaged in the surveillance of political activists since its
inception' (ibid: 150). Its work is essentially (1) record-keeping,
(2) surveillance and (3) making. raids, carried out in order to

counter 'subversion', a concept which, as in Canada, is defined so broadly 'as to justify the inclusion of every politically active person' (ibid: 123).

It gathers and records the following: the names of political activists appearing in the press, of those signing petitions to parliament and of those provided by members of the public through letters; the literature of political groups; address books, letters and cheque-stubs from raids for evidence of 'friendship networks'; information from telephone-tapping and mail-opening, from trials of members of perceived 'subversive' groups, from approaches made to employers, officials, doctors and teachers, from informers (innocent, paid and blackmailed) and from:

> [m]eetings and demonstrations. A report on all demonstrations and any public meetings of significance is prepared either by the Branch officer, or by a CID/uniformed policeman in attendance. The contents of speeches are noted and if made by a 'ring leader' will be transcribed and held for future use. In addition at most demonstrations there is a Branch photographer, and at major ones video-cameras are used to film the whole length of a march.
>
> (Bunyan 1976: 137)

Bunyan estimates that as a result of all this information-gathering the Branch had in the mid-1970s records, comprising an index card if not a file, on nearly three million people. The figure is comparable to that of the eight hundred thousand Canadians that the RCMP Security Service had files on at about the same time (CBC *Ideas* 1989: 9). (In 1987 its successor agency, CSIS, destroyed 115,000 old subversion files 'in a burst of contrition' (*Globe and Mail* 29 November 1989, p. A6).) And the files kept by J. Edgar Hoover's FBI are, of course, legendary. Some indication of what goes into a person's file is afforded by the exposure in 1989 of the RCMP file on June Callwood, a prominent Canadian writer, broadcaster, humanitarian and social activist awarded the Order of Canada. Under 'subversive' is recorded, for example, 'Has a history of aiding groups involved in social issues, etc., regardless of their political affiliation.' Furthermore:

> Her file shows the Mounties spying on her as she took part in anti-Vietnam War protests, women's peace groups and civil liberties meetings, as she attended family planning conferences

and a University of Toronto teach-in on the Americanization of
Canada, spoke to student and Children's Aid groups, organized
hostels for street-kids.
The file makes special mention of her taking part in the
founding of the Canadian Civil Liberties Association.

(Valpy 1989: A8)

Surveillance either arises in the course of a case or is ongoing.
The latter is directed to certain groups such as *ad hoc* committees
(for example, the Vietnam Solidarity Campaign), perceived
'revolutionary' groups ('like the International Socialists, black
groups, trade union branch committees, or claimants' unions')
and 'more liberal organizations' like 'the National Council for
Civil Liberties or community groups' (Bunyan 1976: 138–139).

The information held by the Branch on the active political
community in Britain is in itself a major intrusion into people's
political freedom, but it is the actions of the Branch against
individuals and groups that highlights the danger of a political
police force.

(ibid: 140)

Thus, the Branch conducts raids, most commonly for the purpose
of 'fishing expeditions':

What disturbs my clients, and what they really desire to have
stopped is that police officers can walk into the offices of a perfectly
legal organization, and under the guise of arresting an individual,
proceed to make a clean sweep of all documents, including accounts, collection cards, and to remove them all to Scotland Yard.
(D. N. Pritt, counsel for the National Unemployed Workers'
Movement, in 1932) (Bunyan 1976: 141)

Apart from '[b]lanket surveillance of demonstrations, political
meetings, and industrial struggles' (ibid: 141), the Branch
routinely monitors industry (shop stewards, branch secretaries,
and political activists), universities ('radical' students, left-wing
lecturers), the black community and the emigre community
during visits by foreign heads of state or, doubtless, during war.
And as Bunyan's account of its treatment of David Ruddell makes
clear, it harasses and interferes in the lives of individuals who
peacefully and legally respond to the moral imperative to act in the
service of justice and humanity.

What becomes clear from the historical practice of the British state is that its repressive agencies have been overwhelmingly directed against the extra-constitutional movements of the working class and their revolutionary potential. This is no less true of the present than of the past. The various [repressive] institutions and personnel of the state . . . play their part in the reproduction of the prevailing order which entails the incorporation, containment or elimination of any political movement threatening capitalist dominance.

(Bunyan 1976: 300)

INTERPRETING POLICE PRACTICES: THE CRISIS OF CONTEMPORARY CAPITALISM

Though their roots are historically deeper, the three developments which we have described have each been interpreted in critical criminology as strategies for dealing with the hegemonic crisis in contemporary capitalism. Both the 'repressive state apparatus' (coercion) and the 'ideological state apparatus' (legitimation) – or, more simply, force and fraud – directed at the working class and other problem populations, have been used to manage this crisis (Althusser 1971; see also Cuff *et al.* 1990: 121–124; cf. Gramsci 1971). Structural conflict theorists generally locate the 'crisis' in contradictions that have emerged in what they variously describe as late, advanced, corporate, monopoly, welfare capitalism. By these titles they mean to locate the central features of the global political economy that has become established in the late twentieth century. These contradictions are standardly attributed to:

the general world crisis of capital overaccumulation and overproduction, and reduced rates of profit. A severe international stagflation has resulted in a combination of problems – inflation, profit decline, *and* high unemployment – that were not experienced *simultaneously* in any previous period of capitalist development and all of which have been exacerbated by increased energy costs to the developed economies.

(Frank 1981: 10, cited in Ratner and McMullan 1985: 186)

These changes in the conditions of capitalist production have been consequential for the relations of production in terms of class, gender and race. As major employers have sought to reduce costs by, for example, moving production to low-cost areas and by reducing the size of their labour force, and governments have not only collaborated in this process but have sought to reduce their own costs by privatizing state-run industries and a range of social services, the population in the industrial societies have felt the consequences in the form of increased unemployment, under-employment and part-time employment as well as a deterioration in the range and quality of services previously provided by the 'welfare state'. Despite state efforts to rationalize these steps via an ideology of 'releasing private enterprise', 'expanding choice' and 'rolling back the frontiers of government' these and related changes have brought about a crisis in legitimacy at the level of the political superstructure. That is to say, the ideological supports by which the consent of major segments of the population had been traditionally secured have been eroding. This erosion has been disproportionately distributed through society. It has been particularly serious amongst traditionally 'marginal' populations such as youth and Britons, Americans and Canadians of African and Afro-Caribbean descent and in the regions of old or single manu-facturing or processing industry. Most importantly, it has brought about resistance on a number of fronts. Workers in privatized and 'rationalized' industries, notably the miners in Britain, and blacks in the urban centres of Britain and America, have mounted virtual rebellions against state authority.

The period since the 1960s has also seen a 'crisis' at the level of ideology, though structural conflict theorists would interpret this as ultimately grounded in material or economic conditions. Since the 1960s the United States, Canada and the UK have at different times and to different degrees witnessed massive popular conflict over civil rights, the War in Indochina, nuclear disarmament, women's rights, gay rights, aboriginal autonomy, Quebec independence, Northern Ireland and other sociopolitical issues. Through public protest and large-scale demonstrations and, in the case of Northern Ireland, a 'war of liberation', the ruling ideas about such issues have been challenged.

It is in response to this broad crisis of legitimacy, of ruling-class hegemony, that the state has modified, expanded and refined its social control apparatus. These developments have included the innovations in policing which we have reviewed above, as well as changes in criminal law (Chapter 3), the administration of justice (Chapter 8) and the use of prisons (Chapter 11). As we showed in

Chapter 3 structural conflict theorists interpret crime control measures in terms of the functions of coercion, accumulation and legitimation. Firstly, 'the class control function is always the most essential function that the police serve in a capitalist society'. Within this framework the police 'serve as the front line mechanism of repression' by, for example, strikebreaking, helping divide Third-World and white workers, infiltrating working-class political activities and repressing working-class culture and recreational activities. Moreover, 'the police have *primarily* served to enforce the class, racial, sexual, and cultural oppression that has been an integral part of the development of capitalism' (Center for Research on Criminal Justice 1975: 20, 15, 11, original emphasis).

Secondly, the police function as class controllers is masked by a facade of 'acceptable' public service. They help those in trouble, they solve or, at least, try to solve 'dangerous crimes', they direct traffic and provide the public with information. This is the 'velvet glove' side of policing, a side which is intertwined with that of the 'iron fist'. The Center for Research on Criminal Justice argues that the velvet glove serves legitimation functions which then permit the increase in the level of violent repression. The mystification of the class-control nature of policing, and the mass dissemination of ruling-class ideological justification of the police, such as 'law and order' rhetoric, is in itself repressive, and serves important class-control functions. Thirdly, as a result of its coercive work and its legitimation of both the rule of law and the social relations of production thereby reproduced, the capitalist state, it is argued, fulfils the accumulation function of sustaining the conditions under which the generation of profit can proceed.

Finally, in providing means, illegal or otherwise, of controlling those problem populations that constitute the social dynamite, the police are serving the interests of the state (in the ultimate interest of the capitalist class), namely keeping informed about, and actively coercing, sources of opposition to its rule, opposition emanating from outside (though sometimes from inside) the range of the two (or three) principal political parties whose artificial conflict constitutes what passes for democracy in the United States and, somewhat less narrowly, in Canada and the UK.

Chapter 8

Discipline, domination and criminal justice

In this chapter we begin by elucidating the structural conflict notion of 'class rule in other-than-class terms'. Then we consider how pre-trial and trial proceedings reproduce capitalist class relations and serve ruling-class interests. In the final section we review sentencing studies in the light of instrumentalist and structuralist interpretations of structural conflict theory for what they reveal of the operation of capitalist, patriarchal and neo-colonialist structures of dominance.

CLASS RULE IN OTHER-THAN-CLASS TERMS

In setting out the central concepts of the structural conflict approach in Chapter 3, we said that the state helped to secure ruling-class hegemony by controlling class conflict in other-than-class terms. The very organization of the politico-legal system, including the criminal law, provides a set of means for depoliticizing working-class resistance by representing 'acts of resistance' as crimes. We will briefly consider the following three of these devices:

1 distinguishing the 'political' from the 'criminal';
2 distinguishing 'civil' law from 'criminal' law;
3 casting the criminal law in universal terms.

The 'political' and the 'criminal'

One way we have organized this book has been in terms of the conventional tripartite division of the criminal justice system into the law, the courts and the police. Each part plays a particular role in the system, namely law making, justice administration and law enforcement, respectively. But this arrangement presupposes that the spheres of political action and criminal action (and criminal matters as opposed to civil matters, as we see below) have been separated and can be kept apart. Events teach us that this can be problematic. From the structural conflict perspective this distinction comes to be seen as a device that may be used by the state in 'the administration of justice' in the interests of the ruling class. However the differing contents of the 'political' and the 'criminal' are defined in the political system of the society in question, it is in the application of the distinction that the practice can be seen.

Thus, during the 'Oka Crisis' in Canada/Quebec in the summer of 1990, what Mohawks and native leaders across Canada defined as a political act of self-defence by the armed forces of a nation – the setting up and defending by armed Mohawk 'Warriors' of barricades on disputed land in the environs of Mohawk reserves at Kanesatake and Kahnawake first, to prevent the expansion of an Oka municipal golf course onto claimed Mohawk land, and second, in protest against an assault on the first barricades by Quebec Provincial Police – was counter-defined by the Prime Minister of Canada, the Premier of the Province of Quebec, the Mayor of Oka and government officials generally as a series of criminal acts of mischief, illegal possession of firearms, etc., by terrorists whose relationship to their people was that of an 'extremist minority suppressing dissent' (the Prime Minister, 28 August 1990). In short, one side defined the conflict in political terms as one between 'sovereign' entities where the applicability of the (criminal) laws of Canada was precisely what was at issue; the other side defined the conflict in criminal–legal terms within the jurisdiction of the Canadian state and constitution.

Whatever the relative merits of the two cases the relevant sociological point here is that of the kind of theoretical interpretation of these definitional moves the structural conflict perspective can offer. This would involve, for example, translating the dispute and stand-off into the terms of conflict over control of material matters – land, physical resources, capital – between contending classes. For example, though one drawn from the United States:

> Upwards of half of all known 'domestic' U.S. uranium reserves
> lie within the boundaries of present-day [Indian] reservations,
> as do as much as a quarter of the high grade low sulphur coal, a

fifth of the oil and natural gas, and major deposits of copper and other metals. Loss of internal colonial control over these items would confront U.S. elites with significant strategic and economic problems.

(Churchill 1991: 103)

Instrumentally put, one class would be the ruling capitalist class represented by 'its executive branch', namely the government in power, the other an oppressed under-class led and represented by a particular 'fraction', namely, to return to the Canadian case, the Mohawk Warriors and native leaders and their organizations. In terms of this theoretical description the competing definitions of the dispute asserted by the participants stand as ideological moves in the politics of class conflict. In particular, the government attempt to render the dispute in criminal–legal terms (against an acknowledged background of racial injustice) is seen to be an effort to control class conflict in other-than-class terms.

What does this mean in practice? To the extent that the definition of the situation as one of criminal actions by a terrorist group can be sustained, then the relevant controlling agency is the police. If, as happened, police resources are judged inadequate to maintain control and bring the 'criminals' to justice, then the army may be brought in. But their actions are then seen as essentially police work, that is, assisting or replacing the police in the tasks of law enforcement. When police and/or army deploy high-powered weapons, including tanks and helicopters, and fix bayonets to their rifles, when barricades are charged, persons terrorized, food supplies interrupted, freedom of movement denied, freedom of assembly for peace groups denied, freedom of the press restricted and so on, these actions are ones defined as 'police' work by civil authorities in the (ultimately national) interest of 'law and order'. Or they are counter-defined as acts of 'aggression', including 'invasion' of sovereign territory and the denial of human rights under the terms of international law as found in such documents as the United Nations Charter and the Universal Declaration of Human Rights. In the preamble to the Universal Declaration, for example, 'armed struggle' is recognized as a legitimate last resort for oppressed groups seeking political recognition of their rights. Clearly, in the hands of the powerful, the distinction between the 'political' and the 'criminal' is a powerful tool for shaping social reality. And it serves as a means to rationalize the state's use of coercion in its unending task of reproducing capitalist class relations. It is just such aspects of social organization that the structural conflict perspective alerts us to when we come to examine the 'administration of justice' through the courts.

A comparable analysis of the Canadian state's 'creation' of, and response to, the FLQ (Front de Libération du Québec) crisis of the 1960s and 1970s in terms of the 'criminalization of Quebec nationalism' is afforded in a brief but useful exposition by Corrado (1987: 305–306, 309). It focuses on the invoking of the War Measures Act in the wake of the 'October Crisis' of 1970 and the resort to illegal activities by the RCMP Security Service (which we examined in Chapter 7). He sets it off nicely against a candidate 'interactionist' analysis of the same episode (305, 307–308), using the expressions 'capitalist democratic' and 'pluralist democratic', respectively to describe the two perspectives.

The 1970s and 1980s have witnessed sustained efforts by the Governments of Canada, the USA and the UK to criminalize perceived political opposition (usually movements of economic nationalism) through the use of the label 'terrorist'. Whether it is Canada and the Mohawk 'Warriors' or the FLQ, or the USA and the Governments of Nicaragua, Cuba, Libya, Grenada, Panama, etc. or the PLO or FMLN (Farabundo Marti National Liberation Front), etc., or the UK and the IRA, the political character of such 'opposition' is thus denied or invalidated and its suppression by the forces of national and international 'law and order' becomes justified. Given the horrendous scale of terror, death and destruction visited on such 'opposition', particularly by the actual or proxy forces of the USA ('globocop'), the articulation of the 'terrorist' version of the political/legal distinction has arguably been very effective. That such suppression is itself terrorism, that is 'state terrorism', is an idea only barely entertained in respectable academic circles (Greisman 1984; Chomsky 1987, 1988; Herman and O'Sullivan 1989).

'Civil' and 'criminal' law

The way the laws are written focusses attention on interpersonal predatory behaviour and property offenses. The conduct of individuals in an organizational or occupational context is generally exempted from criminal law: recall from [Chapter 2]

the differences in the anti-opium laws directed at the Asiatic
minority and the Proprietary Medicines Act directed at
physicians.

(Brannigan 1984: 100)

A second distinction that may be construed from within the structural conflict approach as a social control device embedded in the
administration of justice is that between 'torts' and 'crimes':

tort law . . . provides compensation or damages for wrongs
performed negligently or carelessly against persons or property
to whom we owe some duty of care. The most common example
is a civil action between two car-drivers where the plaintiff is
claiming damages for the death of a relative, or for injury to the
plaintiff or his passengers or for property damage or loss of
earnings.

(Parker 1983: 25)

Torts, then, are acts regarded as private wrongs to be settled
between the parties concerned by using, where desired, the resources of the civil law, whereas crimes are regarded as public
wrongs done against 'the state' which the state prosecutes using
the resources of the criminal law.

Legal history cannot provide us with a precise date at which
crime and tort became separate legal concepts . . . Royal justice
and private justice overlapped; royal retribution and private
feud lived side by side. Eventually two jurisdictions developed,
one for wrongs that were deemed 'public' (or crimes) and one
for wrongs that were deemed 'private' (or torts). Even today
there is some overlap between criminal and civil justice; assault,
trespass and libel are both crimes and torts . . . Slowly, crime
and tort developed differing forms and standards of behaviour
that would attract liability. The criminal law concept of responsibility (incorporating *mens rea*, the guilty mind, intention, recklessness or advertence) became distinct from the standard of
tortious liability (which eventually was based on negligence and
inadvertence) . . .
    By the sixteenth century, the categories of crime had become
established in a mould that still exists today – at least in relation
to serious crime. If we read the statutes and commentaries of
that period, we find that treason, murder, rape, arson, robbery
and theft were the most stringently condemned acts. They were

condemned because they threatened the internal security of the group; treason and murder most obviously of all . . . The other serious crimes . . . gained prominence, however, because they also threatened various forms of property rights that had become increasingly important as a result of the rise of a bourgeoisie in industrial and mercantile society . . . Indeed, the history of criminal law is very largely a series of reactions to actual or perceived breaches of public order and panic responses to emergencies that threatened private property and social stability.

(Parker 1983: 33–34, 45–46, 27).

In structural conflict terms this is to say that acts of resistance against ruling-class hegemony – killing or harming political or corporate leaders (= treason or murder), stealing or damaging their property (= theft, robbery, malicious damage), organizing civil resistance on the streets (= breach of public order, unlawful assembly, seditious libel), etc. – were and are assigned criminal status, that is treated as acts against the public good (not against the private interests of capitalist property holders and their collective 'executive branch', the government), to be combated by public servants, namely the police, and prosecuted in the name of the public by the crown. In contrast acts of negligence or inadvertence, that may cause untold death, injury or other harm to individuals, groups or whole populations, were and are treated for most legal purposes as private wrongs for which redress is to be sought by private individuals or groups through civil suits for damages. Torts carry none of the stigma and associated social penalties that attach to 'crimes'. And whereas the resources of the state are available for the prosecution of criminal offences, victims of torts must finance their suits from their own resources. If, then, as Parker's quote suggests, much of the criminal law developed as a means of controlling acts of opposition to capitalist rule, while relegating to torts the wrongs and injuries caused by capitalism itself, it can be seen that the crime–tort distinction is another powerful weapon in the armoury of the ruling class.

In 1974 in the USA there were approximately 100,000 occupationally induced deaths on the job and deaths from industrially induced disease, as well as 390,000 physical injuries. During this same period there were 20,600 murders and non-negligent manslaughters (Reiman, 1979: 75). Clearly, there is a far greater

risk to life as a result of health and safety violations on the job
than there is of dying at the hands of a gunman [sic]. However,
none of these health and safety violations are construed as acts
of murder because the law is wired to criminalize only individuals acting with the intent to kill. [Consequently], [w]hile
executives and businessmen operate unsafe work situations,
market dangerous products and poison the environment, no
one has spent a day in jail for any resulting deaths.

(Brannigan 1984: 101)

Comparable Canadian data (Reasons *et al.* 1981) indicates [sic]
that Canadians are eighteen times more likely to die from
work-related illness or injury than they are to be murdered. Yet,
the problem does not receive as much attention as conventionally defined murder.

(Hinch 1987: 192)

What both Brannigan and Parker fail to bring out in the passages
quoted above is the significance of the crime/tort or public/
private distinction as a vehicle of the patriarchal domination of
women (recall Chapter 1). Despite the fact that the home is the
primary site for the killing of women the criminal law has not
traditionally crossed the threshold from the street to the parlour.
In statute, prosecution and policing the sexual or otherwise
physical assault of wives by their husbands has not been regarded
as a crime. Prior to the recent changes in Canada and the United
States with respect to marital rape and the battered wife defence
that we reviewed in earlier chapters, the situation has been as
Edwards describes it for England and Wales. The crime/tort
distinction

perpetuates the public/private dichotomy which exists in the
substantive law and categorizes violence against wives as private
rather than public. From wife assault to marital rape, the
criminal law has conventionally never been regarded as the best
instrument for dealing with 'family matters'.

(Edwards 1990: 155)

She argues further that the legal redress made available to wives in
England and Wales through civil legislation introduced in the late
1970s has the symbolic function of '*obstruct[ing]* the recognition
of violence in the home as a criminal offence' (Edwards 1990: 155,
original emphasis). However, she does point out that since 1984

wives have become compellable witnesses in prosecutions brought against their husbands. That rape is nevertheless a criminal offence obfuscates what is essentially a patriarchal-cum-ruling-class concern to protect property rights in (their) wives or potential wives or, more precisely, in their 'unspoiled reproductive capacity', essential for the inheritance of accumulated wealth and the perpetuation of the class (Clark and Lewis 1977: 111–132; Parker 1983: 296–302). For the law applied, in effect, only to strangers.

Casting criminal law in universal terms

A third device by which the criminal law may be used to control class conflict in other-than-class terms is one that, initially, appears to provide a counter-argument to the position developed above. That is, it is perfectly clear that, with some sexist and heterosexist exceptions (which probably will not much longer survive), the criminal law is cast in universal terms. Its statutes apply to everybody. For example:

> 283. (1) Every one commits theft who fraudently and without colour of right takes, or fraudently and without colour of right converts to his use or to the use of another person, anything whether animate or inanimate, with intent,
> (a) to deprive, temporarily or absolutely, the owner of it or a person who has a special property or interest in it, of the thing or of his property or interest in it,
> (b) to pledge it or deposit it as security,
> (c) to part with it under a condition with respect to its return that the person who parts with it may be unable to perform, or
> (d) to deal with it in such a manner that it cannot be restored in the condition in which it was at the time it was taken or converted.
> (*Pocket Criminal Code* (Canada) 1982: 143–144)

The statute makes no reference to any 'offender characteristic' such as class or gender or race or age. Capitalists are not favoured over workers. It is designed to apply equally to all. Nothing could be more democratic. As the Prime Minister of Canada said repeatedly during the 'Oka Crisis', we are all equal before the law. But in so far as property is divided unequally in society, and the division is based on social class (defined, let us recall, in terms of the relationship of groupings of individuals to ownership of private property in the means of production), then it may be expected that acts designed to redress the inequality by the direct taking of others' property are rather more likely to be done on the propertied by the relatively unpropertied, than on any other group. This appears, in fact, to be the case (Hagan 1985). We are presenting here a deliberately instrumentalist–Marxist account of the role of the state in conjuring the law. Such an account is open to the left–realist objection that, in fact, 'Most crimes are committed against the working-class poor' (Kinsey *et al.* 1986: 7) by poor working-class offenders. We postpone a reply to this argument until the second section of Chapter 12 when we give a more structuralist account of the developments being discussed here.

In its application, then, a law criminalizing such acts – now called 'theft' – by all persons without discrimination is far more consequential in the protection it affords the holders of private property in the means of production than it is in protecting the largely propertyless members of the proletariat. Their acts of self-predation are of relatively little concern to the powerful, however significant the loss of their meagre property to theft is to workers themselves. It is far more important that their acts of 'political resistance' against the system of class rule which exploits them – acts of redistributing property – are not countered directly by the private forces of the ruling class in what would visibly be a class war, but instead are, through the vehicle of the criminal law of 'theft', re-conceptualized as 'crimes', as acts against the state, indeed, as acts against society itself, to be controlled by the agents of the state, namely the police and the courts. Thereby, their political and class character is removed, and they are seen to be merely criminal, moreover the product of individual pathology. In this way class rule is exercised in other-than-class terms.

The history of theft laws in the Anglo-Saxon tradition can then be invoked in support of this interpretation. When, in 1473, a 'carrier' hired to transport some bales of wool broke them open and took their contents – an act which to that point had not been considered a crime but rather a tort (since the bales were in his possession at the time) – the decision to make this a criminal offence opened the door 'to admit into the law of larceny a whole series of acts which had up to that time been purely civil wrongs' (Hall 1952: 10, cited in Hagan 1980: 605). This reflected the transition from feudalism to mercantile capitalism in which a growing bourgeoisie required protection to carry on trade in what was the most important product of the time. The state, in the form of the King, who was also a vigorous merchant himself, obliged and (various forms of) theft became a crime (Brannigan 1984: 4–5; recall Chambliss on vagrancy from Chapter 3).

As the passage from Parker quoted on p. 171 indicates, this account of the criminalization of offences against property could be matched by a similar account of the origins and functions of 'offences against public order', that other major category of actions that threaten the interests of the ruling class. Once again, for those without private power, for whom collective action at the workplace in the form of strikes or on the street in the form of demonstrations and rallies is their chief means of political action, the criminalization of 'tumultuous' gatherings (= riot or unlawful assembly) and of speech advocating the forceful overthrow of government (= seditious libel) amounts to class control by the state. Universal laws serve particular interests.

We may summarize the three foregoing points and conclude this section by saying that there is much at stake here for class rule, for failure to translate the political into the criminal might, as Carlen (1976: 101) indicates, 'rob the law of either its symbolic or instrumental aspirations and reveal, instead, the conflict and coercion inherent in its societal invocation'. It may be argued that the wider social and political significance of the Oka Crisis resided in the threat of just such a revelation. We saw in Chapter 3 how the laws criminalizing opium served to split the labour movement in early twentieth-century British Columbia, and thereby to secure the hegemony of the capitalist class against a threat to its rule. In Chapter 7 the role of the police in this politico-economic enterprise was described. In the rest of this chapter our goal is to examine how the administration of justice by the courts operates to 'realize' capitalist class relations and ruling-class interests. With the above section as an attempt to illuminate the 'invisible' framework from which they hang, we turn now to the courts themselves.

THE FUNCTIONS OF PRE-TRIAL AND TRIAL PROCEEDINGS

If the contribution of the police to class (or patriarchal or neo-colonialist) rule is to use the mandate of the criminal law to manage, contain and, in general, control 'problem populations' –

to produce, that is, a collection of candidate offenders – then the function of the courts is to render their offences politically harmless, their class (or sexist or racist) character expunged. This ideological task of mystification is done in a variety of ways at the pre-trial and trial stages of court proceedings.

The pre-trial stage

Perhaps the most striking fact about criminal proceedings is that the overwhelming majority of cases – estimates for Canadian, American and British courts range from 80 to 90 per cent – are settled without a trial by the defendant pleading guilty. Perhaps the second most striking fact is the extent to which offenders are convicted of offences they did not strictly commit, or, at least, offences that are different from that or those with which they were originally charged. In Chapter 9 we rehearse an organizational explanation for these facts. In this chapter, however, we argue that pre-trial arrangements – for it is in the pre-trial stage that these matters are decided – are ways of de-politicizing the offences by preventing them from coming to trial. Pre-trial procedures remove the possibility of these acts being seen as defensible, that is, through the admission of guilt, and systematically obfuscate and mystify the offences by reducing them to lesser offences, or, in the case of girls and young women, by sexualizing or 'therapizing' offences.

There is the myth, widely believed, that modern industrial societies like Canada, the USA and the UK are awash with crime, and that such crime is overwhelmingly violent in nature, consisting of offences against the person such as murder, sexual assault and robbery (that is, theft with violence). The truth is, that when traffic offences, including impaired driving, are removed from the total, the vast majority of recorded offences are minor property offences. The contradiction is explained by the role of the courts which has the effect of making the property offences invisible and the serious offences against the person visible. Because the minor offences are routinely plea-bargained, they are settled by a guilty plea without a trial. There is little or no publicity. The relatively few cases of this type the press does pick up on will be those with a particular angle that makes them a little out of the ordinary and therefore newsworthy. It will be the noteworthy offender, the unusual method, the spectacular arrest, that is, cases with just those features that are not routine that will come to public attention. But the public will have little sense of the sheer volume of routinely dealt-with property offences committed by predominantly poorer people. Instead, what is publicized and shapes the content of public consciousness is the tiny minority of cases that, because of a not guilty plea, do come to trial. Of these it is the murders and sexual assaults that provide the fodder of local and regional crime reporting in the news media. These offences are not readily seen in class terms. (We take up the purpose they do serve in the next section on the trial stage.) This mystification of crime is an important ideological function of the criminal justice system and its attendant media of communication (cf. Fishman 1980: Chapter 6). The mechanism of plea bargaining is one crucial device on which it depends for making invisible the essentially property-based nature of routine crime, and therefore obscuring its class character.

To this must be added the making invisible of the crimes of the powerful, that is, ruling-class crime. We have seen already how that is partially achieved through the defining of the potentially harmful acts of the powerless as 'crimes' and the potentially harmful acts of the powerful as 'torts'. For those acts of businesspeople and corporations for which there are criminal sanctions such as fines and imprisonment, 'much of the legislation . . . has not been put in the [Canadian] Criminal Code' (Snider 1988: 304). Examples of such Federal Statutes are the Combines Investigation Act, the Food and Drug Act, the Weights and Measures Act and the Hazardous Products Act. In the case of the Combines Investigation Act, for example, the regulatory body (the Combines Investigation Branch) may choose whether to proceed through the criminal courts or by issuing a report upon an investigation and holding hearings to communicate the results to the public. What must be emphasized here is the miniscule enforcement of such acts, the tiny frequency of convictions and the entirely nominal nature of the sentences (Goff and Reasons 1978). Business crime – what is euphemistically called 'white-collar crime' – as part of the exploitation of one class by another is thereby rendered invisible. We should add, in anticipation of an argument we make in Chapter 12, that when the occasional case is allowed to surface it is made to serve the purpose of showing that after all the law falls on the rich and the poor alike.

Our third point is more speculative since we know of no studies that bear directly on it. As studies of plea bargaining, such as that by Sudnow reviewed in Chapter 10, show, the offence for which one is convicted may be (1) only one of those for which one was charged ('saturation charging' being standard police practice in Canada), (2) a lesser, 'included' offence than the one charged or (3) a lesser, 'unincluded' offence than the one charged. Thus, to anticipate Sudnow to illustrate (3), one may be initially charged with 'molesting a minor' but convicted, on a guilty plea, of 'loitering around a schoolyard' where one may never have been anywhere near a schoolyard. (Compare the slightly different circumstances where an appeal is involved. *Time* magazine (8 April 1985, p. 32) reported, in connection with the Bernhard Goetz case: 'When Bernhard was twelve, his father was accused and convicted on charges of molesting two 15-year-old boys. The elder Goetz appealed the verdict and later pleaded guilty on a reduced charge of disorderly conduct.') The point is that in each case a distorted lessening of the nature and gravity of one's actions is achieved. As Blumberg (1976: 160, fn. 24; emphasis added) says, writing of the American courts, 'The vast range of crime categories which are available facilitates the patterned court process of plea reduction to a lesser offense, *which is also usually a socially less opprobrious crime.*'

This has a number of consequences. Firstly, one's agency is partially removed from one's actions. (This may also be accomplished without plea bargaining, simply through the dismissal of charges. It is a tactic one suspects is used by prosecutors to forestall attempts by (anti-nuclear, women's rights, gay rights, anti-war, anti-racist, prisoners' rights . . .) demonstrators charged with some public order offence from pleading not guilty and using the trial as an occasion to publicize their cause.) Secondly, if one is victim of a sexual assault and the offence is plea-bargained to, say, common assault, the nature of one's victimization is removed; the sexually-violent character of the crime is 'disappeared'. Moviewatchers will recall such a case from *The Accused.* Thirdly, there is evidence that, even prior to charging, paternalistic concern for the welfare of adolescent female offenders on the part of police and court personnel results in a diminishing of the seriousness of whatever criminal act has been committed and the substituting of a preference for treating the young person as incorrigible or, if evidence can be found, of being sexually promiscuous and thereby in need of protection rather than prosecution. What we are saying, then, is that the lessening and changing of offences in the plea-bargaining process involves a process of alienation, in which persons are separated from their actions, the character of those actions – including the real conditions in which they arose – is mystified and the result is discarded from the system as so much junk. Since defendants are overwhelmingly working class this alienation clearly has a class character. For victims of sexual assault it may also have a sexist character. Whether, in the case of female crime, its character is also patriarchal (Allen 1987) is a matter we take up below.

We derive our fourth point from the study by Ericson and Baranek (1982) of *The Ordering of Justice*, referred to at greater length in Chapter 9. From a detailed consideration of the organizational and legal factors that enter into 'plea negotiation' they conclude as follows.

> In light of such practices as police 'overlaying' higher and multiple charges, and routinized agreements for withdrawal of dual charges arising from the same incident, it is extremely difficult to ascertain what a 'deal' or 'bargain' consists of . . . Furthermore, given the greater number of elements which go into judicial determinations of guilt and innocence, and sentence, it is also difficult to say whether someone in any particular case might have 'got off more lightly' by pleading not guilty than by agreeing to a guilty plea arrangement, or vice versa . . .
>
> The question of whether a 'deal' or 'bargain' is obtained must be answered ultimately in terms of the perceptions of the various actors . . . To the extent that the criminal control agents reach an agreement that merely reflects the going rate . . . , and to the extent the accused is nevertheless made to believe that he got a bargain . . . , the term 'plea bargaining' can be seen as another source of *mystification for keeping the accused in order.*
>
> (Ericson and Baranek 116–117, emphasis added)

The trial stage

Since trials are the exception rather than the rule in the criminal justice system we will not dwell on them. To do so is to risk joining in with what structural conflict theorists would call the ideological picture of the nature of justice offered by system apologists, news media, television dramas and movies, and fostered by the allocation

of courtrooms themselves. Thus, for example, in our local jurisdiction, only one of eight courtrooms deals with the myriad
routine crimes disposed of by guilty pleas without trials, while five
courtrooms are reserved for trials (plus one for traffic offences,
and one for 'set dates'). Trials, then, are always going on, and, of
course, are always being reported. They then come to play a much
bigger part in the 'social construction of justice' than their frequency as a proportion of all cases would arguably warrant.
Indeed, they provide recurring occasions for the 'dramatization of
evil', for the creation of 'folk devils', whether of the 'crazed (serial
or mass) killer', 'vicious rapist', 'wicked (abusing) mother', 'young
slut' or 'youth gangs' variety. They become stages on which are
played out the ritual moral dramas of good and evil, guilt and
innocence, trust and betrayal, fear and loathing, sexual jealousy,
family secrets, generational conflict, the war of the sexes and so on.
Persons are cast as individuals or as representatives of standard
social types. Trials, then, have important symbolic functions even
as they serve to discipline the accused and those like him or her.
(One often feels, watching the standard round of US network
made-for-TV movies with their predictable dose of violence against
women, that they somehow serve as a vehicle for the disciplining
of women, reminding them of, and keeping them in, their place.)
The epitome of this process are jury trials.

They symbolize the fight between 'good' and 'evil' and assure
citizens that the system is working as it should (whether this is
true or not). Thus, jury trials have considerable ideological
impact on the society. They are, as Silberman put it, our equivalent of the medieval morality play (Silberman, 1980: 382); the
'focal point of the ideology of democratic justice' (McBarnet,
1981: 79). The fact that they reproduce existing class and status
relationships – middle-class White males tend to become fore-
men, not Blacks, Native peoples, women, or lower-class people
– and that they are capable of incredible prejudice against
certain types of defendants in certain locales, such as Blacks in
the southern states or Native Indians in Kenora – does not
detract from their importance in the criminal justice system.
The prominence they have achieved in the media, as part and
parcel of the whole public myth surrounding what happens in
the courts, however, promotes a picture of the criminal justice
system that is not borne out by the facts. It is now overwhelm-

ingly clear that, jury or no jury, virtually all the elements in the criminal justice system, from the initial encounter with the police to the *denouement* in court, work to the systematic disadvantage of the accused. The case against the accused is constructed, at considerable expense, by paid agents of the state out of the seemingly inexhaustible public purse; that of the defence is pure private enterprise, (with the partial and limited exception of legal aid), whereby one receives the defence one can afford. But beyond this, as McBarnet (1981) and Ericson and Baranek (1982) have pointed out, the prosecution has access to information the defence cannot obtain until the court date; it has trained experts and forensic laboratories to construct evidence; it can compel witnesses to testify and reward recalcitrant ones (with immunity from prosecution, for example); and it has comprehensive powers of search and seizure. Even the most affluent defendant is hard put to overcome the structured, systematic, and comprehensive advantages which reside on the side of the Crown.

(Snider 1988: 306–307)

SENTENCING AND DOMINATION

How is ruling-class domination effected through sentencing? Structural conflict sociologists have approached this question from both instrumentalist and structuralist orientations. Instrumentalists have looked for discrimination against workers and women and racial minorities in the form of heavier sentences for the same offence. That is, the supposition is that judges' sentencing practices would be the vehicle by which the state, acting in the interests of capital, men and whites, coerces the working class, women, natives and blacks through legal punishment. To test this it would be necessary to show that judges take such extra-legal or 'non-legitimized' (Hagan 1991: 175–176) factors as class and sex and race into account at sentencing so as to produce more punitive outcomes for the dominated groups.

The results of such studies as have been done do not generally or clearly support the instrumentalist thesis. Firstly, it is necessary to say that much of the observed disparity in sentencing outcomes is accounted for by such legal or 'legitimized' factors as seriousness of offence and prior record. Secondly, where, as in Canada, the legal system gives judges wide discretion in the type and length of sentences to be imposed, and a national basis for regulating sentencing has not existed, it is not surprising that considerable variation occurs (Griffiths and Verdun-Jones 1989: 336–337). Hogarth (1971), for example, has shown very wide disparities in the sentences handed down for the same offence by different Ontario judges. However, he also found that individual judges' sentencing patterns were predictable on the basis of their sentencing philosophies. Thirdly, where studies have produced results showing the influence of class, gender and race the variation has not all been in the predicted direction. That is, while there is evidence that the poor and unemployed, women, natives and blacks have received more severe sentences than their richer, employed, male, white counterparts when legal factors are held constant, there is also evidence that the dominated groups have been treated more leniently.

While these results clearly pose a problem for the instrumentalist thesis, they are more readily accommodated, not to say expected, in structuralist terms. If capitalism, patriarchy and neo-colonialism really are in control, and if the job of the state is to reproduce the social relations whereby those types of domination are exercised, then both severity and leniency of sentence are explainable in the right structural context. There are two points. The first point is that, as Sharrock (1979: 136) says in criticizing Marxist interactionists (see Chapter 9) looking for signs of a struggle for dominance in doctor–patient encounters, 'Someone who is genuinely and firmly in control does not have to contest that fact with those he [sic] controls – that he does not have to contest it is one of the things, surely, that being in control means.' That is, the state through the courts does not need to discriminate in order to rule. Indeed, structuralists would argue that to the extent that rule is more efficacious when based on consent then it is in the interests of the rulers that justice be 'fair', that is that it comply with formal legal rules of due process and equality before the law. This way it secures authority for itself, and is seen to be authoritative. If, as Marxists of all persuasions argue, the whole system is substantively rigged in favour of power in the first place then formal fairness will produce the desired results anyway, and without the threat posed by cases of gross inequality in sentencing giving the whole game away. As Michael Shapiro said to one of the authors in answer to his question at a conference on 'Discourses of Power' in Arizona in 1987, 'authority is power's way of cutting the costs'.

The second point is, then, that the social relations of subordination be reproduced through sentencing simply by judges mirroring the social presuppositions of the wider society. We consider class, gender and race in turn.

Class

In sentencing studies class has rarely been conceptualized and measured in Marxian terms. Rather, the employment status of the offender has been examined. Here, it appears that judges see unemployment as a mitigating factor in some circumstances and as an aggravating factor in others. In either case the dependent and manipulable status of the unemployed is preserved. Some evidence of the perceived structural conditions under which unemployment becomes an aggravating factor in sentencing comes from a study reported by Box (1983). He argues that it is in times of economic hardship that inequality is the outcome of judges' sentencing decisions. Writing of the United Kingdom in the early 1980s Box says:

> Thus the growth of unemployment, which is itself a reflection of deepening economic crisis, has been accompanied by an increase in the range and severity of state coercion, including the length of imprisonment. The increased use of imprisonment was not a direct response to any rise in crime, but was rather an ideologically motivated response to the *perceived* threat of crime posed by the swelling population of economically marginalized persons. Whether this perception was based on 'fact' is unclear for the literature on unemployment and crime (Box and Hale 1982; Tarling 1982) comes to an ambiguous conclusion. But what is clear is that this perception was *real* in its consequences. Unemployment levels have and are having an effect on the rate and severity of imprisonment *over and above* the effect produced by changes in the volume and pattern of crime (Box and Hale 1982). The unemployment-effect on prison population is not a result of the courts mechanically responding to increased 'work-load'; it is essentially produced by the judiciary acting in terms of its beliefs on the relationship between unemployment and crime and what might deter potential unemployed persons from committing crimes.
>
> (Box 1983: 212, original emphasis)

Box and Hale (1982) show that in England and Wales from 1949 to 1979 'for every 1,000 increase in youth unemployment 23 additional young males get sent to prison *after the effect of crime rates and court workload have been controlled*' (Box 1983: 216, original emphasis). The condition is exacerbated for black and other ethnic minority young men. And what is the purpose of this preference for imprisoning the 'problem population' of young, working-class urban (black) males (and increasingly females)? Given, as we shall see, the extent to which the crimes of the powerful go more or less unprosecuted and unpunished, then the purpose cannot be to control serious crime.

> Rather [governments] are more concerned to instil discipline, directly and indirectly, on those people who are no longer controlled by the soft-discipline-machine of work and who might become growingly resentful that they are being made to pay the price for economic recession. Whilst the powerful are getting away with crimes whose enormity appears to sanctify them, the powerless are getting prison.
>
> (Box 1983: 219)

Gender

The same argument is applicable to the results of sentencing studies with respect to gender. As with unemployment both mitigation and aggravation have been found. Thus:

> After controlling for a large number of legal and extra-legal variables, and examining their effects on different stages in the criminal justice process, [Nagel] concluded that her data failed to reveal any: 'evidence that females were more harshly treated . . . females charged with a crime were significantly less likely than males similarly charged to spend any time behind bars . . .' (Nagel 1981: 111).
>
> However, she also found that this conclusion did not apply across the spectrum of offences, for where a female's offence exhibited 'inappropriate sex-role behaviour' the penal outcome tended to be harsher.
>
> (Box 1983: 173)

Essentially the same assessment has been afforded more recently by Smart (1990: 79).

Again, as with unemployment, both results are open to the same structuralist interpretation. Sentencing decisions, whether lenient or severe, reproduce patriarchy by embodying paternalism towards women. On the one hand leniency is deemed appropriate for women who are seen as primarily mothers whose essentially domestic lives should not be interrupted by imprisonment. On the other hand 'courts act to protect "traditional" women by punishing those who are "unconventional"' (Box 1983: 173).

Box goes on to say that given 'the variability in the methodological adequacy and the contradictory results of [much] research [on female crime], it would be wise to avoid dogmatic assertions' (ibid). We recommend Box's chapter, 'Powerlessness and crime – the case of female crime', in his *Power, Crime, and Mystification* (1983), to be followed by Smart's (1990) valuable feminist explanation and evaluation of this state of affairs in criminology, the chapter on feminist criminology in Downes and Rock (1988 (1982)) and Valverde's (1991) review of the literature.

Race

A parallel situation obtains in the case of race. The overall result of many sentencing studies, particularly in the United States, is that in aggregate there is no appreciable disparity between blacks and whites in sentencing outcomes. However, the aggregate result conceals two contrasting patterns of differential sentencing. For the same offence, with legal factors held constant, blacks receive both more severe and more lenient sentences than whites. Again both differences can be explained as the outcome of the same structure of subordination. Thus, for example, when blacks kill blacks they are treated more leniently than when whites or blacks kill whites. 'Niggers' not being regarded as quite fully human or quite fully civilized, their loss does not count as highly as that of whites, and self-predation is after all only an expectable reversion to type. Racism similarly may be said to account for the scandalous infant mortality rates among blacks in the United States. On the other hand when black males rape white women, only lynching and castration are really good enough. According to Amnesty International (1990), reporting a 1990 comprehensive study by the US General Accounting Office, the race of the victim continues to be a factor in the imposition of the death penalty in the United States. Those who murder whites are more often executed by the state. As we have seen in the sections above, under the structuralist Marxist interpretation the administration of justice is designed to protect valued property. The case of the treatment of the aboriginal peoples in Canada is not dissimilar, if not so dramatic. It is not unusual for judges and magistrates practising in 'the North' to treat native offenders more leniently than they would whites. But in the 'South', albeit predominantly in rural jurisdictions, the poverty of native offenders sentenced to pay a fine for minor offences like being drunk and disorderly results in their supplying a vastly greater proportion of the inmates of prisons than their numbers in the general population would predict. It is not necessary for the judiciary to be racist. In a racist society just by doing their job they keep the bothersome natives off the streets.

After this brief review of sentencing in terms of 'structures of dominance' based on class, gender and race, we return to a more general consideration of this topic. Alongside the apparently merely reproductive function of sentencing needs to be placed the consequences of earlier decisions in the criminal justice process. As we have seen in part in earlier chapters class and gender and race get built into the formulation of the law and into police practices; for example, patriarchy is implicated in the way police respond to calls (Chapter 5). This remains true as we proceed through the police decision to record a reported occurrence as an actual offence or 'unfound' it (USA, Canada) or write it off as 'no crime' (UK) (Bottomley and Coleman 1981: Chapter 4), the judicial decision to prosecute or not, the plea negotiation, the arguments of counsel in trials, the decision to convict by judge or jury and the working up of pre-sentence reports by probation officers (Allen 1987). While clearly there is much more that can be said about these topics we will conclude with two observations, one about patriarchy, the other about capitalism.

For the range of crimes of violence against the person, where the person is a woman or a girl, traditionally there has been a stark contrast between the penalties available – for example, life imprisonment in many jurisdictions for rape – and the actual sentences meted out to the paltry few who 'survive' the attrition through the system (Clark and Lewis 1977). A similar contrast may be drawn between the inflammatory rhetoric that accompanies the drinking-and-driving problem and the nominal sentences traditionally received by the few who are ever convicted (Gusfield 1981:

Chapter 5). For Gusfield this feature of drinking-and-driving warrants the title 'moral fault without censure'. The point of the legal rhetoric (recall Chapter 4) is not to deter offenders but to symbolically man the moral boundaries of proper conduct. It is tempting to say that the rape or sexual assault laws are similarly symbolic in so far as: (1) their deterrent effect appears negligible, such assaults being not only 'frequent' but virtually endemic; (2) police have standardly unfounded or written off some 30 per cent of reported cases; (3) victims have standardly felt they were on trial rather than the accused; and so on.

But this is to ignore the way the laws have been framed and applied. Thus, at least four categories of women could not for all practical legal purposes be found to have been raped, namely wives (by statute), prostitutes (by virtue of their occupation), women with a sex life (= 'unchaste', 'promiscuous') and women on a date with their attacker. In its prosecution the law became a device for policing such women conceived as moral types, rather than punishing and deterring those who did or would violate them. Where, however, enforcement is pursued and punishment is severe is in the case of the violation of 'respectable' women. Such women are valuable patriarchal property. The protection of such property is the purpose of the prosecution of this law.

The second observation shows the class basis of sentencing, not in terms of disparity in sentences for the same offence but for different offences. Glaring examples of inequality reside in the gap between typical sentences for standard Criminal Code (Canada) offences compared with those for white-collar crimes:

> Item: The average prison sentence for robbery is 38.9 months; that for income tax evasion (which nets the culprit 10 to 20 times as much, on average) is 1.4 months (Mandel, 1983; cited in Brannigan, 1984: 108).
>
> Item: The Department of Revenue reveals to the Supreme Court of Canada that people who steal from the government through tax fraud are not prosecuted if they can pay up when caught. In other words, only the relatively poor offenders are charged (Tepperman, 1977: 163).
>
> Item: No employer in Ontario has been imprisoned for stealing from employees by paying wages below the legal minimum, denying vacation pay, termination pay, or the overtime pay required by law (Snider and West, 1980: 225).

Item: Merchants who stole from customers by employing inaccurate scales were fined an average of $204.26 per charge between January 1974 and June 1976, and none were imprisoned (Snider and West, 1980: 229, recomputed).

(Snider 1988: 304)

Chapter 9

Justice and symbolic interaction

In this chapter we shall be considering symbolic interactionist work on the administration or 'construction' of justice. We begin by introducing the interactionist tradition of inquiry into the role of 'accounts' in social action, with particular reference to excuses and justifications offered by defendants in court. We then consider lawyers' application of conceptions of delinquents in courtroom interaction before turning to studies of the organizational context of the work of lawyers and judges in plea negotiation and sentencing. Fourthly, we examine the professional dominance thesis in relation to lawyer–client and court–defendant interaction.

'ACCOUNTS' AND COURTROOM INTERACTION

It is perhaps not surprising that symbolic interactionists have paid particular attention to the use of 'accounts' in their studies of courtroom processes since the court is a prime site where persons can be expected to explain themselves, justifying their actions, offering excuses for their behaviour, etc. Indeed, it is partly on such accounts of their conduct, in response to allegations, that the court's verdict and the judge's sentence (if any) will be based. Accordingly, in this section we shall consider symbolic interactionist work on accounts with particular reference to their role in courtroom interaction.

Probably the earliest symbolic interactionist work on the connection between accounts and conduct is that of C. Wright Mills and Sutherland, though what they had to say was rather brief. In his article, 'Situated Actions and Vocabularies of Motive', Mills (1940) referred to socially defined and available 'vocabularies of motive' as permitting the 'release' of the energy required to perform an action. These 'vocabularies' were 'good reasons', 'justifications', 'excuses', etc., in terms of which action could be said to make sense both prior to and after its occurrence. Sutherland (1939) made use of a similar notion in his theory of differential association and, in particular, his theory of white-collar crime (Sutherland 1949). In the former he proposed that a person 'becomes delinquent because of an excess of definitions favourable to violation of law over definitions unfavourable to violation of law'. These 'definitions' referred not only to techniques of committing crime, but also to 'a collection of motives, rationalizations, excuses and justifications for committing crimes'. In his study of white-collar crime Sutherland indicated that an 'ideology' for illegal business practice is learned which 'helps the novice to accept the illegal practices and provide rationalizations for them'.

The first major symbolic interactionist study in this genre was Cressey's (1953) work, *Other People's Money*. After interviewing numerous persons convicted of embezzling from their places of employment, Cressey theorized that in addition to being in positions of financial trust and experiencing 'nonshareable financial problems' embezzlers employed 'vocabularies of adjustment' which permitted them to engage in embezzling behaviour. Such permission not only preceded these illegal acts but it was also necessary, argued Cressey. This was because the offenders conceived of themselves as essentially non-criminal. Vocabularies of adjustment or rationalizations such as the characterization of the act as only 'borrowing' enabled the embezzler to take the money and at the same time preserve a sense of him or herself as non-criminal, at least for the initial acts of embezzlement.

The explanatory role into which motives and rationalizations were cast in the work of Mills (1940), Sutherland (1949) and Cressey (1953), and the conception of the criminal and delinquent as basically conformist and in need of linguistic constructs through which they could accommodate crime with a conventional identity, were continued in the work of Matza on *Delinquency and Drift* (1990 (1964)). Matza's aim is to counteract the misleading tendency amongst criminologists to envisage the delinquent as essentially different from conformist youth and as committed to their delinquency. Such a view is that of the 'positive delinquent', says Matza – one who is committed to their misdeeds and constrained by the values and norms of a 'delinquent subculture'. Not so, says Matza. Rather than being committed to delinquency, the delinquent 'drifts' into situated acts of delinquency by virtue of a collection of ideas which permit its occasional occurrence. These ideas include five 'techniques of neutralization' which excuse or justify delinquent acts. These are (1) the denial of the victim, (2) the condemnation of the condemners, (3) the denial of responsibility, (4) the denial of injury and (5) the appeal to higher loyalties. They enable a kind of 'moral holiday' for the youth, an episodic release from the constraints of conformity. Thus, the 'denial of responsibility' permits the youth to say he or she did not mean it to happen, that it was an accident. The denial of the victim permits the delinquent to say he or she 'did it in self-defence'. The condemnation of the condemners involves pointing to the 'far worse' crimes committed by more conventional and typically more powerful persons and groups (for example, 'alcohol is far more harmful, so why bust us for marihuana?') The 'denial of injury' permits the claim that 'no one was hurt'. Finally, the 'appeal to higher loyalties' provides for the explanation that the delinquent act was 'required' or 'demanded' in some way by a 'higher authority'.

These symbolic interactionist studies were later subjected to conceptual clarification in an article by Scott and Lyman (1968) entitled 'Accounts'. They indicate that, for the most part, this corpus of work was referring to one of two varieties of 'accounts': excuses or justifications. Thus excuses admit wrongfulness but deny responsibility whilst justifications admit responsibility but deny wrongfulness.

In later studies the role of accounts has been examined not in relation to how they facilitate criminal behaviour in the first place but with respect to their role after the offender has been charged and put on trial for such behaviour. Two studies are of particular note here. The first, by Taylor (1972), is concerned with sexual offenders' accounts of their crimes. The second, by Emerson (1969), examines the use by delinquents of excuses and justifications in the juvenile court.

Taylor: sex offenders' accounts of their motives

Taylor's study is interesting because it not only provides a description of the range of accounts used by sexual offenders, it also examines the relative acceptability of those accounts for the courts. As far as the former is concerned, accounts range from the involuntary to the voluntary. Involuntary accounts cited factors which were beyond the individual's control at the time of the offence and they deprecated the role of a conscious motive for the assaults. Out of a total of ninety-four accounts offered in the study, forty-one thus cited some form of 'breakdown in mental functioning' such as temporary insanity, a blackout or fit or some kind of cortical disturbance. Twelve explained the behaviour in terms of an 'inner impulse' such as instinct or an overwhelming desire which 'compelled' the offender to act against his will. In this regard offenders spoke of being 'sex-mad' and 'over-sexed', mere spectators while their irreversible and uncontrollable urges took over. Another twelve 'involuntary' offenders spoke in terms of 'defective social skills'. For them their assaults were a 'mistake'. They thus claimed things like 'I didn't know what I was doing', 'I just stumbled into the situation', and 'I didn't mean to frighten her. I was trying to ask her to go out with me'. Voluntary accounts, on the other hand, admitted the active role played by the offender in the commission of the offence. Six accounts 'implicated the victim', saying they were tempted and willingly went along with the temptation, seven reported a desire for special experiences, three confessed a wish to frighten or hurt the victim and another five reported a refusal to accept the normative constraints surrounding sexual relations; they insisted on the importance of allowing 'free play'. One of these last stated 'I'll do it to anybody. It's all a laugh to me.'

Turning to the relative acceptability of these accounts, Taylor found that with respect to twenty-six magistrates questioned there were marked differences in acceptability. The magistrates were offered the various categories of accounts and were asked how likely they thought it was that the statement was true and how likely it was that the remark would be made by a sexual deviant. This was done in relation to three offences: rape, indecent assault and indecent exposure. The relative acceptability was consistent across these three offence categories. Thus the most acceptable accounts were those mentioning 'involuntary factors' whilst the least acceptable were those of the voluntary variety. Thus:

Account	Number of judgments of acceptability as true
Defective social skills	49
Breakdown in mental functioning	40
Inner impulse	38
Wish to frighten or hurt	36
Implicating the victim	34
Desire for special experiences	26
Refusal to accept normative constraints	22

These results show that magistrates are more likely to accept as true those accounts which cite 'involuntary' factors.

Emerson: typical delinquencies in the juvenile court

Symbolic interactionism has had a long-standing interest in the use of social types, classifications and labels in social interaction. This is in keeping with its concern for illuminating the 'actor's point of view'. As we shall show in the next chapter, this interest in 'typification' is one which it shares with phenomenology and ethnomethodology, but with certain key differences in approach. We review these differences in the next chapter. It remains true, however, as we noted in Chapter 5, that ethnographic studies in symbolic interactionism and ethnomethodology are often quite similar since their authors frequently draw on both of these traditions (see Hawkins and Tiedeman 1975). A major example of this is the work of Emerson on *Judging Delinquents*. He examines the interactional practices and the typifications used by court staff in dealing with alleged juvenile offenders.

With respect to the typifying work of the court he found that an initial distinction could be drawn between those cases typified as involving 'trouble' and those not. Of course, all youths brought before the court are regarded by someone as trouble; every complaint is a plea for the court to do something about the defendant. However, Emerson found that the court has its own ways of judging or typifying trouble. For the court 'trouble' is a 'predictive construct'. It is the 'inferred potential for committing serious delinquent acts'. Trouble relates to the type of person the offender is, not simply to the type of offence he or she has committed. The nature of the offence may assist in typifying the trouble but it will not be the only criterion. Serious offences create a 'presumption of trouble', but trouble is also predicted on the basis of the presence of adverse patterns of behaviour and social circumstances which typically precede delinquency.

The court's focus on the offender rather than the offence flows from its commitment to treatment rather than simple sanctioning of the juveniles who come before it. As Emerson puts it, the court's concern is not so much 'what happened' but 'what is the problem here'. Once it has decided that it has trouble on its hands, it looks in greater depth at the juvenile's overall behaviour, personality and family and social circumstances. There then occurs what Emerson calls a 'second sorting' which involves establishing or typifying the juvenile's 'moral character' (recall Sacks on the assessment of moral character, in Chapter 6).

Assessments of moral character provide for the kind of special handling that cases require. That is, assessments of moral character differentiate kinds of trouble and provide accounts for the delinquent behaviour. Three general types of moral character were distinguished by the court: the 'normal', the 'hard-core' and the 'disturbed'. The juvenile with a 'normal' moral character was seen as being like most kids, acting for basically normal and conventional reasons, despite some delinquent behaviour. Those seen as 'hard-core' were typified as criminal-like delinquents, motivated by malice and hostility, consciously pursuing illegal ends. The 'disturbed' moral character belongs to those who were driven to acting in senseless and irrational ways by obscure motives and inner compulsions. These distinctions echo those described in Cicourel's earlier (1968) study of juvenile justice.

The significance of the categories of juvenile moral character is that they provide institutionally relevant means for explaining the juvenile behaviour and they provide justifications for the court's actions. Thus, to decide that a youth is 'disturbed' is to account for his or her behaviour and to provide the relevance of psychiatric care, whilst to typify the youth as 'hard-core' explains the behaviour as a product of that kind of criminally motivated actor who needs punishment and restraint. The decision that the juvenile is 'normal' explains the behaviour as the result of conventional motives and provides justification for routine handling, for example, probation.

If these are the types of moral character used by the court in examining and dealing with individual cases the question is then raised as to how moral character is decided. Emerson suggests that in general it is a product of social interaction and communicative work involving the delinquent, his or her family, enforcers, complainants generally and the court. In particular, it involves two types of social process. The first is the presentation by the prosecuting and defence lawyers of different versions of moral character. The second is the use of protective strategies by the juvenile.

There are two types of character presentation used by the lawyers: pitches and denunciations. Pitches are directed to obtaining a more lenient disposition than would initially seem appropriate. They tend to emphasize the sterling moral qualities of the defendant. Denunciations, on the other hand, seek a more severe disposition than could be expected. They aim to soil and discredit the juvenile's character. Both focus on the delinquent act and both emphasize the delinquent's general behaviour, including personal and social background, arguing that these provide evidence of moral character. Successful pitches manage to depict the act as a typical product of a normal actor and thus establish the normality of the youth's biography. Successful denunciations establish the present act as that typically committed by delinquents of a criminal-like character and they manage to construct a delinquent biography that unequivocally indicates someone of such character.

In presenting both pitches and denunciations the lawyers focus on (1) the offence and (2) the defendant's biography. With respect to the offence, they make use of the notion of 'typical delinquencies' (see Sudnow in Chapter 10). These consist of the typical features of regularly encountered delinquent acts and delinquents, embodying the court's experience with and commonsense knowledge of the situations and settings of delinquent acts. Each typical delinquency or delinquent is composed of typical elements or features. For example, the typical shoplifter is a mild type, not a serious delinquent, with no previous record, from a well-to-do family, who takes goods for kicks, is seldom in trouble, not a thief at heart, succumbing to the temptation of the moment. On the other hand, the typical handbag snatcher is a pretty serious delinquent, known to other courts, maybe on parole or probation and is aggressive. Furthermore, typical delinquencies as a whole were divided into three classes by the court. Thus, for example, the 'normal' assault is a fight comprising a street scene, young boys, fists (weapons only in the 'heat' of battle) and equal contributions by both parties. By contrast, the 'criminal assault' is an attack on a stranger, typically motivated by robbery, and is vicious, causing serious harm, sometimes murder. The 'disturbed assault' has no apparent motive, involves strangers, and is typically an irrational outburst. The job for the denouncer, if he or she is to be successful, is to demonstrate that the features of a typical criminal assault were present. For a successful pitch, the task is to show that those of the normal assault were present.

With respect to the defendant's biography, denunciations seek to place the delinquent act at or near the ultimate stage in the youth's delinquent career, that is, a hopeless case. Pitches demonstrate that the youth has rehabilitation prospects, that the person's delinquent involvement is inconsequential, and that they are growing out of it. Both denunciations and pitches attempt to do this first by 'establishing a pattern'. The denouncer therefore presents a history of both official and unofficial prior delinquency, uses reports to accentuate the significance of the present incident and emphasizes the youth's bad attitude, trouble at school, truancy and bad companions. The pitch's pattern-making, on the other hand, involves minimizing the significance of prior trouble, the youth's cooperation and good attitude. Secondly, the denouncer and the pitcher refer to 'family background and sponsorship'. Here both try to show the presence or absence of the typical background and circumstances associated with the type of delinquency which they are recommending to the court.

Emerson's work shows the importance of typification in judging delinquents. However, before leaving it we must emphasize that this is not to say that dealing with delinquents is solely a one-sided cognitive process. The juvenile does at least have the opportunity to provide a version of the events leading to the court appearance. Emerson thus refers to three types of 'defensive strategy' employed by the juveniles in courtroom discourse: (1) the plea of innocence, (2) justifications and (3) excuses. These are the sort of accounts we discussed earlier in the chapter on the role of accounts in symbolic interactionist work. Coleman (1976) provides a useful symbolic interactionist analysis of 'grievance accounts' in traffic court, an analysis that may be compared to the ethnomethodological studies of traffic court interaction by Pollner, whose work we examine in Chapter 10.

THE ORGANIZATIONAL IMPERATIVES OF COURTROOM WORK

As Peter Berger (1963) says in his famous, if now somewhat dated, short *Invitation to Sociology*, the discipline has a reputation for debunking official and 'respectable' images of society. A large part of this reputation is owed to the ethnographic (that is, descriptive) studies by symbolic interactionists of a huge variety of everyday settings, both those that are nominally 'exotic' (nude beaches, massage parlours) and those that are, superficially, closer to home (buses, shopping malls, factories). Indeed, in some quarters, such work has been accused of amounting to advocating partisanship on behalf of the 'underdog'. As Cuff and Payne (1984: 129–131) argue, however, this effect arises, not from some 'political' intention on the part of the inquirer, but from symbolic interactionist studies adhering to their own methodological principles, namely, to tell the story from the 'inside', as the participants to the setting see it, that is in terms of their 'definitions of the situation'. Inevitably, this will mean giving equal weight to viewpoints that standardly are not heard – the prostitute's, the janitor's, the bus-driver's, the drug-pusher's, the 'deviant's'. This attitude is expressed, for example, in the title of an article by Stoddart (1982) which we cited in Chapter 5, 'The enforcement of narcotics violations in a Canadian city: heroin users' perspectives on the production of official statistics.' Indeed, for most members of a modern society with its highly variegated division of labour the work settings of others are, in many cases, 'foreign' territory. Just to learn how such settings routinely operate can be a source of news. We pass through or by the doctor's office, the bus, the mall, the office building, the factory, the bar, the hospital. How is it for those who spend their working lives there? How does it really work?

The criminal justice system has been no exception to this debunking phenomenon. We saw in Chapter 5 how, in order to do what they regard as good police work, police were seen to have recourse to extra-legal features of an encounter to select that which was criminal. Similarly, we shall see that in order, as they see it, to make the court system work legal personnel engage in a variety of practices that lie outside the strict legal description of their jobs. This is not something they see themselves as having an option about. That is, they feel compelled in order to fulfil the mandate contained in their job descriptions, indeed their professional vocation, to be responsive to what we will call the 'organizational demand characteristics' or 'organizational imperatives' of the work setting itself. The expression 'demand characteristic' comes from experimental psychology where it refers to those features of an experiment which are influencing the results but which are not intended parts of the research design. Thus in the court system the desired outcome, namely justice within the law, must be achieved not only according to the rules of due process and according to the facts of each case, but with due respect for the following inescapable organizational matters: the resources available, the time at hand, the working relationships that must be sustained between setting co-inhabitants, the division of labour, the flow of cases, the availability of witnesses, the sentencing practices of particular judges, the presence of interpreters and so on. According to Blumberg (1976 (1967)) the court's 'problem' can be reduced to the dilemma of managing huge caseloads while preserving due process. He describes the court's 'solution' as comprising 'a large variety of bureaucratically ordained and controlled "work crimes", short cuts, deviations, and outright rule violations adopted as court practice to meet production norms' (ibid: 150).

Blumberg mentions the following 'stratagems' to dispose of too-large caseloads:

> threatening a 'potentially harsh sentence . . . as the visible alternative to pleading guilty, in the case of recalcitrants'
> 'tailoring' of probation and psychiatric reports to meet organizational needs, or to be 'at least responsive to the court organization's requirements for the refurbishment of a defendant's social biography, consonant with his new status'
> judges' pressing into service '[s]tenographers and clerks, in their function as record keepers . . . in support of a judicial need to "rewrite" the record of a courtroom event'
> using bail as a 'weapon . . . to collapse the resistance of an accused person'.
>
> (Blumberg 1976 (1967): 150–151)

As these practices suggest it is appropriate to think of court personnel as a 'closed community'. Such a community embraces all who are 'regulars' in that setting, including the judges, crown attorneys, the Office of the Clerk of the Court, the Probation

Division and the press. It also includes the defendant's lawyer, especially if s/he is a court-appointed duty counsel (Canada) or public defender (USA): 'The accused's lawyer has far greater professional, economic, intellectual and other ties to the various elements of the court system than he does to his own client' (Blumberg 1976: 149). Consequently, the defendant is regarded as an 'outsider', one who in Blumberg's phrase is the 'mark' in a legal 'con game'. 'Goffman's (1962) "cooling out" analysis is especially relevant in the lawyer-accused client relationship' (Blumberg 1976: 154).

If the court's problem is too many cases, the court community comes together to solve it by focusing on getting the defendant to plead guilty, thus avoiding a trial and all the work, expense and time that involves. A '*plea bargain*' is '[a]ny agreement by the accused to plead guilty in return for the promise of some benefit' (Griffiths *et al.* 1980: 159). The standard benefits on offer are as follows:

reduction of a charge to a lesser or included offence
withdrawal of other pending charges or a promise to do so
a promise about a sentence recommendation (type, severity)
a promise not to oppose the defence's sentence recommendation
a promise not to charge friends or family
a promise to proceed summarily in dual offences
the shortening of 'dead time'
concealment of actual criminality (e.g. from parole board)
freedom from further investigation of prior offences
(from Griffiths *et al.* 1980: 159–160; Skolnick 1975 (1966): 175)

According to Klein (1976) defendants mostly do 'deals' directly with the police. Police benefits are cited as recovery of illegal or stolen property (such as explosives, firearms or drugs), the improvement of clearance rates and the maintenance of the flow of information. Indeed, on occasions such as the Olsen case and the Kirby case, both in 1981–82 in Canada, the police will buy information from defendants or witnesses. Brannigan cites data from 'A Longitudinal Study of the Cumulative Effects of Discretionary Decisions in the Criminal Process' carried out by the Centre of Criminology of the University of Toronto in the middle and late 1970s showing police pressing their views in particular cases on the prosecuting crown attorney. Indeed, according to one of the major reports on this study – the only large-scale (and interactionist) study of such matters in Canada – 'detectives frequently participated in plea discussions and were often acknowledged by the defence lawyer and crown attorney to be the key participant because they had the most intimate official knowledge of the case and thus were deemed to be in the best position to decide the limits of negotiation' (Ericson and Baranek 1982: 115). According to Tepperman 'the process of turning arrests into conviction statistics usually takes place in a prosecutor's office' (1977: 82) and takes place between an accused person's lawyer and the prosecutor (1977: 80). But in the end it appears to be the defence lawyer, whether retained privately or through legal aid who must sell the deal to the client and so get the guilty plea from him or her (Blumberg 1976: 162–163; Snider 1988: 296). 'In sum, police, crown attorneys, and lawyers collaborate in collectively achieving an outcome that serves their respective interests' (Ericson and Baranek 1982: 123).

The actual discussions that may or may not result in an agreement as to plea are not standardly conducted in open court (although, especially in the United States, they must be reported there) but 'in various "low visibility" contexts out of court. Charge alterations, possibilities for evidence submission, and ranges of sentencing are discussed in a variety of locales, e.g. in the courthouse corridors and offices, in the judge's chambers, at a lunch counter, and over the telephone' (Ericson and Baranek 1982: 111). There are structural limits to the scope of 'bargaining' set by, for example, mandatory minimum penalties for certain repeated convictions and, conversely, by the considerable sentencing discretion in the hands of the judge in Canada: a reduced charge may not mean much if the judge can give the same sentence for it as for the original charge.

In addition to the limits framed by the penalty structure, and by sentencing practices of judges, there are substantial influences coming from other sources. Chief among these is the charging practices of the police, which frame what the other parties have to discuss once the case reaches the court stage . . . Alschuler (1968) states, 'The charge is the asking price in plea bargaining, and the drafting of accusations is therefore an integral part of the negotiating process.' . . . [O]ur observation of the police in constructing cases against our accused respondents (Ericson, 1981, 1982) led us to conclude that an established practice was to charge every accused in a case with everything possible as a means of creating a maximal starting position for plea discussions. This was undertaken even on some occasions when the police explicitly stated that some of the charges against some of the accused would clearly not be upheld in court.

(Ericson and Baranek 1982: 115)

Furthermore, much that is relevant to plea discussions is tacit. That is, as in many an organization, 'silent bargains' are struck between various players as to what will be the preferred course of action in some given state of play. When such circumstances arise, nothing need be said; matters are simply understood. Again it is arguable to what extent participation in these 'games' is optional:

> Prosecutors establish reciprocal relationships with those who are able to reciprocate, resulting in the neglect of those who are unable to do so. Reciprocity is largely confined to those defence lawyers who have been admitted to the social circle, dependent as it is on the quality of their relationship with the prosecutor. Reciprocity results in discrimination, for benefits are limited to those lawyers who happen to be suppliers of benefits. Lawyers who do not supply their 'quota' of guilty pleas and contest every case are subjected to 'the bare bones of the legal system'.

(Grosman 1969: 80; cited in Griffiths et al 1980: 161)

This admittedly 'impressionistic' result from Grosman's interview study of crown prosecutors in the county of York, Ontario is nevertheless supported by a parallel observation in Sudnow's (1976 (1965)) study of 'sociological features of the penal code in a public defender office' in a metropolitan California community, a study we examine in greater detail in Chapter 10. The first of the practices Blumberg cites (see p. 198) whereby defendants are induced to plead guilty refers specifically to 'the case of recalcitrants'. In Sudnow's court 'recalcitrants' are called 'stubborn defendants'. 'These are cases for which reductions are available, reductions that are constructed on the basis of the typicality of the offense and allowable by the D.A.. These are normal crimes committed by "stubborn" defendants' (Sudnow 1976: 136). Stubborn defendants are those who insist on pleading not guilty. For the team of the public defender and the district attorney the question here is not one of guilt or innocence, but of 'reasonableness'; they take the guilt of the defendant not to be in question.

Consequently, when the case of such a defendant who will not play the game gets to court, the defence provided by the public defender amounts to what Sudnow calls minimum 'adequate legal representation'. That is, while the lawyer will

> conduct his part of the proceedings in accord with complete respect for proper legal procedure . . . [H]e will not cause any serious trouble for the routine motion of the court conviction process . . . In 'return' for all this, the district attorney treats the defendant's guilt in a matter-of-fact fashion . . . [and] 'puts on a trial' (in their way of referring to their daily tasks) in order to, with a minimum of strain, properly place the defendant behind bars. Both prosecutor and public defender thus protect the moral character of the other's charges from exposure.
>
> (Sudnow 1976: 139–140)

> The routine trial, generated as it is by the defendant's refusal to make a lesser plea, is the 'defendant's fault': 'What the hell are we supposed to do with them? If they can't listen to good reason and take a bargain, then its their tough luck. If they go to prison, well, they're the ones who are losing the trials, not us'.
>
> (Sudnow 1976: 138)

In short, the 'punishment' for the stubborn defendant of minimum, adequate legal representation seems quite akin to that of 'the bare bones of the legal system' visited on the lawyers who will not play the game.

THE PROFESSIONAL DOMINANCE THESIS AND THE LAW

The 'professional dominance thesis' was originally developed to explain the social organization of medical care (Freidson 1970). It is a 'structural' thesis. Gross features of the phenomenon in question, namely the provision of medical care, are seen to be consequences of a certain arrangement of the social structure, namely that medicine is organized in the form of a profession and that profession has come to dominate the provision of that care. But from the beginning the thesis has received an interactional interpretation. Not only is professional power institutionalized in that the relationship between service provider and service seeker is carried on as one between a 'professional' and a 'client', but, it is argued, that power is exerted and expressed in the forms of 'control' by which the doctor dominates the patient in the consultation itself (Scheff 1968; Strong 1979: 128ff.).

So interpreted the thesis is attractive to those looking for the sociological missing link – the bridge between micro- and macro-levels of analysis. Indeed the result has been what Robert Dunstan (1980: 74) calls 'interactionism for Marxians', an area of inquiry in which the two perspectives have somewhat converged. (There have also been important contributions from that area of linguistics known as 'discourse analysis' or 'pragmatics', and in the work of West (1984) and others an important gender component has been added.)

The thesis has been extended from medicine to more or less the whole range of professional/client 'service encounters'. In its general form the thesis holds that such encounters are

arenas of conflict, struggle or, at least, negotiation
over the definition of the situation, the interactional agenda and the time and resources available
between contending parties with competing interests in the matter at hand.

The professional service provider is portrayed as one concerned to define the presenting 'complaint' in terms that suit his or her professional, bureaucratic or, indeed, ruling-class interests: the professional is interested in the disease rather than the patient's health, a manageable classroom rather than the student's education, a smoothly operating courtroom rather than justice for the defendant. To enforce those interests, and this is where the specifically interactional claims arise, the professional is said to employ various strategies for controlling the service encounter. Among these are specifically sociolinguistic ones. Particular significance has been accorded to interruptions, questions and silences (Eglin and Wideman 1986).

The following is a characteristic statement of the thesis as it applies to lawyer–client interaction.

In contrast to the traditional depiction of lawyers as providing loyal disinterested service to clients, analysis of one lawyer–client interaction in a legal aid office revealed that the lawyer used language to control the client's presentation of the case, and to define it in terms of convenience to the organization rather than the expressed wishes of the client. Three types of

linguistic strategies relating to the control of talk were
examined: (1) management of structural features; (2) choice of
instrumentality; and (3) management of interactional features.
Structural strategies of interruptions and topic control served to
display the lawyer's expertise, while preventing the client from
enhancing his status. The form of the directives controlled the
client's responses, forcing him to react to the lawyer's assertions
rather than serving as the primary source of information, while
the use of performatives and other elements of the formal
register served to highlight the lawyer's control. Frequent challenges to the client's adherence to the maxim of quality by the
use of repetitions, requests for outside confirmation, reformu-
lations, repeat questions without waiting for a reply, and
unfounded presuppositions combined with the other features
to establish a dialogue that is very much like cross-examination.
(Bogoch and Danet 1984: 249)

While the above is stated for the case of lawyer–client interaction
in a legal office virtually identical claims have been made for the
character of spoken interaction in the courtroom between judge
or lawyer and defendant (Danet and Bogoch 1980; O'Barr 1982).

Particularly prominent in professional dominance studies have
been analyses that have attempted to show that it is through the
professional's use of interruptions and particular kinds of
questions that power and control are exercised. By interrupting
the client or defendant or witness, by being the one who asks the
questions, and by asking particularly yes/no questions, the professional (lawyer or judge) is said to control topic choice, topic
development and answerer's options. Thereby the defendant is
coerced.

Of course, before it can be assessed whether or not questions
and interruptions do produce these interactional effects they have
to be identified as such in the record of the talk to be analysed.
This is where problems begin to arise for this Marxian-
interactionist enterprise. The mere identification in the transcript
of some syntactic form such as an interrogative or declarative does
not guarantee that the one is doing the work of 'asking a question'
and the other 'answering'. For questions can be asked without
using interrogative syntax, and utterances with such a form may be
doing an accusation rather than asking for information. As
Dunstan says:

The proposal that almost every one of a lawyer's turns will have 'the illocutionary force of a request for information' [Danet and Bogoch, 1980] appears to be patently insensitive to the work done in and through 'questioning'. As has been pointed out elsewhere, such turns are only 'minimally describable' as questions for they are also variously produced and treated primarily as accusations, counter-denials, displays of disbelief, repair initiations, pre-sequencers, and so on [see Atkinson and Drew in Chapter 10, this volume]. Furthermore, in only a small fraction of instances are the questions asked in cross-examination genuine requests for information. It is, as consultation of trial manuals will reveal, a primary 'rule' for cross examination, that one should never ask a question to which one does not know the answer.

(Dunstan 1980: 64)

Similarly, there is no syntactic or other coding rule which will uniquely capture interruptions, since interruptions are a form of deviance and symbolic interactionism itself teaches that the identification of deviance rests on the interpretive judgments of participants, not observers. Overlapping talk, for example, may result from simultaneous starts by both parties to the talk or may constitute what conversation analysts call 'third-turn overlapping repair'. In neither case is interruption involved. Nevertheless, without regard for this fundamental point Bogoch and Danet (1984) proceed to code their case for interruptions.

Their initial finding is that 12 per cent of utterances are interrupted by the other speaker, and that 'the difference in the rate of interrupted utterances between the speakers is not great (14 per cent for the client and 9 per cent for the lawyer)' (ibid: 254). This surprises them since the literature would lead one to expect that the lawyer 'who is the superior in the interaction' would interrupt more often. However, they realize that not all interruptions are alike, and distinguish two types, 'cooperative' and 'competitive', the former occurring at the end of utterances and signalling co-participation, the latter in mid-utterance and signalling attempts to control.

The distribution of these two sorts of interruptions between the lawyer and the client is highly revealing. While over three-quarters of the interruptions of the client's speech occurs in mid-utterance, reflecting the lawyer's bid for control, 70% of the interruptions of the lawyer's speech occur at the end of her utterance, most likely indicating active cooperation by the client.

(Bogoch and Danet 1984: 255)

The authors display the following example of each type, where overlaps are indicated by square brackets.

COOPERATION

Lawyer: What happened [to you]
Client: [He asked me] to leave

COMPETITION

Lawyer: Private? A private complaint?
Client: Yes yes [it]
Lawyer: [The man] who is the attacker, what's his name?

Notice (1) that without the lawyer's next utterance in the first case it is impossible for the reader to know how the lawyer took the claimed interruption. (2) Again, without the client's preceding utterance it is impossible to know whether, as seems likely from the client's answer, the completion of 'What happened' could be projected by the hearer; were that so then it is quite common for next speaker not to wait for the end of the turn but to come right in at the first point that understanding has been achieved and so produce overlap with the end of the current speaker's turn. It is doubtful in such interactional circumstances whether anyone would find this to be an interruption.

In the second case notice: (1) that the client answers the lawyer's question perfectly adequately, whereupon the floor quite legitimately returns to the questioner for the next turn; (2) that the answerer chooses to try to extend the turn produces the overlap with the questioner's next turn; (3) after one word in overlap answerer drops out. If this is an interruption by questioner it is immediately acceded to by answerer. Competition would seem to be noticeable by its absence.

This is not how it appears to Bogoch and Danet who go on to assert that the lawyer's 'interruption' denies opportunity to the client to 'display his knowledge of legal matters', 'indicates that what he had to say was not worth hearing' and asserts the lawyer's 'right to control the topic' (ibid: 255). These claims are advanced without any evidence presented from the client's talk of struggle, challenge or competition that might indicate that he shares the analysts' perception and evaluation of the situation. Bogoch and Danet conclude by noting how like courtroom cross-examination this encounter is and clearly find it thereby objectionable. That this is a collaborative accomplishment of the two parties, that they produce the interactional features of an interview or consultation (not unlike the medical sort), that socialization of the client to the standard format for such an encounter may be a feature of it (see Hughes (1982) for the medical case), and that it is specifically a feature of (first) legal interviews that the lawyer *does* 'cross-examine' the prospective client are considerations not to be found in their account.

The foregoing critique of elements of the interactional version of the professional dominance thesis as applied to one form of legal encounter has drawn on ideas from a species of ethno-methodological conversation analysis that deals with the organization of turn-taking in conversation and related speech exchange systems. We examine this approach in detail in the next chapter (Chapter 10) as it applies to courtroom interaction, and so will not say anything further on that topic here.

Chapter 10

Ethnomethodology in court

Ethnomethodologists have a long-standing interest in the administration of justice. Garfinkel's jury study is a classic piece in this area. As it is representative of 'early' EM we reviewed it in Chapter 4 on EM studies of the law. (Recall that for EM the law *is* its application.) More recently, the courtrooms and corridors of the halls of justice have been a focus for each of the three 'main strands' of ethnomethodological inquiry which we identified in Chapter 1: mundane reason analysis, membership categorization analysis and conversation analysis. In this chapter we shall consider how each of these strands has been exemplified in courtroom studies. Thus, we shall firstly introduce mundane reason analysis and show its application to the determination of 'fact' in courtroom proceedings. Secondly, we examine ethnomethodological studies of the role of typifications, descriptions and membership categories in plea negotiation in the courts and in hearings in the US Congress to determine the warrantability of criminal proceedings. Thirdly, we consider conversation analytic studies of courtroom interaction and show how the concepts of speech exchange system, preference organization and adjacency pair elucidate the social interaction and practical reasoning therein. However, before engaging these studies, and by way of a 'critical' introduction, we consider the critique of symbolic-interactionist and structural-conflict courtroom analyses offered by Atkinson and Drew (1979) and that of Becker's labelling theory by Pollner (1974b).

AN ETHNOMETHODOLOGICAL CRITIQUE OF 'CRITICAL'
AND LABELLING-THEORETICAL ACCOUNTS OF
CRIMINAL JUSTICE

For ethnomethodology, the accounts of the symbolic interactionist and structural conflict perspectives exhibit (at least)
three fundamental shortcomings. The first of these is their failure
to examine the interactional detail of courtroom processes. As
Atkinson and Drew put it:

> symbolic interactionism and, more recently, Marxism have
> probably been the major influences to date, so that the main
> emphasis of court-room studies has tended to be on what courts
> are claimed to do to defendants (e.g. intimidate, bewilder,
> oppress, alienate, label, stigmatise, etc.) rather than on the
> details of how they work. Indeed, the fact that courts work at all,
> and apparently do so rather smoothly, appears to have been
> regarded as a passing and essentially uninteresting matter of
> fact.
>
> (Atkinson and Drew 1979: 3–4)

Secondly, in criticism of those who presume that courts are a
vehicle for dominating, oppressing and alienating the underclasses, women and minorities, it is argued that such character-
izations of courtroom processes are simply versions the provenance of which is external to court settings, and the consistency
of which with participants' orientations is thoroughly problematic.
Atkinson and Drew continue:

> some model of social order and social interaction will inevitably be
> used by researchers in constructing descriptions and explanations
> of how court proceedings are experienced in different ways by the
> participants involved. In other words, existing theories of social
> order and action have to be invoked and applied as a resource in
> developing characterisations of court-room interaction and in
> making them intelligible for others. On the face of it, this may
> seem perfectly reasonable and unproblematic, but it does raise an
> important issue about the use of social scientific theories and
> methods for the study of some substantive area such as court
> proceedings, namely that the impression can all too readily be
> given that the knowledge so employed is firmly established,
> uncontested, definite and valid.
>
> (ibid: 4)

In other words, there is a danger inherent in such work, namely that theoretical frameworks will be imposed on the data rather than the data being inspected with a view to uncovering what the members themselves are oriented to. The kinds of glosses which the symbolic-interactionist and structural-conflict approaches deploy in characterizing courtroom interaction and which we described in the preceding two chapters have this kind of character and hence they stand in a problematic relationship to the members' own orientations.

Thirdly, in his study of 'Sociological and common-sense models of the labelling process', Pollner draws attention to the ethnomethodological 'heuristic' to 'treat social facts as accomplishments', an injunction we identified as one of four cardinal features of the perspective in Chapter 1, 'Where others might see "things", "givens" or "facts of life", the ethnomethodologist sees (or attempts to see) *process*: the process through which the perceivedly stable features of socially organized environments are continually created and sustained' (Pollner 1974b: 27). He also draws attention to an 'ostensible congeniality' between the ethnomethodologist and the 'labelling theorist' in this regard since the latter, as we have seen in Chapters 5 and 9, have treated 'deviance' and 'crime' as created through definition and social interaction. This ostensible congeniality is, however, misleading because there are, from an ethnomethodological point of view, fundamental contradictions within the labelling perspective's conception of crime and deviance as matters of definition. These contradictions are exemplified in Becker's (1963) work on 'types of deviance'.

According to Pollner, Becker's work embodies a confusion between two models of deviance: the common-sense or mundane model and the constitutive model. This confusion is displayed in his four 'types of deviant behaviour': 'conformity', 'falsely accused', 'secret deviance' and 'pure deviance'. The parameters for generating these types are (1) whether or not some behaviour is 'rule-violating' and (2) whether or not that same piece of behaviour is 'socially labelled as deviant'.

Thus, 'conformity' is behaviour which neither violates a rule nor is socially labelled or perceived as deviant. 'Falsely accused' behaviour, on the other hand, does not violate a rule but *is* perceived as deviant. The 'secret deviant', similarly, is one who breaks a rule but is not perceived as deviant. Finally, the 'pure deviant' is perceived as deviant and breaks a rule.

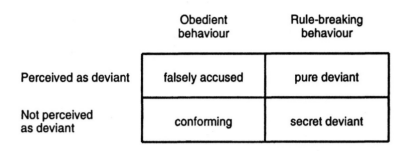

Figure 10.1 Four types of deviant behaviour (Becker 1963: 20)

The problem with this typology is that it contradicts the ostensible commitment of labelling theory to the constitutive or 'sociological' model of deviance. Thus, if deviance is a matter of definition or labelling, then both 'secret deviance' and 'falsely accused' are illogical categories of deviance in the way Becker has conceived them. In the case of secret deviance this is because if 'no one notices' the act, that is, if it is not perceived as deviant, then it cannot be deviant, at least not in terms of the labelling perspective's basic assumption about the nature of deviance, that is, that it is essentially a matter of definition. One cannot 'break a rule' without having been perceived as having done so. The case of the 'falsely accused' reveals a similar contradiction: on the premise that deviance is a matter of definition, then there can be no 'false accusation' since the accusation is definitive of the deviance in the first place. One is what one is accused of, so that any appeal to 'what is really the case' is irrelevant.

Logic aside, however, it is quite clear that Becker does seem to have a point. It seems reasonable to claim that people break rules but do not get caught for doing so and we might feel rather uncomfortable with the view that we are what the authorities and other crime definers say we are. This reasonableness and discomfort stem from our common-sense knowledge of crime or, more precisely, our use within our common-sense frame of reference of the mundane model of crime. Becker's point, then, rests upon such a model. Becker, like the common-sense members of the community, takes for granted that certain acts are criminal; that their criminality exists independently of social reaction and definition. This may be common-sensically sound, but it is sociologically confounded.

The general point is that, for the ethnomethodologist, common-sense, everyday, practical reasoning is to be treated as a topic
of inquiry, not as a taken-for-granted resource. More specifically,
then, the common-sense or mundane model of deviance needs to
be treated in line with this study policy. As such, how the model is
used becomes the focus of attention. We examine Pollner's work
on judges' use of 'mundane reason' in the next section.

MUNDANE REASON IN COURT

We touched briefly on the subject of mundane reason in Chapter 6
when we examined the police use of an assumed objective 'thing'
called crime, and when we considered the deployment of 'factual
knowledge' as an interactional device in interrogations. In this
section we shall be examining this approach in greater detail.

'Mundane reason analysis' is the third distinctive form of contemporary ethnomethodological inquiry which we mentioned in
Chapter 1. Even though it is possible to trace the origins of this line
of ethnomethodological inquiry to Schutz and Garfinkel's early
work (which we reviewed in Chapter 4), and to find continuities
between it and the work of, say, Berger and Luckmann (1966) on
the 'social construction of reality' and that of other phenomeno-
logically inclined sociologists (Psathas 1973; Luckmann 1978), it is
the work of Pollner which has featured most prominently in the
analysis of mundane reason. It is therefore to his work that we shall
turn.

Pollner: the azande poison oracle and the idiom of mundane reason

In his study of 'mundane reasoning', Pollner (1974a) argues that
the objectivity and intersubjectivity of our everyday social realities
are assumptions which provide for and are confirmed by a variety
of reasoning practices. These assumptions comprise what Pollner
calls the 'idiom' of mundane reason.

In order to allow us to appreciate the relativity of these assumptions about our social world and hence about the 'things' within it,
Pollner describes the presuppositions and reasoning practices pertaining to Azande witchcraft. He shows that even in the face of
events which to Western eyes might seem to constitute contradictions of their beliefs the Azande make use of a collection of

'secondary elaborations' of their basic beliefs which serve to forestall any doubt. The Azande believe in oracles, witchcraft and magic. When they want to make an important decision they take a substance from the bark of a tree and give it to two chickens. They determine in advance that if the first chicken dies it will mean 'yes' or 'no' to a question which they want answered. It is believed that an 'oracle' will speak through the fate of the chicken. The chicken's death or otherwise is entirely dependent on the oracle, not on the chemical properties of the substance taken from the tree. As a check on the oracle's workings, whatever was taken, with respect to the first chicken, as a sign of a 'yes', is now reversed in the case of the second. If the first's death meant 'yes', the second's continued life means 'yes'. If the first died and the second lived, it is surely the case that the 'oracle speaks'. But sometimes the second does the opposite. If the first died, the second dies too. If the first lived, the second lives also. Does the oracle therefore not speak? Is the Azande faith in its very existence shown to be worthless by this apparent 'failure'? Not at all; the Azande bring into focus their 'secondary elaborations' of belief and account for such 'failures' in terms which serve to confirm their basic beliefs in witchcraft, oracles and magic. Thus, such 'contradictions' are explained away in terms of such occurrences as the exercise of malicious witchcraft which results in an 'interference' with the workings of the oracle. The 'river' of magic notions which informs the everyday life of the Azande thus continues to flow undisturbed.

Just as it is possible to examine the assumptions pertaining to 'strange' belief systems such as the Azande's, it is also possible, with a little effort, to examine the taken-for-granted beliefs and assumptions which comprise the world of everyday life in our own society. The suggestion is that these are no more 'factual' and resting on incontrovertible bedrock than those of the Azande. Of course, 'reality' for us is as apparently objective as 'reality' is for the Azande. But we can perhaps learn from studies of strange belief systems and thereby come to view our own as 'anthropologically strange', and as relative to and contingent upon a plethora of self-sustaining practices like those of the Azande (cf. Winch 1970). It is this which motivates Pollner's work on 'mundane reason'.

'Mundane reason' consists of the assumption, and reasonings based thereupon, of the 'objective' existence of the features of the social world. In particular, it refers to the use of the assumption that deviance (and crime, more specifically) is something which exists independently of 'subjective' views. Instead, it exerts a 'constraining' influence' on such views. We react to something as crime because it *is* crime, not because we have constructed it that way. We therein mask from ourselves our own presumptive and hence creative and assumptive work.

The use of mundane reason – the assumption of objective deviance – is examined by Pollner in the context of the traffic court. He suggests that a central component of mundane reason is the assumption that not only does deviance exist independently for the individual but that each individual assumes that it exists similarly for others. Deviance, is, in other words, not only objective, it is intersubjective. We shall demonstrate the use of mundane reason with respect to, firstly, the resolution of 'reality disjunctures' in court and, secondly, judges' use of the mundane model of crime.

Pollner: resolving reality disjunctures in traffic court

Pollner examines how 'disjunctures' in the traffic court are dealt with. Are they grounds for calling into question the presumption that the producers of the disjunctive descriptions are inhabitants of separate realities? Are they both correct? Can they both be telling the truth even though they can be heard to contradict each other? The answer is 'no'. The disjunctures are explained, accounted for, by pointing to 'exceptional' observational conditions which obtained at the time of the 'disputed' event. Pollner argues that it is through such accounts that the 'belief' in the commonly shared world is sustained.

For example, puzzle: how could a defendant claim that he did not exceed 68 miles an hour and an officer claim that he did? Solution: faulty speedometer. Puzzle: How could a defendant claim that the vehicle in front of him and not his camper held up traffic and an officer claim that it was the camper? Solution: The camper blocked the officer's vision. Puzzle: How could a defendant claim that drag racing did not occur at a specified time and place when an officer claims that it did? Is it possible that drag racing did and did not occur? Is it possible that drag racing did and did not occur at the same time? Are they both right? Solution: The officer was actually referring to a different time.

In each of these cases neither judge nor defendant brings the intersubjectivity of the events into question. Rather, they look for a solution to the disjuncture. They hold that if 'other things were equal' the persons would corroborate each other. If the various obstacles, mistakes and pieces of faulty equipment had not prevented it then a uniformity of perception would have prevailed. To reiterate, the central focus of this type of analysis is members' use of assumptions about the objectivity and intersubjectivity of the social world and its constituent 'facts' and features. Essentially, the focus is on how these assumptions are part of the process through which social facts are constituted as objective and intersubjective in the first place. Pollner's work on practical reasoning in traffic courts shows how the 'mundane model' of crime informs legal and judicial thinking about crime and is thereby constitutive of crime in the courts (see also Eglin 1979).

Pollner: mundane judicial reasoning

Pollner asserts that Becker's typology of deviance, described in the first section, is not a sociological conceptualization of deviance because it presumes that deviance (or crime) exists independently of its recognition or 'labelling'. Rather, it is a picture of the possible relations that a mundane reasoner can see as existing between (1) the response of the community and (2) what is presumed to be real deviance – where this is defined by some method other than the immediate response of the community. Thus, in a world of real deviance the community may succeed or fail to recognize it. Where it fails, we have 'secret deviance', the 'dark figure of crime'. Where it succeeds, we have 'pure deviance'. Where it 'recognizes' deviance when in fact there was none, we get cases of 'false accusation'. In the traffic court, the judge's conception of the relational possibilities which derive from the interaction between (1) law enforcement officials and (2) violators/non-violators of the law reproduces this typology.

For example, the judge 'knows' there is no one-to-one correspondence between citations and offences which warrant a citation: offences are increasing but some are undetected. These undetected deviants are secret deviants. The judge 'knows' that the police make mistakes: they cite someone for an infraction they never committed. Such persons are falsely accused. Pollner's critical point is that both of these possibilities rest upon an assumption of objective deviance or conformity.

Similarly, from the judge's point of view police discretion refers to action taken by police which consists of not citing deviant persons. This presupposes the independent character of the deviant. The judge's mandate is provided by the presumption of objective deviance and the presumption that sometimes the identifiers of it 'get it wrong'; thus the judge is required to adjudicate on the relation between the alleged crime and what really happened. Contestation and accusation make sense only if it is presumed that guilt and innocence are independent of the methods by which they are determined. Similarly, for a defendant to accuse the police of capriciousness or inconsistency, it must be presumed that rule-violations are objective stimuli to which the police ought to respond in an objective, that is, corresponding manner. With respect to evaluations of court verdicts, the question of 'correctness' presumes that the court's judgment corresponds with or fails to correspond with actual or real crime/conformity. According to mundane reason some defendants, after all, 'get off' and others who 'get away with it' don't even become defendants. Their 'crimes', however, might well be deemed to warrant the attention of realist criminology.

From *within* the crime-making enterprise, then, the mundane or common-sense model is invoked as a method for describing the enterprise – the enterprise conceives itself as confronting an order of events whose character as deviant is presupposed as independent of the response of the community. The participants in the law enforcement enterprise make use of a mundane model of deviance or crime. From a sociological point of view, however, the use of the mundane model is a constituent feature of the process through which 'deviance' or 'crime' is realized as such.

It will be recognized that the mundane and the constitutive models of deviance correspond to what we have alternatively characterized as the 'realist' and 'interpretivist' conceptions of crime, discussed in Chapter 5. Furthermore, they and the confusion between them, are widely used in the field of criminology. Thus, the 'realist' or mundane model is used in generating the positivist critique of official statistics on crime and criminals and in justifying self-report methodologies in search of the 'dark figure' of crime. Such a model is used to warrant claims that the criminal justice system is biased and inequitable in definitional activities.

STUDIES IN TYPIFICATION AND CATEGORIZATION: THE ROLE OF 'KNOWLEDGE' IN ACCOMPLISHING JUSTICE

It was shown in Chapter 6, and in Emerson's work in Chapter 9, that 'typifications', or common-sense knowledge of the social structures (Chapter 4), play a crucial role in law enforcement. It was seen that typifications of acts, actors and contexts provided a scheme of interpretation for the identification of suspects and offenders and, by implication, the exclusion of other persons from law enforcement scrutiny. This emphasis on 'typification' reflects the importance of Schutzian phenomenology in the early development of ethnomethodology.

Thus, to reiterate, Schutz's programme of inquiry was based upon the methodological presupposition that the social reality of everyday life, and other realities, was based upon certain assumptions and taken-for-granted knowledge shared by the participants. In particular, Schutz, following Husserl, proposed that society's members experience their social realities with a 'natural attitude'. The social world is not doubted, it is as it appears to be. It is assumed that if one were to change places with one's fellow human beings, then the world would look much the same from the new vantage point. We would see the same 'objects' from 'there' as we do from 'here'. This world, furthermore, is experienced through typifications, which is to say our knowledge of the world which structures our experience of it is organized as a collection of typifications or social types.

It is perhaps worth taking a paragraph to explicate the connection between Schutz's natural attitude, mundane reason and typification. Mundane reason is Pollner's way of talking about the natural attitude. Typification (and categorization) can be said to embody mundane reason. When persons typify objects and other persons in the world they subsume the unique under abstract headings. They can be heard to speak of these objects and persons as instances of general types; they 'anonymize' them. In so doing, they treat the typified as the same for the practical purposes of talking about them as others in the 'same' category. This, of course, presumes that the features of one object or person correspond with the features of another or with the general category of such objects or persons, and this means that the interpretation that two things are the same, and hence whether they are subsumable under the same category, requires that the features of

the things themselves are examined and used as the grounds for
the typification, rather than the constituted processes whereby
'sameness' is identified. The typification, in other words, is dependent on the features of the thing. Of course, were this assumption
not made, then the issue of 'sameness' would be meaningless. In
the very use of everyday categories and typifications, then, the
presupposition that the things can be of the same type or category,
and hence have features that are independent of how they are
recognized, is reproduced. The use of such a presupposition pre-
serves a distinction between the character of the thing in question
and the description produced for it (Hester 1991).

In the first part of this section we take up this theme of typification through an examination of its role in plea bargaining. We
shall be considering firstly Sudnow's (1976 (1965)) classic study of
the use of the concept of 'normal crime' in the work of lawyers in
pre-trial negotiations about pleas, followed by Maynard's (1984)
analysis of lawyers' use of 'defendant attributes' or 'person-
descriptions' to justify proposed dispositions.

Sudnow: 'normal crimes' and plea negotiation

Students of the criminal justice system have often explained the
existence of plea negotiation or bargaining in terms of its
functions. As we saw in Chapter 9 it is held that if a majority of cases
were not dealt with through the defendant pleading guilty to the
offence(s) with which he or she is charged then the court system
would become inoperable. If every alleged offender exercised
their right to trial and pleaded not guilty then there would be just
too many trials for the court system to cope with. Plea bargaining
expedites the efficient processing of cases. However, whilst it is a
relatively easy task to point to the functions served by this legal
activity the precise procedures through which plea negotiation
actually takes place are by no means as obvious. It is to these
procedures that a number of ethnomethodologists (Sudnow 1976
(1965); Lynch 1982; Maynard 1982a, 1982b, 1984, 1988) and
ethnomethodologically informed scholars (Brannigan and Levy
1983) have directed their attention. For the purposes of exempli-
fying the work of typification the studies by Sudnow and Maynard
are most relevant here.

Plea negotiation typically involves a reduction in charge, or
some other 'favour' of the sort reviewed in the previous chapter in

return for a guilty plea. As we saw in that chapter these negotiations take place between the prosecutor and the defence attorney
and, of course, the defendant (and frequently the police). Sudnow's research examined how reductions in charge were arrived
at. His analysis provides a prime example of the importance and
use of typifications in legal work.

Basically, Sudnow found that plea negotiations occur only in
cases which are 'routine'. Their routine character is related to
whether or not they are 'normal' for the type of crime which the
defendant is alleged to have committed. By 'normal' is meant the
typical, the usual, the commonplace. Lawyers and judges have to
deal with thousands of cases each year. Over the course of their
work they come to recognize common or typical features of these
crimes for the jurisdictions in which they work.

For example, burglaries have typical features. If the features are
present in any particular case then it is a 'normal' burglary. In the
district where Sudnow did his research, the 'normal' burglary was
committed by regular violators, did not involve weapons, involved
low-valued objects, little property damage, lower-class establish-
ments, blacks as both offenders and victims and independent
operators who typically had a 'non-professional' orientation to
their crimes. Assaults similarly are normal or otherwise depending
on the presence of a known collection of typical features such as
those pertaining to location of the offence, the relationship
between victim and offender, the degree of injury, and so on.
There is even a 'normal' child molestation. Thus, the normal child
molestation is that offence which is committed either by middle-
aged strangers to the victim or by lower-class or middle-class
fathers of the victim, who typically have bad marriage circumstances and are multiple offenders. The offence itself typically
involves no actual physical penetration or lower tissue damage,
and involves mild fondling, petting and/or stimulation.

Equipped with these preconceptions of what constituted the
normal or typical for any type of crime the lawyers routinely
typified each and every case. Those they considered normal were
dealt with routinely. This meant that in return for a guilty plea the
offender could be offered a standard reduction in charge. For
each type of crime there existed a corresponding typical reduction
in charge. Thus, a case of child molestation would be reduced to
loitering around a school yard, and a case of burglary would be
reduced to petty theft, to the extent that they were both perceived

as exhibiting the normal or typical features of such crimes. Where such features were absent, where the offences displayed unusual features, then the alleged offences could not be so routinely processed and the defendant was therefore less likely to be offered a 'plea bargain'. Ethnomethodological studies such as Sudnow's show that people routinely use descriptions or typifications to accomplish certain tasks. As such, describing itself is a form of social activity, a way of acting. This insight has been developed by Maynard in his study of how in 'actual decision making, descriptions of defendants partially constitute the activity of warranting or justifying proposed dispositions' (Maynard 1984: 151).

Maynard: defendants' attributes in plea bargaining

On the basis of close examination of tape recordings of plea-bargaining sessions between attorneys in an American court system Maynard shows how (1) both public defender and district attorney use defendant attributes such as sex, age, marital status, number of children, religiosity, occupational status and ethnicity along with other features of the circumstances of the case to determine what offence, if any, took place, and thus to justify proposed dispositions; (2) the meaning of any attribute depends on its relationship to the collection of others and (3) both these matters are assessed in terms of how the case would look in court, before a jury (Eglin 1987: 206).

Consider, for example, the following extract in which the public defender (PD) responds to the district attorney's proposal 'that the defendant should spend 75 days in jail on the present charge' (Maynard 1984: 157) of drunken driving.

> PD2: See, here's his problem. The guy lives and works in South Beach, he's got a good job, well, least he's working, he supports his family, wife and kids, and it's his third drunk driving offense. And, uh, if he does 75 days straight time, he's going to lose his job, his wife's going to be on – kids, you know – family's going to be on welfare.
>
> (Maynard 1984: 157)

Maynard makes two central observations in relation to this extract. The first is that the public defender's descriptions are not merely or disinterestedly descriptive but are selected for their interactional utility, specifically to counter the position taken by the district attorney and solicit a penalty which is not only more lenient but which would avoid the undesirable outcomes projected by '75 days in jail'. He subsequently argues for weekends in jail. The second observation is that these descriptions do not stand in relation to each other as independent items in a list but rather are related to one another contextually. That is to say, the meaning of each descriptive item informs and is informed by each of the other items. Thus, 'it is not just that he is "married" and has "children", but that his family will be affected if he serves "seventy-five days" in jail' (ibid: 158). The number of days is not significant in itself but, contextually, in terms of the defendant being 'employed' and having a family, wife and kids to 'support'.

Like Sudnow, Maynard uses such examples as this to show that defendant attributes are 'salient in negotiations because they are used to construct the person as a good or bad character, thereby providing a way of seeing the alleged offense as a "real" crime or not' (ibid: 160). This practice is a specific form of the 'documentary method of interpretation' (Garfinkel 1956a, 1967) in which the meaning of any of a collection of particulars, such as the person descriptions above, is determined by a presumed underlying pattern such as a 'good character', just as those particulars determine the meaning of the underlying pattern. The descriptions form part of a 'gestalt contexture' built up around each case and not separable from it, in which background and foreground, context and particulars, mutually constitute one another.

Coming via descriptions to a determination of 'what sort of a person the defendant is', and thus what his or her actions amount to and what punishment if any they deserve, leads the attorneys, in the absence of a Sudnow-like normal crime reduction scheme, to a collaborative search for a suitable offence on which to settle the plea bargain. This is quite reminiscent of and formally similar to the skid-row police officer's problem Bittner (1967a: 710) identifies (Chapter 6) as 'whether, when someone "needs" to be arrested, he should be charged with drunkenness, begging, or disturbing the peace'. And there is a quite obvious parallel with the world-orderly considerations informing the US (and UK) decision to go out and 'arrest' Iraq in the Gulf Crisis of 1990–91.

Maynard's conclusion is one that directly addresses the overall thesis of this book. If we are to understand which actions get constituted as crime and what crimes they are constituted as, we cannot avoid examining 'common sense reasoning and the use of attributes to typify offenders and acts for deciding guilt or innocence' (Maynard 1984: 163). Furthermore, he acknowledges the necessity 'to examine the typification process in relation to other aspects of the negotiational environment' (ibid), such as argument and counter-argument, participants' concerns for formal and substantive justice and the anticipated defensibility of particular cases in court. Lastly, he recommends a focus on 'how discourse is organized within the criminal justice process' (ibid). He is here echoing the position of Atkinson and Drew (1979) whose work is considered in the final section of this chapter.

Halkowski: 'role' as an interactional device

We indicated in Chapter 1 that one of the key differences between ethnomethodology and other sociological approaches centres around the distinction between topic and resource (Zimmerman and Pollner 1970). Ethnomethodologists treat as topics that which other types of sociology take for granted as resources in their investigative work and in their explanations. One such resource, especially popular in functionalist and symbolic interactionist accounts, is the concept of 'role'. This concept refers to 'the set of behaviours appropriate to a particular social position or status' (Halkowski 1990: 565). Traditionally, it has been used, as an 'analytic tool to account for social order'. However, ethnomethodology reminds us that 'members of society invented the concept "role" as a useful, practical part of their language' and that 'rather than treating "role" as a self-evident, social scientific resource for analysis . . . [they] should take it as a *topic* of study' (ibid). The payoff from this is intended to be a greater understanding of how members of society organize their social worlds through the use of such notions.

This view of 'role' as a topic of inquiry is evident in Halkowski's study of the Iran–Contra Congressional hearings. Such hearings are part of the American criminal justice system in so far as they may be used to determine if criminal charges should be laid in matters of political significance usually involving members of the government. Much of the talk in the Iran–Contra hearings concerned how people's actions should be seen (see Bogen and Lynch 1989). Halkowski describes how the concept of role in lay usage is a technique for engaging in what he calls 'category shifting work'.

Categorizations of persons and actions used in the hearing (and elsewhere) can be used to construct and to avoid accusations. This is because categories imply devices. Category shifting is a means whereby members impute and avow motives and define the character of their own and others' actions.

The case in point concerns the shredding of documents containing financial records pertaining to the 'residual funds being used to support the Nicaraguan resistance'. The issue for the hearing is whether the witness 'obstructed justice' by destroying documents required by an 'official inquiry' of the Attorney General's office. We shall consider the following portion of the transcript of the hearing.

CC = Committee Counsel (Mr. Nields)
W = Witness (Lt. Col. Oliver North)

```
 1   CC:   =are you he:re telling thuh committee. (.hh)
 2           that y:ou don't remember. (.hh)
 3           Whether on November twenny first there was a
 4           document in your files reflecting presidential
 5           approval of the diversion.
 6          (0.8)
 7   W:     As a matter of fact I'll tell you specifically
 8           that I thought they were all go:ne.
 9          (0.3)
10           Because by thuh time I was to:ld
11          (0.5)
12           that some point early on November twenny first
13          (0.3)
14           that there would be an INnquiry.
15->         Conducted by:: (.) Mister Meese,
16          (0.6)
17           I assured (0.3) Admiral Poindexter
18          (0.2)
19           in correctly it- it see:ms,
20           that A::LL (.) of those documents no longer
21           existed.
22          (0.2)
23           and so that is EARly (0.3) on November
24           twennyfirst,
25          (0.2)
26           because I believe thuh decision (0.3) to make an
```

```
27          inquiry
28          (.)
29->        to have thee Attornally-Atttorney General
30          (0.4)
31->        or Mister Meese in his ro:le as friend ta thuh
32->        President
33          (0.30
34          conduct a fact finding excursion,
35          on what happened in September an November
36          Nineteen Eighty F:I:VE,
37          (0.6)
38          I asssured the Admiral,
39          (0.3)
40          don't worry (0.4) its a:ll taken care of.
41          (0.2)
42    CC:   You('d) all [ ready shredde ] d 'em.
43    W:                 I thought
44          (0.2)
45    W:    That's right.
```
                                        (Halkowski 1990: 566)

There are three different references to Mr Meese (the Attorney
General) in this passage. The first is to 'Mister Meese' (line 15).
The second is to 'thee Attornally-Attorney General' (line 29). The
third is to 'Mister Meese in his ro:le as friend ta thuh President' (lines
31-32). The question for Halkowski is 'why does the witness refer
to the same person in three different ways?

His analysis is couched in terms of membership categorization,
a form of ethnomethodological inquiry we considered in some
detail in Chapter 6. He suggests that the first reference does not
implicate a membership categorization device, but the second and
third references do. That is, 'Attorney General' implicates the
device 'cabinet members' or 'law enforcement officers'. 'Mister
Meese in his ro:le as friend ta thuh President' implicates the device
'relation to the President': 'friend'/'not friend'. These categorizations are used in conjunction with action–descriptions, namely
'make an inquiry' (lines 26–27) and 'conduct a fact finding
excursion' (line 34). Halkowski observes that:

> with his person–reference repairs, as well as with his action–
> description repairs, the witness is shifting from one categori-
> zation device to another; from devices that might be implicated

by the categorizations 'Attorney General' and 'inquiry', and repairing those referents with categorizations that implicate the device 'relation to the President'.

(Halkowski 1990: 569)

The interactional utility of this 'category/device shifting' procedure is that:

> with these descriptions the witness makes Meese and his actions seeable as non-official. The witness thereby also proposes a description for his own actions. While he might be seeable as destroying documents that were being sought by the 'Attorney General', he refers to Meese as a 'friend of the President'. Depending on which description of Meese and his action prevails, the witness either impeded an internal 'fact finding excursion' or was involved in the 'obstruction of justice' and the destruction of evidence needed by an official inquiry.

(ibid)

It is said that once a person has been referred to by a category, which implies, by definition, a device, then one way or method for eliminating the initial device's implicativeness for the characterization of one's actions, motives and character is by offering an alternative device. This can be done by offering another category. In this particular case the method of category/device shifting has been deployed to avoid imputations of criminal wrongdoing. Further ethnomethodological analyses of a related episode to do with the Iran/Contra criminality, namely the Bush/Rather interview on CBS News in 1988, can be found in a special section of *Research on Language and Social Interaction* (Pomerantz 1988/89).

LANGUAGE AND SOCIAL INTERACTION IN THE COURTROOM

The court has also been the site of interesting research by that branch of ethnomethodology known as conversation analysis. We have already discussed this approach, particularly in Chapter 6. Here we shall return to its concept of the 'speech exchange system' as an analytic device for examining members' methods for organizing discourse in ordinary conversational and in specific institutional settings.

In their book *Order in Court*, Atkinson and Drew (1979) make use of the concept of the speech exchange system in an examination of the social organization of social interaction in the court, with particular reference to the conduct of trials. A speech exchange system, as we showed in Chapter 6, refers to the practices and procedures which participants in discourse use to organize the allocation of turns or 'turn-taking'. These systems, according to conversation analysts such as Sacks *et al.* (1974) may be arranged along a continuum with 'informal' systems at one end and 'formal' ones at the other. An informal speech exchange system would be that of ordinary conversation. This is characterized, as everybody knows, by one speaker talking at a time, with a minimum of gap and overlap between speakers. Most speech exchange systems share these features. However, they differ significantly in other respects. For ordinary conversation there is an absence of 'pre-allocation' in the order of turns, the type of turn taken, the size of the turn and the direction of the talk. These features of ordinary conversation are decided on a turn-by-turn basis; they are negotiated organizational outcomes of the conversation itself. For other speech exchange systems, as they become more 'formal' this 'local management' of the features of turn-taking is not the case. Instead, there appears to be extensive pre-allocation of such features. Thus, for debates each 'side' takes its turn to, typically very extensively, present its case or argument without interruption from the other. There is, then, a modification of the ordinary conversational rule that a person may select themselves to speak at the end of the previous speaker's sentence (or other 'transition relevance place'). In ceremonies of various kinds there is a strict pre-allocation of who says what and when. In the marriage ceremony, for example, the bride and groom must wait their turn before saying 'I do' and it is the priest or other person conducting the ceremony who alone has the right to the declarative turn, 'I now declare you husband and wife . . .'. Starting up a conversation by introducing 'irrelevant matters' would 'disrupt' the proceedings and threaten its character as a marriage ceremony. In between ceremonies and ordinary conversation is the speech exchange system of classroom discourse where the pupils have restricted rights to speak. It is typically the teacher who selects the pupils to speak, and often they have to 'bid' for a turn by putting their hands up, rather than the other way round. Furthermore, as Mehan (1979) shows in his book, *Learning Lessons*, the teacher not only selects the pupils to speak but also takes an 'evaluative' turn in which they comment on the pupil's response to their selection, before taking another selecting turn.

In the context of the courtroom the rules of ordinary conversational speech exchange are modified to the extent that there is a pre-allocation of turns between the lawyers and the witness or defendant. When the latter enters the witness box he or she is obliged and is oriented to speak according to the rules of courtroom discourse. These provide that it is lawyers who have the right to select others to speak and not the other way round. In particular, it is the lawyers who ask questions and it is the witness or defendant who must answer them. There is, then, not only a predetermined order of speaking, there is also a pre-allocated distribution of turn types.

This restriction on the witnesses' and the defendants' rights to speak may well, from a structural conflict point of view (as we have shown in Chapter 8), be interpreted as 'domination' and 'degradation'. However, more interesting from an ethnomethodological point of view is how these rules of courtroom discourse are actually used and oriented to by the participants themselves.

In this regard, Atkinson and Drew have shown how the achievement of various ordinary conversational tasks is made into a more complex procedural matter by the existence of these restrictions on the organization of discourse. To fully understand this, they indicate that many utterances produced by consecutive speakers may be characterized as 'adjacency pairs'. This means not only that the utterances are positioned adjacent to each other but also that the occurrence of the 'first pair part' makes relevant the production of the 'second pair part'. Thus, if someone asks a question of another person, then that person is expected to provide an answer in the next turn (unless they 'delay' answering with a question of their own, thus producing what conversation analysts call an 'insertion sequence'). If the answer is not forthcoming it is 'noticeably absent' for the conversationalists, thereby indicating their orientation to the rule that persons selected to provide answers should do so at the appropriate conversational juncture. Now, many adjacency pairs are of this sort. That is, there is only one proper response to the first part of the pair. However, for other adjacency pairs there is more than one acceptable alternative. Invitations, for example, may be followed by acceptances or rejections, just as requests may be followed by grantings or refusals. If these alternative responses are studied it becomes clear that they are constructed differently. They are, in particular, characterized by a 'preference system' which is to say that some responses are 'preferred' whilst others are 'dispreferred'. Preference is a matter of turn construction. Preferred responses are done immediately following the first pair part whilst dispreferred responses are subject to such turn-constructional features as delay (pauses, hesitations, turn prefaces such as 'well' and 'er . . .'), 'token' preferred responses, transition markers ('but') and accounts, before the dispreferred response is actually produced. Thus, with regard to invitations, acceptances are 'preferred' and so they are done straight away. Rejections, on the other hand, are dispreferred and so we get utterances like 'er well, I'd like to but I'm afraid I'm very busy at the moment' in response to an invitation.

What does this have to do with courtroom discourse? Well, we have seen that rules of courtroom procedure mean the pre-allocation of certain types of turns to the lawyers and the witnesses and the defendants. The lawyers must ask questions and the witnesses and defendants must provide answers. This means, firstly, that whatever it is that the speakers want to do with their turns they must do so via the question-and-answer format. This is especially significant for the lawyer conducting cross-examination. It means that if the lawyer wishes, for example, to accuse the defendant of lying, then this must be done in the form of a question or questions. Furthermore, given that the preferred response to an accusation is one which avoids it in some way (for example, a denial, a justification, counter-accusation, and other forms which amount to an avoidance of self-blame) then it is likely, as Atkinson and Drew (1979: 112) put it, 'that the recipient of an accusation will then make a denial, or perform one of the actions including justifications, excuses, which seek to avoid or reduce self-blame'. This has implications for the management of an accusation. Thus, as Atkinson and Drew say:

> Given that a denial is an anticipated next utterance on the part of the recipient, the accusation may be constructed so that a simple 'flat denial' can be seen to be unsuccessful; for if a 'flat denial' were always to work there would be little point in ever making an accusation . . . Therefore a counsel may seek to forestall such straightforward defeat of an accusation by doing some work to set an accusation (prior to its being declared or otherwise acknowledged), work which might be regarded as

achieving the grounds for the accusation and thereby orienting in advance to the possible basis for a denial. Such work can include the production of 'facts', and a description of events, etc., from which the inference that the witness did X . . . can be made – and designing questions to get the witness's (or defendant's) confirmation of or agreement to those facts.

(Atkinson and Drew 1979: 114)

For the defendant to deny the accusation, then, means that he or she will have to not simply produce a denial, but also to address the accusatory implications of the 'facts' from which the accusation is formulated. If the defendant fails to do this then such failure will be noticeably absent and 'accountable grounds for holding that the witness has "failed to answer the accusation", or for inferring that he has not understood the accusation properly' (ibid: 115). The adjacency pair format, then, and the preference organization pertaining to accusations–denials means that the lawyer will be constrained to 'prospectively manage' the accusation. He or she 'may be expected to manage question–answer sequences so as to establish progressively the facts, etc., out of which the accusation is built, before actually declaring that he is accusing the other person of doing X' (ibid).

Chapter 11

Crime and punishment

So far in this book we have considered law creation, law enforcement and the administration of law in terms of the approaches of symbolic interactionism, structural conflict theory and ethnomethodology. We have devoted a chapter to the contribution of each of these perspectives to each of these topics. The difference between this chapter and those preceding it is that each of the three approaches is deployed within this one chapter. Our topic is crime and punishment.

There is a vast range of punishments available to the courts, from fines to the death sentence. Our concern is not with all of this range; instead we shall focus mainly on sociological work with respect to one particular form of punishment, namely imprisonment. This is because, once again, it is not our concern to document exhaustively the full range of research on a substantive topic, but to draw on it selectively in order to exemplify our chosen ways of doing sociology. It is sociological work on prisons and the experience and impact of imprisonment which provides most adequately for this task.

We begin with structural conflict theory and consider its accounts of the development of the prison, the functions of the prison as an institution and of the various practices of control within it (with particular attention to those applied to women), and the authoritarian response to the current 'crisis' in prisons, especially in Britain. Turning to symbolic interactionism, we review accounts of the social organization of prison life in terms of the inmate social system or prisoner subculture, and we examine labelling theory's account of the impact of imprisonment. Finally, we take an ethnomethodological perspective on the classic topic of the convict code.

THE STRUCTURAL CONFLICT PERSPECTIVE

The development of the prison

It is only relatively recently that the prison became a dominant form of social control. In this section we consider how this came about. In recent years a number of celebrated and influential books have been written on this subject, most notably those of Ignatieff (1978), Foucault (1977) and Melossi and Pavarini (1981). We shall consider briefly the work of Ignatieff and Melossi and Pavarini; the major focus of our attention, however, will be on the earlier 'classic' in this field, namely the work of Rusche and Kirchheimer (1939) on *Punishment and Social Structure*. Before doing so, we wish to 'set the scene' by presenting Cohen's (1985) excellent discussion of the 'Great Transformation' of which the development of the prison as the major form of punishment was a central part.

According to Cohen (1985), the 'Great Transformation' in methods of social control occurred around the end of the eighteenth and the beginning of the nineteenth centuries. This transformation involved four major changes in the social control of deviance in general and crime in particular. The first was an increase in the involvement of the state 'in the business' of deviancy and crime control, an involvement which was eventually to mean the development 'of a centralized, rationalized and bureaucratic apparatus for the control and punishment of crime and delinquency and the care or cure of other types of deviants' (Cohen 1985: 13). The second major change was the differentiation of deviants. This entailed an increasing differentiation of deviants from each other as they were classified into separate types and categories. It also meant the association of each type of deviance with a particular body of 'scientific' knowledge which was applied by recognized and accredited 'experts', who eventually developed monopolies in the care and control of deviants in their field (ibid). A third major change was segregation. This process consisted of the increasing segregation of deviants into 'asylums' – special institutions for each type of deviant – 'penitentiaries, prisons, mental hospitals, reformatories and other closed, purpose-built institutions. The prison emerges as the dominant instrument for changing undesirable behaviour and as the favoured form of punishment' (ibid). The fourth change is in the 'object' of punishment: the mind rather than the body. This meant 'the decline of punishment involving the public infliction of physical pain' (ibid: 13–14). A plethora of 'positivist theories emerge' (as discussed in Chapter 1) 'to justify concentrating on the individual offender and not on the general offense' (ibid: 14). There are three models which have been used to explain these changes and hence, specifically, to account for the development of the prison as the dominant form of crime control. The first is an 'idealist' model which conceives of the development of the prison in terms of penal 'ideas', especially those of 'reformers' who were influenced by the Enlightenment philosophers of the eighteenth century. Penal changes are characterized by 'uneven progress' in the application of ideas to the improvement of penal practice. The second model is a structural consensus or functionalist model which views the prison and, more generally, 'asylums', as functional solutions to problems of societal disintegration and deregulation. According to Rothman (1971) they were established with 'good', if 'complicated', intentions which had 'disastrous' consequences. The third model, deriving from the structural conflict tradition, is the 'discipline and mystification' interpretation of penal change (Cohen 1985). It is with this interpretation that our concern lies.

The discipline and mystification interpretation of changes in penal practice claims that the transformation of the criminal justice system 'was not what it appeared to be, nor should the subsequent history of institutions like the reformed nineteenth century prison' (Cohen 1985: 21) be regarded as failure. Rather, according to this view, the prison in particular and the criminal justice system in general were, and have continued to be, successful but not in terms of conventional notions of 'reform' or 'progress'. As Cohen points out, they have instead been successful in the sense of fulfilling very different social functions. These functions are the requirements of an emerging and developing capitalist social order which 'needs' the persistent repression of the unsocialized and recalcitrant members of the working class. Furthermore, even the reformers themselves were mystified into believing that the social control system was 'fair, humane and progressive' (Cohen 1985: 22).

As we have seen in earlier chapters, the structural conflict or discipline and mystification story has both instrumentalist and structuralist versions. The former is a historical materialist account which assumes that it is changes in political economy which under-pin changes in penal practice. There is little room for ideas, intentions and choices in this story since everything that occurs is seen as required by the needs of the capitalist system. Ideas are assumed to conceal the real interests and motives behind the system. They are a facade to make acceptable the exercise of otherwise unacceptable power, domination and class interests. The works of Rusche and Kirchheimer (1939) and Melossi and Pavarini (1981) exemplify this story. The structuralist version, on the other hand, is less reductionist in two senses. Firstly, it accords a greater independence to the interests of the state in the for-mation of penal policy and practice, and secondly, it conceives of ideology as a significant vehicle for domination and control in itself. The works of Ignatieff (1978) and Foucault (1977) approach this less reductionist and more structuralist version of the develop-ment of punishment.

Rusche and Kirchheimer's study begins much earlier than the eighteenth century since they also account for the historical development of other forms of punishment. They consider three historical periods: the early middle ages, the later middle ages and the modern period, dating from the beginning of the nineteenth century. In considering these three periods they examine the relationship between three things: (1) forms of punishment, (2) social, economic and political changes and (3) penal ideology. Their thesis is that changes in the mode of production create new class interests and therefore changes in the forms and ideologies of punishment to support those interests.

In the early middle ages when much of European society was feudal in character the population was small and there was a high demand for labour. The dependency of 'lords of the manor' on their peasant workers or serfs, together with the growth of towns which for economic reasons attracted workers away from the land, meant that landowners had to treat their serfs with care. Punish-ments were therefore relatively benign. Order was maintained largely through traditional and religious authority. Where offenders did stray from the right and proper path they were 'persuaded' to return to the fold through the imposition of fines and penance. Jails were only used to hold persons until their fines were paid. Justice was largely a local matter. The state remained a distant authority. Such a system served well the interests of the landowners.

In the fifteenth century certain changes took place in the political economy which 'required' the invention of new forms of punishment. We have already alluded to this history in Chapters 3 and 7. Thus, the population began to increase. This in turn led to the exhaustion of fertile land and an unsatisfied demand for grain. Landowners turned small tenant farmers off their land to make bigger profits. As unemployment rose landowners were able to pay lower wages. As poverty increased the unemployed peasants streamed to the towns but the townspeople enacted Poor Laws which, as we saw in Chapter 3, criminalized the activities, not to say mere presence, of persons now defined as 'beggars' and 'vagrants'; such laws were designed to keep out these and other members of the 'dangerous classes'. The classic trilogy of class struggle, unemployment and 'crime' was thus formed. The poor turned to 'crime' as a means of survival. The authorities then responded by enacting harsh criminal law to deal with this perceived threat to social stability and to protect the interests of the new commercial class emerging at this time. Thus the methods of punishment which became routine at this time were execution, mutilation and flogging.

The sixteenth century witnessed further changes in the political economy which in turn led to new forms of punishment. These changes included the growth of towns, increased demand for consumer goods, growth of the financial system, expansion of trade and markets and the conquest of foreign territories. All these added up to the Age of Mercantilism. However, at the same time the population began to decline, which meant a decline in the labour pool. This in turn led to a rise in wages and a consequent decline of manufacturers' and merchants' profits. The commercial class therefore appealed to the state for help. Attempts were made to increase the labour pool by increasing the birth rate through tax breaks for early marriages and large families, laws prohibiting the clergy from sanctioning unwed mothers, condemnation of the customary one-year period of mourning and attempts to stop infanticide. When these were less than successful laws were passed forbidding the migration of labour, fixing maximum wage levels, establishing working hours of between 12 and 16 hours a day, prohibiting worker associations and work stoppages and encouraging child labour. Most important, however, was the introduction of state-sponsored systems of forced labour. Thus, law violators and others under state supervision were drafted into the 'Houses of Correction'. The acute labour shortage became linked to the perceived 'plague of the beggars' and laws were broadened to define vagrants to include all who refused to work at prevailing rates. By the end of the seventeenth century the 'Houses of Correction' became, in response to economic conditions, a significant part of penal policy. In them prisoners were forced to work and thus develop the habits of industry. The Houses were run either by state administrators or by private contractors. Either way, the inmates were used to aid private enterprise at a time of labour shortage.

The relationship between economic interests and penal practice is particularly clear-cut in the cases of galley slavery and transportation. Thus, galley slavery grew out of the need for rowers to propel sailing vessels in the Mediterranean. Many European powers used galley slavery as a form of punishment not only for 'senior offenders' but also for beggars and the 'unworthy poor'. At the height of demand for oarsmen the courts in France, for example, were instructed by the Crown to convict criminals more quickly and judicial administrators organized hunts for potential felons who could be sentenced to galley slavery. The standard sentence for galley slaves was between 10 and 12 years so that maximum utility could be obtained from them. Galley slavery declined only when refinements in the art of navigation eliminated need for it.

Transportation – the shipping of convicts to distant colonies – emerged when labourers were needed to exploit territories acquired through the practice of imperialism. At first, as 1992 reminds us, the colonial settlers tried to enslave the native populations but these groups tended to resist and were killed off in colonial wars. Those natives who were enslaved often died as a result of harsh labour and exposure to European diseases. The importation of convict labour was thus an attractive alternative. Not only was it a solution to the labour problem in the colonies but it also avoided depleting the labour pool in the home country. Throughout the eighteenth century thousands of convicts were thus sent to the colonies, typically for a fixed period of time after which they obtained their freedom. Many stayed and became independent farmers and planters. Transportation ended as a form of punishment when it became clear that the importation of African slaves was more profitable. African slaves were considered more valuable because of the indeterminate length of their servitude and because of their average smaller size than European convicts. This meant that more of them could be packed into the slave ships.

We mentioned earlier the influence of the Enlightenment philosophers on the penal 'reforms' occurring at the end of the eighteenth century and, in particular, on the development of the prison. Whilst they recognize the role of these 'thinkers' in the process of penal change, Rusche and Kirchheimer nevertheless stress that these have to be seen in the context of the political and economic changes occurring at the time. Thus, the late-eighteenth and early nineteenth centuries saw the birth of the Industrial Revolution and consequent changes in the mode of production. It is against this background that the development of the prison has to be understood. There was, in effect, a coincidence of the rationalizing influence of the reformers with the economic interests of those with most to gain from the new industrial order.

The Industrial Revolution meant a declining need for labour as industrial production was increasingly mechanized. At the same time the population of industrializing countries began to increase. Work became scarce, unemployment rose and again the poor turned to 'crime' as a means of survival. The authorities responded with demands for a return to harsh punishment, with imprisonment the chief form. Within the prisons the inmates were subjected to harsh regimes designed to discipline them. It was believed that they should learn through exposure to routines, 'proper' habits of industry and submission to authority. Given the reserve labour pool and the development of the factory system there was no economic payoff in exploiting the labour of prisoners. Work instead became a means of punishment: prisoners were required to carry stones from one place to another, work pumps which returned flowing water to its source, use tread mills and, perhaps slightly more satisfying, grind pebbles into sand.

For Rusche and Kirchheimer, then, the prison serves several important functions for the industrial capitalist social order. It makes docile the recalcitrant members of the working class, it deters other, potential criminals, it teaches habits of discipline and order and it reproduces the hierarchy so integral to the system of capitalism.

In terms similar to Rusche and Kirchheimer, Melossi and Pavarini (1981) argue that the concept of discipline is central to understanding the emergence of the prison as the dominant form of punishment at the time of the Industrial Revolution. The system requirement, they claim, is for a 'socially safe proletarian', someone who has 'learnt to accept being propertyless without threatening the institution of private property'. The prison is therefore like a factory. It is the function of the prison to produce such persons for the capitalist industrial order. Instead of producing goods it produces disciplined workers.

In his *A Just Measure of Pain* Ignatieff's (1978) focus is not only much narrower than that of Rusche and Kirchheimer, it is also less reductionist and instrumentalist. His aim is to account for the emergence of the penitentiary in England in the period 1770 to 1840. At times his account is quite similar to that of Foucault. However, as Ignatieff emphasizes in his subsequent reflections (Ignatieff 1983) on his own, Rothman's and Foucault's work, there is also an instrumentalist strain running through Foucault's writings on the disciplinary power of the state. In contrast, Ignatieff attempts to explain the emergence of the penitentiary 'without imputing conspiratorial rationality to a ruling class' (1983: 77).

A Just Measure of Pain stresses firstly how the reformers and 'classical' philosophers of the eighteenth century forged a 'new disciplinary ideology'. Beccaria, Fielding, Howard, Bentham and Romilly were central figures in what subsequently became known as 'classical criminology' (to which we briefly alluded in Chapter 1) and the reformist ideas for reshaping the criminal justice system associated with it. 'Just' and 'equitable' measures of pain (through imprisonment) were to be administered in carefully calculated response to the severity of, and 'pleasure' derived from, 'crime' (our scare quotes). The ideal of this new system was reform through punishment, not careless retribution as had been the case when the body rather than the mind had been the penal object. Philanthropic campaigns to build prisons and reform the old criminal justice institutions were launched. They offered a new 'strategy of class relations' although they did not express themselves in this way. Thus, 'in return for the humanity of minimal institutional provision, the disobedient poor were drawn into a circle of asceticism, industriousness and obedience' (Ignatieff 1983: 87). It was argued that 'they would return to society convinced of the moral legitimacy of their rulers' because 'prison reform was to be humane and just punishment which would convince the offender of the moral legitimacy of the law and its custodians' (ibid).

The reformers gained support for their 'disciplinary ideology' from the 'evangelical, professional, mercantile and industrial classes' who were 'seeking to cope with the dissolution of a society of ranks and orders and the emergence of a society of strangers' (ibid). These members of the bourgeoisie were also victims, either directly or indirectly, of the 'crisis years of early industrialization', especially after 1815.

The 'crisis' was manifested in three main ways. Firstly, there was a breakdown in social relations because of the casualization of the agricultural proletariat in the southeastern agricultural counties. This led to rising rates of vagrancy, pauperism, petty 'crime' (our quotes) and riots. Secondly, there were riots and rising rates of juvenile 'crime' (our quotes) in London, a state of affairs with which the existing constabulary could not cope. Thirdly, in the northern industrial regions, labour-markets tied to single industries like cotton were vulnerable to the cycles of demand in international trade. In 'bad years' this led to a breakdown in labour-market discipline. In these circumstances the new policy of mass imprisonment was seen as a potentially effective response to the breakdown in public order.

Even though there may have been a coincidence of interest amongst the reformers and the bourgeoisie it is important to remember, as Ignatieff reminds us, that the reformers did not justify their programme as a response to the problems of labour discipline during this time of crisis. The reformers' ideas antedate these discipline problems by a substantial period of time. Consequently, it would be incorrect to reduce the emergence of the penitentiary to the economic interests and problems of the bourgeoisie at this time of crisis. On the other hand, of course, it is difficult to imagine that the reformers would have succeeded in implementing their programme 'if the authorities had not believed they were faced with the breakdown of a society of stable ranks and the emergence of a society of hostile classes' (Ignatieff 1983: 90).

Foucault (1977) has also suggested that the development of the prison offered a new strategic possibility, namely that of isolating the 'criminal' working class from the rest of the working class, incarcerating the former so that it could not corrupt the industriousness of the latter. This strategy was apparently based upon a ruling-class consensus about the utility of exploiting the divisions within the working class between its 'rough and respectable', 'poor and pauperized' and the 'criminal and working' members (as we noted in Chapters 3 and 7). Even though Ignatieff agrees that this strategy of divide and rule may have succeeded, the reasons for its success were not that the ruling class 'manufactured' class divisions through these penal practices but rather that they exploited differences which were already present in the working class. As he puts it: 'the strategy of mass imprisonment is better understood in class terms as an attempt by the authorities to lend symbolic reinforcement to values of personal honour which they themselves knew were indigenous to the poor' (Ignatieff 1983: 91).

In sum, then, in Ignatieff's account we find that the rise of the penitentiary is explained not solely in instrumental terms. Ignatieff does not, as Rusche and Kirchheimer do, account for the emergence of the prison solely in terms of its instrumental 'functions' for the industrial capitalists. Rather, it is a more structuralist account and seeks to incorporate an independent domain of ideas into its explanatory approach. To be sure, the emergence of the prison is not then explicable in a simplistic idealist fashion. Ideas are important, it seems, when viewed in conjunction with the forces of economic interests and problems of class relations. As Ignatieff puts it,

> the new carceral system was not the work of an overarching strategic consensus by a ruling class, but instead fell into place as a result of a conjuncture between transformation in the phenomena of social order, new policing needs by the propertied, and a new discourse on the exercise of power.
>
> (Ignatieff 1983: 95)

The functions of the prison

The work of the structural conflict theorists and their thesis that the function of the prison is one of discipline and mystification has also been applied to the contemporary prison. Thus, Fitzgerald (1977) compares what he calls the 'official functions' of the prison with those which are visible from a structural conflict point of view. From the official point of view, the functions are reformation and rehabilitation, protection of society, deterrence and punishment. Of course, of these the only one which is successfully achieved is the last. Thus, prisons do not rehabilitate or reform, they do not protect society because prisoners typically learn from each other how to be 'better' criminals, and they do not seem to be very effective deterrents because of the extremely high rates of recidivism. However, from a structural-conflict point of view prisons do appear to be quite successful in some respects. Thus, Fitzgerald points out they serve a 'sanitation function' in so far as they remove from view those unproductive and recalcitrant elements created by the social structural arrangements of capitalist society. Furthermore, by sentencing individual offenders the prison permits the 'individualization' of crime and therefore strengthens the individualistic ideology so central to capitalism. Criminals are thus defined as 'failures' in the 'normal' competition characteristic of capitalist society. This serves to mystify the political character of eliminating such persons. The prison may also be said to serve a 'distraction' function in so far as the massive incarceration of largely petty offenders from underprivileged and minority groups diverts attention away from the 'criminality' of the rule-makers and the 'crimes' of the powerful. Punishment of lower-class offenders also serves to distract attention from acts which are much more harmful to the population at large but which are not criminalized. Finally, prison can be seen to serve a 'symbolic function' in that it represents what is currently conceived as 'good' triumphing over 'evil'. As such it serves to deter would-be challenges to contemporary conceptions of social and legal order. The inmates themselves are socialized into a passive acceptance of the hierarchical divisions in society, symbolized in the relations of domination and subordination between them and the 'authorities'.

Social control within the prison

Within the prison, the inmates are subjected to a variety of social controls. Firstly, there is the daily routine. Thus, inmates are subject to restrictions as to how they will organize their daily lives. Their autonomy is removed. Meals, work, recreation, visits are all governed by official rules. The right to privacy is removed as letters are read and cells subjected to search and surveillance at the discretion of the guards. Secondly, there are special, additional punishments for those who resist the incursion of authoritarian rule: solitary confinement may be administered and, until recently, for exceptionally disruptive prisoners the 'control units', often sensorily deprivational, may be used as part of a programme of behaviour modification. Drugs are used for much the same purpose. Daily doses of tranquillizers, from the mild sedatives like valium and librium, to the 'heavy' drugs like thorazine, are commonly used instruments for order maintenance. Thirdly, at prison disciplinary hearings and parole review boards inmates are deprived of a number of the legal rights (such as legal representation) available to persons at other stages in the criminal justice process. The prospect of parole is itself a form of social control, critics having likened the system to the imposition of indeterminate sentences.

Whilst the above observations apply to both men's and women's prisons a number of features of women's prisons in particular have been identified as contributing to the reproduction of the oppression of women in society. A specially notable example of criminological work which makes this point is that of Carlen (1983) in her study of a women's prison in Scotland. This has been described by Sim *et al.* (1987: 15) as the 'first radical analysis of the state of women's imprisonment in the United Kingdom'. She notes that:

> women's imprisonment in Scotland is imprisonment in the general sense that it has all the repressive organisational features common to men's prisons; at the same time, it is a form of imprisonment specific to women in that it has repressive features not to be found in men's prisons.
>
> (Carlen 1983: 76)

These repressive features are expressed in 'the penal discourses and the extra-discursive practices of the women's prison'; they comprise 'contradictory definitions both of legitimate womanhood and the conditions engendering it'. As Carlen puts it:

> The features of the disciplinary regime . . . elevate, fracture and realign opposed ideological elements of the prisoners' subjective experience until they have been constructed as women both irrevocably within and irretrievably without adult female subjectivity. Women prisoners are contradictorily defined as being: both within and without sociability; both within and without femininity; and, concomitantly . . ., both within and without adulthood.
>
> (Carlen 1983: 90)

With respect to the first of these features – sociability – Carlen describes the peculiar regime of restricted and enforced sociability

required of the inmates. Each was allocated to a 'quasi family' unit
of seven prisoners. Within this unit they were then subjected to
rigid surveillance and control; they were not allowed to speak to
the members of other units, they were locked up separately each
evening at 6.30 p.m., conversations were constantly monitored by
prison officers, with both the 'mode' and 'topic' of conversation
being continuously subject to the approval of the officer on duty;
they were required to be sociable with the other members of their
unit without being allowed to develop conversation considered
'normal' outside the prison; their mealtime talk and behaviour was
constantly monitored; they were forbidden to engage in mundane,
everyday activities such as giving each other a light, sharing information or sharing privileges and skills. In short, the women were
required to be sociable with the members of their unit but they
were denied the 'normal' interactional routines for achieving this
sociality. This contradiction produced not 'normal' sociable
women but tense and distrustful inmates; it contributed to, rather
than alleviated, the destruction of the women's sense of autonomy
and self-direction. As Carlen points out, the 'irony' of this coercive,
enforced and circumscribed sociability is that it leads to greater
isolation, a debilitating isolation 'outwith [sic] both sociability and
privacy' (ibid: 96). Furthermore, as the majority of these women
inmates had experienced 'debilitating' family environments prior
to ending up in prison this 'family' discipline within the prison
worked as a vehicle for the reproduction of their core features:
domination and isolation.

If the women were expected to relate in terms of an enforced
and artificial sociality, they were also subjected to a contradictory
regime with respect to their 'femininity'. It is by now well established within sociology that gender identity is a social accomplishment or 'construction'. However, in the women's prison, the inmates were expected to 'be feminine' whilst many of the standard
means for achieving this were denied to them. These deprivations
included the enforced wearing of uniform dress, limited means of
'improving' their appearance with makeup, degrading sanitary
conditions, lack of access to a doctor and lack of privacy in medical
matters, rigid control over their hair, their bodies and their
clothes. All this signified, according to Carlen, a contradiction
between 'the official and discursive claims that women are "helped
to regain their self-respect" and the extra-discursive institutional

conditions wherein the self-respect is further battered and bruised, if not altogether destroyed' (ibid: 106–107).

Finally, there is the contradiction in the area of 'adulthood'. The inmates were officially supposed to be learning to behave 'more like adults' and yet the everyday organizational arrangements of the prison entailed treatment of them more like children. In general, Carlen points to the hierarchical character of the prison as a form of social organization which necessarily inhibited autonomy and independent decision-making. More particularly, she indicates a number of degrading social practices: the inmates were given meaningless and unchallenging work to do, they were required to use specific address terms when talking to staff (for example, utterances to include the address term 'miss'), particular forms of deportment were required of them (they were frequently told to keep their hands out of their pockets), they were persistently instructed in appropriate conversation and etiquette and they were subjected to close surveillance of their leisure activities and mealtimes. All of these practices add up to an assault on their self-worth as adults; they are demeaning and they contradict the official line that the women were being assisted in the process of 'becoming adult'.

Together, furthermore, these three contradictions can be seen to embody an institutional reproduction of the very conditions of being repressed and dominated which these women had experienced prior to entering prison. There, as Carlen describes at some length, they had been subjected to patriarchal repression, often of the most brutal form. These practices served to 'keep them in their place' rather than helping to 'improve' their position in society.

The prison 'crisis'

In Chapters 3, 7 and 8 we have described how recent developments in law creation, in police methods and in the courts have been interpreted by structural conflict theorists as responses to a crisis of capitalist political economy and hegemony. The prison, too, has been a scene in which a greater repression has been observable. In this section we shall consider briefly the features of this development and relate them, in structural conflict fashion, to developments in both the wider criminal justice system and the political economy at this historical juncture.

Sim (1987) identifies the most important features of the 'crisis' within prisons which has emerged over the past decade or so. These include a 'crisis' of overcrowding in disgusting, insanitary conditions, conflict between rank-and-file prison officers and their bosses (the Home Office, prison governors) and others (social workers, probation officers and teachers), and conflict between prison officers and the prisoners themselves, manifested in injuries to both sides, demonstrations against officer brutality and a series of disturbances, protests and 'riots' especially in long-term maximum security prisons. In addition, prisoners have turned increasingly to the law itself as a means of challenging existing treatment policy within prisons, resulting, for example, in winning the right to be legally represented at prison disciplinary hearings (though, as Sim (1987) points out, this right has since been subverted by the authorities). Finally, it has been increasingly recognized, as we have already indicated above in our review of the official functions of the prison, that incarceration does little to prevent recidivism. In fact it tends to achieve precisely the reverse. (We take up this matter below when we consider the contribution of labelling theory with regard to the impact of imprisonment.)

The response by the state to the crisis of overcrowding has been described by Sim (1987) as 'classical and predictable'. That is, in the face of rising rates of 'indiscipline' the state intensifies repression and coercion. New prisons have been and are being built and the old ones have begun to be refurbished. But far from relieving overcrowding these measures have simply created more capacity for more prisoners; they have permitted the use of imprisonment as a punishment option to an even greater extent than before. As the new places have been provided, they have been filled up so that the overcrowding has remained. Similarly, where alternatives to custody have been used, as in the increasing use of 'community control' (fines, suspended sentences, weekend imprisonment, community service orders, electronic tracking, etc.) the result has not been a diminution of the prison population. Rather, as Cohen (1985), and Hylton (1981) and Scull (1984) have shown, the 'decarceration' movement and the alternatives to custodial control have, in fact, meant an increased penetration of social control into the community, where 'offenders' who previously might have escaped the attentions of the authorities are now being drawn into the ever-widening net of control.

In response to what Sim (1987) calls the 'crisis of containment'

– the confrontations, disturbances and protests – the state has reinforced and consolidated prison security measures. This has been achieved partly through the application of advanced technology. In addition, as Sim points out,

> the authorities have introduced and extended various techniques aimed at controlling, neutralizing and isolating those individuals who are regarded as difficult, recalcitrant or subversive. The use of psychotropic drugs to control the behaviour of prisoners has been a major area of controversy in British prisons in recent years, as has been a number of cases of prisoners who have died in custody either through violence or through lack of care by the prison authorities. The introduction of a special squad of prison officers trained in techniques of riot control – the Minimum Use of Force Tactical Intervention Squad (MUFTI) – has further consolidated this drive towards maintaining order and control inside. It has been intimated recently that all prison officers are trained in the techniques of riot control. The prison authorities have also used various forms of segregation in the form of solitary confinement, segregation units and control units to isolate those regarded as difficult.
>
> (Sim 1987: 197)

If the prison system is both expanding and becoming more repressive the key sociological issue for the structural conflict theorist is why this is happening at *this* historical juncture. What socio-structural/political economic conditions provide for a plausible account of these developments? In part, the increased repression in prisons is understandable as one more constituent feature of the array of authoritarian measures introduced in recent years, particularly under the Thatcher governments from 1979 onwards. As we have shown in Chapters 3, 7 and 8 various Acts of Parliament have extended state power whilst the instruments of state power, especially the police, have been strengthened with disproportionate amounts of public expenditure. The expansion of the prison system fits neatly into this picture. It also has benefited from the shift in resources towards law and order expenditure. In instrumentalist terms, this shift and the authoritarian response which it enables are designed to support the interests of those who have most to gain from current political–economic arrangements. The *laissez-faire* capitalism and monetarism characteristic of the right-wing governments in Western societies in the recent past has resulted in increasing class conflict as whole sections of society become 'problematic' for the preservation of social order. Where there is 'resistance' this is met with increasingly coercive instruments of control. Prisons have a central role to play in controlling these problematic and 'surplus' populations. As Box puts it:

> during times of economic crisis, state coercion increases in response to the perceived threat, real or imagined, of public disorder including crime waves. The judiciary, being an integral part of the state control apparatus, makes its contribution to this increased level of coercion by imprisoning more, particularly those typifying the actually, or potentially, disruptive problem populations. This judicial response is one the state, by adopting a posture of non-interference with the independence of judiciary, gratefully allows to occur.
>
> (Box 1983: 217)

Whilst it is possible to relate instrumentally these changes in the penal system to (1) the increasing authoritarianism of the criminal justice system as a whole and (2) the move to a *laissez-faire* economy, it is also important to consider them in structuralist terms. Indeed, as Sim (1987: 206) reminds us, 'there is no straight "fit" between economy, class and state'. Structuralist interpretations, as we have suggested, are less reductionist than instrumentalist accounts in two senses. Firstly, they tend to accord a greater independence to the interests of the state in the formation of penal policy and practice, and secondly, they display a conception of ideology as a significant vehicle for domination and control in itself. The constituents of the 'deep decisive movement towards a more disciplinary, authoritarian kind of society' (Hall 1980) are '*not* invariably tied to the economic sector' (Davis and Stasz 1990). They can be seen to involve an extension of state power *tout court* and the reconstitution of 'the whole of society . . . as a field of social relations structured in dominance' (Centre for Contemporary Cultural Studies 1982). Furthermore, as Sim remarks,

> it is also important to acknowledge that these developments in penal policies and criminal justice practices could be seen as indicative of the government's desire to establish a much more integrated and less informal process of justice in England and Wales which would approach problems of crime and public

order in a manner which is rational, professional and ultimately ruthless.

(Sim 1987: 205)

In other words, then, the state can be seen to have its own 'authoritarian agenda' and 'vision of order' (Ignatieff 1978) which cannot be simplistically tied to the immediate interests of the economically powerful.

In addition, far from being 'economically rational', in structuralist terms the expansion of the prison system and the containment of increasing numbers of 'offenders' within can be seen to contribute to the contradictions of capitalism. We note briefly three ways in which the growth of punishment described above embodies 'structural' contradictions. Firstly, by expanding the prison system and by incarcerating ever-increasing numbers of prisoners within it the state contributes to the problem of overcrowding in prisons which the expansion was designed (in part) to alleviate. Secondly, at a time of fiscal crisis, and with cuts in public expenditure high on the political agenda, it is contradictory to spend more and more money punishing people. Such a policy serves to deepen the fiscal crisis. Thirdly, given the crime-producing tendencies of incarceration the expansion of the prison system serves to create more and more criminals, a process which, incidentally, costs more and more to control.

SYMBOLIC INTERACTIONISM AND THE PRISON: THE SOCIAL ORGANIZATION OF PRISON LIFE

Symbolic interactionists, unlike the structural conflict theorists discussed above, have been mainly concerned with cultural aspects of imprisonment and with the impact of incarceration on the prisoner's sense of self and subsequent criminal 'career'. The former concern has generated an extensive literature on the 'convict code' and 'inmate subcultures'; the latter is a reflection of the wider symbolic-interactionist interest in the development of the self in social interaction. In this instance, its focus is on how the conditions of prison life and the experiences they shape contribute to the building of a criminal identity and the persistence of criminal behaviour. We shall discuss each of these interactionist concerns in turn.

Once an offender is sentenced to a period of incarceration

there occurs a series of events during which his or her social status is transformed from that of an individual citizen within the community to that of an 'inmate'. Goffman (1961) has described the entry into the correctional institution as a process of 'mortification' by which the individual is likely to be stripped of his usual appearance and of the equipment and services by which he maintains it. The individual's prior self-conception is systematically reduced via a 'series of abasements, degradations, humiliations, and profanations of self' (ibid: 14). These may include fingerprinting, photographing, rectal (and vaginal, if a woman) inspection, haircutting or shaving, being allocated a number, bathing and disinfecting and the removal of 'civilian' clothes and their replacement with institutional uniform. Admission procedures comprise a 'status degradation ceremony' (Garfinkel 1956b) in which the former identity of the offender is destroyed and a new identity established. Following processing into the institution the new inmate enters the world of the prison, which includes its own 'social system', an unwritten code of conduct, various social roles and very often a special vocabulary. This inmate social system or subculture has been the subject of considerable criminological attention. It is to this literature that we shall now turn to see what light it has shed on prison life. We rely principally on Wieder's (1974: 120–125) review as it is his own contrasting ethnomethodological study of the convict code which we shall examine in the final section of this chapter.

The content and role of prisoner subcultures

One of the earliest and now classic studies of prisoner subcultures is the work on *The Prison Community* by Clemmer (1940). According to Clemmer the 'convict code' was: 'one of the fundamental social controls amongst the inmate population. It revolves around two propositions: "Don't help the officials" and "Do help your fellow inmates".' For Clemmer, 'prisonization' was socialization to the convict code.

> Thus, Clemmer's prisonized inmate would not snitch, would regard officials as his [sic] enemy and would show this by, for example, not talking to them except about 'business', and would assist his fellow inmates by helping them avoid detection in their deviance.
>
> (Wieder 1974: 121)

In *The Society of Captives*, Sykes (1958) presents the theory that the inmate social system is developed to cope with the 'pains of imprisonment'. These pains consist of a collection of 'deprivations':

[firstly,] the deprivation of liberty, particularly the freedom to see one's family and friends;
[secondly,] the deprivation of goods and services, particularly those necessary to maintain a cherished self-identity;
[thirdly,] the deprivations of heterosexual relationships;
[fourthly,] the deprivation of autonomy, particularly not being allowed to make decisions about how daily activities will be allocated;
and [fifthly,] the deprivation of security, particularly the close physical proximity of persons with records of violent aggression.

(Box 1981: 216)

In the face of these deprivations the inmate subculture affords self-protection to the inmate. It provides a means whereby the inmate can develop 'status' within the prison and it supplies a 'world view' or 'frame of reference' in terms of which the inmate can define and interpret his or her situation. Central to this viewpoint is the belief that it is the 'captors' who are the 'evildoers' since they are immoral, unjust and incompetent in contrast to the inmates who are their 'victims'. Sykes also shows that the convict 'code is embedded in a system of social types', with 'each social type representing a pattern of compliance with or deviance from the code' (Wieder 1974: 122). For example, the 'rat' is an inmate who violates the 'do not snitch on fellow inmates' rule, the 'gorilla' is one who exploits fellow inmates by threatening and using violence, whilst the 'real man' is the inmate who exemplifies compliance with the code. 'He is able to "take it". He has strength . . . and "confronts his captors with neither subservience nor aggression" [Sykes 1958:] (p. 102)' (Wieder 1974: 123–124). Sykes suggests that by evaluating each other in terms of the social type 'real man' (that is, in terms of exemplary commitment to the code) the inmates are able to 'reduce the pains of imprisonment and can achieve a sense of self-respect' (Wieder 1974: 124).

Similar findings have been made by Garabedian (1963, 1964). His account (1964) reflects that of Sykes by addressing the social types provided by the code. He thus identifies 'square johns', 'politicians', 'right guys' and 'outlaws' and describes the types of behaviours which are associated with each of them. 'Commitment' to the convict code is exemplified by such behaviours as breaking the prison rules, avoiding contact with the officials and refusing to participate in staff-sponsored programmes. Because they were more likely to engage in such behaviours, the 'outlaw' and 'right guy' were viewed as more committed and hence were held in greater esteem within the prisoner community than those typified as 'politicians' and 'square johns' (Wieder 1974: 124).

Several studies in this genre have indicated that there tends to be more than one type of subculture within prisons. Thus Irwin and Cressey (1962) and Irwin (1970) point to the existence of the 'thief subculture' and the 'convict subculture'. The former consists of the norms and values which are said to be characteristic of professional thieves and other career criminals. It is also seen as a subculture which is imported into the prison from outside. The latter, the convict subculture, on the other hand, is viewed as arising in response to the conditions found within the prison. This is the subculture of the hard-core, long-term and institutionalized inmates. According to Box (1981: 217) this subculture pertains to that company of 'men who have spent most of their lives, including their youth, in state institutions'; these are inmates who have been, for the most part, 'ineffectual criminals, but who, because of their experience in prisons and similar institutions, know exactly how to work the system'. From this group of inmates, a neophyte prisoner might learn how to manipulate other prisoners and how to hustle but he or she is not likely to learn how to be a more effective criminal. On the other hand, the thief subculture referred to by Irwin and Cressey (1962) is carried by those 'who are essentially criminals and only incidentally prisoners' (Box 1981: 217). Although estimated to be a smaller percentage of the total prison population than the 'convicts' this second group has higher social standing both within and outside the prison. As Box (1981: 217) points out, if the neophyte inmate becomes a member of this section of the prison community the possibility of learning the 'folkways, mores and customs of a criminal way of life as well as learning to cope with the pains of imprisonment' may open up.

Other studies, notably Jacobs (1974), have also found that the subcultural diversity of prisons is further complicated by the presence of gangs formed along racial lines. In his study of a 'Big House' in California, for example, Jacobs located three major racial divisions: blacks, whites and hispanics. The culture of these gangs was imported from outside the prison, was adapted to prison conditions and eclipsed in importance the distinctions between the 'thief' and 'convict' subculture, though clearly within the racial groupings a distinction could still be made between inmates in terms of their identity as high-status criminals or low-status convicts.

Finally, we note that in the classic ethnographies of women's prisons by Giallombardo (1966), Heffernan (1972) and Ward and Kassebaum (1965) both similarities and differences in prison culture were observed. Several social roles or social types similar to those found in men's prisons were evident with respect to commitment to or compliance with the inmate subculture. In Giallombardo's study (1966), for example, those who violated the 'no informing' rule were typed as 'snitches', those who 'made trouble' for other inmates were labelled 'jive bitches', whilst those who were seen as largely accidental criminals or pro-administration inmates were regarded as 'squares'.

There were also important differences in the inmate culture of women's prisons. In general, violence and aggression were less common in the women's prison. Homosexuality in the men's prison was typically the product of violence and coercion whereas in the women's prison it was entered into more voluntarily. Females tended to establish 'pseudo-families' amongst themselves, with the participants playing the various family roles of 'parent' and 'relative' and so on. There was less solidarity amongst female inmates and the economic system which provided for the production, exchange and distribution of goods and services, often of an illicit nature, was less common in the women's prison. Finally, women inmates tended to be less committed to the convict code than their male counterparts.

The impact of imprisonment

It was mentioned earlier that as the inmate enters a prison a process of 'self mortification' is set in motion as he or she is degraded and suffers the pains of imprisonment. This process has received particular attention from the symbolic interactionists or labelling theorists for whom, as we saw in Chapter 5, the development of the self as a social construction is a central feature of the approach. We also suggested, following Matza (1969), that the offender may, through interaction with agencies of social control, pass through a series of 'career' steps or stages which culminate in

the development of a deviant identity or sense of self. We considered the first two of these stages: ban and transparency, and
apprehension and labelling. We can now turn to the third and
fourth stages: incarceration (or exclusion) and post-prison stigmatization.

Being incarcerated or, as Matza puts it, being 'excluded' is
viewed as a part of a process of social interaction with agencies of
social control through which the offender undergoes a change in
self-conception from being someone who, amongst other things,
happens to have committed a crime, to being someone for whom
the facts of their criminality become their most important 'identifier'. Obviously not all offenders reach this stage but for those who
do the chances that they will become 'secondary deviants' are
high. It is well known that prisons function as 'universities' (or at
least 'schools') of crime and that inmates are likely to learn further
means and motives for committing crime. More important,
however, is the fact that it is extremely difficult for an inmate to
sustain a conventional self-image within prison. His or her mere
presence in such an institution is living proof, reaffirmed on a daily
basis, that he or she is a criminal. The pains of imprisonment,
furthermore, add up to a concerted assault and a shattering impact
on the offender's sense of conventional identity. The initial
'shaping' (Pfuhl 1980: 170) of the inmate as an object 'that can be
fed into the administrative machinery' (Goffman 1961: 16) on
entry to the prison persists throughout the period of incarceration. The various controls identified in the previous section are
designed to further 'mortify' the inmate and 'to bring obstrep-
erous, boisterous, or otherwise unruly (that is, those who threaten
organizational procedures) clients back into line' (Pfuhl 1980:
171). The upshot is a further diminution of the inmate's prior
sense of self, its replacement with an institutionally countenanced
label and, in all likelihood, a smouldering sense of injustice.
Together with these processes, turning to either of the inmate
cultures is likely to accelerate the development and confirmation
of the offender's sense of criminal identity.

The fourth and final stage is 'post-prison stigmatization and
social rejection'. As Erikson (1964 (1962): 16–17) has indicated,
'the deviant often returns home with no proper licence to resume
a normal life in the community.' Often the family and the community are reluctant to accept the deviant back into the fold.
Along similar lines, Box (1981: 229) has suggested that there are

four reasons which can explain why an ex-convict comes to the conclusion that a normal, straight life is just not feasible. The first is 'atrophy of interactional skills'. Thus, long-term prisoners especially lose the ability to carry out normal, everyday interactional routines, let alone find and keep a job. The second is 'social discrimination'. This depends on the community's knowledge of and view taken about the type of offence for which imprisonment occurred. If social discrimination does occur, the greater are the chances of the person re-offending. Thirdly, there is 'job-rejection'. As Box (1981: 232) has pointed out, 'the best established fact about recidivism is that it is closely associated with unemployment'. It is well known that ex-prisoners have difficulties obtaining legal work. To the extent that they do, they are much more likely to re-offend and to have their sense of criminal identity confirmed. Finally, there is 'surveillance by the police'. As Matza (1969) indicates, the police routinely suspect and rely heavily on ex-offenders as a method of solving crimes. Such treatment serves to confirm the ex-offender's social identity as a criminal and may help to propel him or her into further criminality.

In conclusion:

> The bulk of the prison population consists of secondary deviants. Their lives and activities are centred around the problem of deviance and their more or less accepted deviant identity. They became secondary deviants because, having been selected for apprehension from a much larger population at risk of being apprehended, they were severely punished and, on release, discovered that the costs of conformity were too high. Behaving themselves involved putting up with a bad or no job, little money and no prospects; it involved having a poor social life and denying themselves the company of other criminals, who might at least sympathize and understand their problems. It's just too much.
>
> (Box 1981: 234)

ETHNOMETHODOLOGY AND THE CONVICT CODE: NORMATIVE AND INTERPRETIVE APPROACHES TO PRISONER SUBCULTURES

Ethnomethodology draws our attention to the difference between normative and interpretive approaches which studies of prisoner subcultures exemplify. This difference becomes most apparent when the ethnomethodological work of Wieder (1974) is compared to the material on inmate subcultures examined above. Thus, despite varying levels of subscription to interactionist premises, the work of Clemmer, Sykes, Garabedian, Goffman, Jacobs and others all imputes a kind of causal role to the inmate culture. Each of these studies uses the concept of the inmate or convict code to explain the behaviour of the prisoners. It is compliance to the code, these theorists argue, which accounts for their behaviour, in particular their deviant behaviour, within the prison. Inmates and their actions are seen to be governed by a set of rules. The inmates are conceptualized as rule-followers. The code, then, becomes a sociologist's method for explaining behaviour which appears problematic to him or her. In contrast, the work of Wieder is concerned not with producing a sociological explanation of convict conduct in terms of compliance with a code but rather with examining how the inmates themselves make use of the code in the course of their natural social interaction. Wieder finds that the 'code' as a corpus of rules or norms is invoked in residents' conversations with other residents and with staff, in staff-initiated conversations with residents and, interestingly enough, in conversations among staff themselves, at the halfway house where the research was done. The code is used as an interpretive and as an interactional device, which is to say that the inmates are able both to define and perform actions by making reference to the code. Interestingly, one task they perform is that of accounting for their own conduct in terms of conformity to the code. As such, the prisoners are conducting themselves rather like 'folk sociologists' except that they are not searching for social scientific explanation but instead are engaged in ordinary everyday social interaction.

It is this contrast between using everyday language and culture as a resource in the construction of social scientific theories and treating the use of language and culture as a topic in its own right which distinguishes the normative from the interpretive paradigm in sociology (Wilson 1970). From an interpretivist position (and here we would include both ethnomethodology and the ideally interpretive form of symbolic interactionism) language and culture are not determinants of social action; rather, they are simply materials used in constructing social action.

Wieder lays out the report on his study of the convict code in two parts. In the first part he describes the regularities in resident behaviour that sociologists traditionally would want to explain, and provides a standard normative explanation in terms of compliance with the maxims of the convict code. In the second part, however, he conducts an ethnomethodological examination of the accounts of their behaviour offered both by residents and staff in the course of interaction and by such sociological explanations as he himself provides in part one.

The regularities in the conduct of residents consist of six patterns of deviance which Wieder (1974: 76–97) describes as follows:

1 'doing distance'
2 'doing disinterest and disrespect'
3 'passive compliance'
4 'doing requests and demands'
5 'doing unreliability as informants'
6 'doing violations'.

Examples of the last include not showing up for 'group', not looking for work, using drugs (the residents were all ex-narcotics felons) and jumping parole. These patterns of deviance are massively regular, are 'independent of production cohorts', are chronic topics of staff concern being departures from the official order and are seen as 'caused' by the code by all concerned, including sociologists.

Wieder describes the code itself as a set of eight maxims:

1 Above all else, do not snitch.
2 Do not cop out.
3 Do not take advantage of other residents.
4 Share what you have.
5 Help other residents.
6 Do not mess with other residents' interests.
7 Do not trust staff – staff is heat.
8 Show your loyalty to the residents.

(ibid: 115–117)

He then shows how the patterns of deviance may be explained by regarding them as 'caused by', 'governed by' or 'following from' the code maxims. Thus the first four patterns are explained by the eighth maxim, the fifth pattern by maxims one, two, five, six and seven and the sixth pattern is 'protected, supported, and encouraged by the code, though . . . not directly prescribed' (ibid: 119). Like Sykes and Garabedian earlier, Wieder also shows how the categories of convict/resident (for example, kiss ass, snitch, gorilla, merchant, ball-buster, real man, square john, politician, outlaw) are also defined in terms of the identities that the code makes available, and are in that sense explained by it. What makes his study ethnomethodological is the analytical step which makes up part two. For the code is not simply an outside sociological observer's construct for explaining residents' deviant conduct, but is used in the very course of interaction by all parties to the setting as a way to perform actions and simultaneously display what those actions are. In Wieder's terms 'telling the code' is multi-consequential as a form of action and multi-formulative of the (identity or meaning of) the action itself, its immediate inter-actional context and of the surrounding social structures. For example, consider the utterance 'You know I won't snitch' which 'often terminated a relatively friendly line of conversation' (ibid: 168) between staff or researcher (Wieder) and residents. Wieder explicates its multi-formulative character as follows. It:

1 told what had just happened – e.g., 'You just asked me to snitch',
2 formulated what the resident was doing in saying that phrase – e.g., '. . . My answer is not to answer',
3 formulated the resident's motives . . . – e.g., 'I'm not answering in order to avoid snitching' . . . [and] . . . formulated the sensible and proper grounds of the refusal [the code],
4 formulated . . . the immediate relationship between the listener . . . and teller . . . [by invoking] the[ir] persisting role relation-ships . . . – e.g., 'For *you* to ask *me* that, would be asking me to snitch',
5 was *one more* formulation of the features of the persisting role relationship.

(Wieder 1974: 168–169)

'Beyond the multi-formulative character of this single utterance, it was also a consequential move in the very "game" that it formulated' (169). The resident, in saying 'You know I won't snitch':

1 negatively sanctioned the prior conduct of staff or myself . . .
2 called for and almost always obtained a cessation of that line of the conversation . . .
3 [consequently] left me or staff ignorant of what we would have learned by the question had it been answered . . .

4   signaled the consequences of rejecting the resident's utterance
    or the course of action it suggested. By saying, 'You *know* I *won't*
    snitch' . . . the resident warned that the conversation would
    turn nasty if staff or I did not retreat from the question . . .
    [and] pointed to the consequences for himself if he were to go
    ahead and answer the question . . . [which] could include
    beatings and even death.

(ibid: 169–170)

Thus the code could be used for stopping a conversation or changing a topic, declining a suggestion or order, urging or defeating
a proposed course of action, and for accounting for one's feelings
or actions in an acceptable way – that is, for demonstrating one's
competence as a reasonable and moral person. The code was
particularly useful to staff as an excuse for the failure of house
programmes, as an interpretation of residents' complaints and, in
general, as a method of managing their circumstances.

'Telling the code' was useful to staff by converting problematic
acts of residents into instances of a familiar pattern, into acts
which were connected to plausible ends and other activities,
into acts which were rational or reasonable, and into acts whose
occurrence was not dependent on the specifics of any given
staff–resident encounter or relationship.

(ibid: 156–157)

In short: 'The code, then, is much more a *method* of moral
persuasion and justification than it is a substantive account of an
organized way of life' (ibid: 175).

Chapter 12

The functions of crime control

A question we have yet to address, but which is arguably the most fundamental in criminology, is 'why is there crime at all in society?' We have argued throughout the book that the possibility of crime depends on given acts being proscribed by the criminal law, that is, that crime depends on law, and on particular instances of action being identified and interpreted as crimes, that is, that crime depends on crime-processing agencies, conventionally the police and the courts. But these matters presuppose that 'society' should define any acts in the first place as criminal. Why does criminalization occur at all?

The answer to this question depends on which sociological perspective is used. We are concerned here with the answers provided by those sociologists employing the structural-consensus or structural-conflict approaches. They have seen the question as inviting a 'functionalist' answer. That is, criminalization is said to occur because it serves some societal purpose, provides societal benefits and contributes to social order. Consensus and conflict accounts differ in just what these purposes, benefits and contributions consist of, or just what population they serve. They agree, however, that criminalization is analysable in terms of its beneficial (and detrimental) consequences. We begin with the consensus account as classically displayed in the work of Durkheim and Erikson.

THE FUNCTIONS OF CRIME: THE STRUCTURAL CONSENSUS ACCOUNT

The structural consensus analysis of the functions of crime is similar to this perspective's analyses of a wide range of social phenomena, including religion, the family, and the school. The basic approach is to identify the consequences, both positive and negative, which these phenomena have for the society as a whole. The underlying assumption is that society can be viewed as if it were an organism, such as the human body, with each of its constituent elements having some function to perform in the overall survival and stability of the whole. Sociologists have long sought a technical means of identifying and distinguishing the functional and dysfunctional aspects of human activity. As would-be social 'physicians' they have attempted to diagnose the diseases of the social body and to identify the 'health-promoting' features of social life. An early example of this sociological health consciousness can be found in Durkheim's distinction between the 'normal' and the 'pathological'. He defines as 'normal' those social practices which are both widespread in societies of a given type and are not disruptive of societal stability. Crime is therefore considered as 'normal' because it is not only widespread in societies of all types but it also does not interfere with the overall stability and functioning of the social organism. This rather surprising conclusion is defended on the grounds that the degree of our moral outrage about human actions is not proportional to their 'objective' social harm, a view endorsed in the more recent writings of the structural conflict criminologists. We reserve our greatest disapprobation for those individuals who murder others, argues Durkheim. However, it is not clear that society is endangered as much by this source of loss of life as it is by other sources built into the everyday practices of the military, government departments and corporations, and, as feminists would argue, of patriarchal social institutions. As we showed in Chapters 3 and 8 our society does not view as criminal many of these practices even though they cause harm and injury. Whereas, as we know, the structural conflict theorists see in this state of affairs a reason for complaint, Durkheim argues that there is good reason why society should criminalize those acts which offend our moral sensibilities irrespective of their objective harm. Indeed, both Durkheim and those who have used a similar approach, proceed to identify a number of positive benefits for society as a whole which accrue from the existence of crime. We shall consider two of these.

Crime and the maintenance of moral boundaries

The idea that crime has a maintenance function with respect to moral boundaries relates to the mutual intelligibility of crime and conformity. Without the one there can be no sense of its opposite. The two need each other as good needs evil, as light needs dark. If society itself in the Durkheimian view is a moral phenomenon then it needs immorality to make morality visible. Moreover this is not a task that is ever completed. Reminders are continually required.

> There was certainly a sense in which, for Durkheim, society existed in the minds of its members, for a society could not exist without (1) extensive agreement on morality among its members, and (2) some awareness on the part of these members of the fact of agreement between them. Without this common morality, a society could not possess a unity. However, the mere existence of agreement on morality is not enough to unify a society. Sentiments can and will become attenuated unless they are exercised. Durkheim tended to look upon human states of mind as somewhat akin to muscles: they tend to atrophy if they are not used . . . Durkheim treats many states of mind as analogous to this. We may feel strongly against murder. But if no one is ever murdered in our society, eventually we shall cease to feel so strongly against it. If our feelings *are* to be kept alive and strong, they must be provoked and stimulated, that is, *exercised.*
>
> (Sharrock 1984: 88–89, original emphasis)

In view of this, then, it is relatively easy to see that public trials and punishments can serve as not only reminders but also celebrations of the morality. In this sense, the 'criminal' serves not only a useful purpose but also a necessary one.

> We are faced with a conclusion which is apparently somewhat paradoxical. Let us make no mistake: to classify crime among the phenomena of normal sociology is not merely to declare that it is an inevitable though regrettable phenomenon arising from the incorrigible wickedness of men; it is to assert that it is a factor in public health, an integrative element in any healthy society.
>
> (Durkheim 1982: 98)

Thus Durkheim proclaims the necessity of crime for society. However, it appears that this is not an empirical claim about the relationship between two independent phenomena, namely crime and social order, but one that arises from the very way in which Durkheim conceptualizes 'society'. That is, it is a conceptual assertion, a matter of definition. For if, as we argued at the beginning of Chapter 2, society is for Durkheim in essence its moral rules, then it is definitionally impossible for there to be society without deviance (crime), since morality and deviance require each other.

> Imagine a community of saints in an exemplary and perfect monastery. In it crime as such will be unknown, but faults that appear venial to the ordinary person will arouse the same scandal as does normal crime in ordinary consciences. If therefore that community has the power to judge and punish, it will term such acts criminal and deal with them as such.
>
> (Durkheim 1982: 100)

Crime, then, is not just beneficial but essential to society, at least in the Durkheimian view. Such a view has not, however, been without its critics. Box (1981) and Roshier (1977), for example, have called into question two aspects of Durkheim's work. Firstly, they have pointed to the fact that it is misleading to speak of the functions of 'crime' as such because this implies that there is some objective thing which can be non-problematically identified as 'crime'. As we have pointed out in earlier chapters 'crime' is always a matter of definition or 'criminalization'. That is to say, certain acts become criminalized through the enactment of laws and through the enforcement of those laws with respect to particular instances of behaviour. Without enactment and enforcement there can be no criminal behaviour as such, only, at best, potential criminal behaviour. This means, then, that if anything is functional for society it can only be the social reaction to and definition of behaviour as 'crime', rather than the behaviour itself. Indeed, though Durkheim fails to articulate it in so many words, this 'social reaction' approach to crime is implicit in his analysis of the society of saints and the significance of punishment. It is the 'judgment', 'identification', 'stigmatization' and 'punishment' of the 'deviant' act and 'deviant' person that is central to Durkheim's account.

As with the other three perspectives discussed in this book it is possible to trace the implications of this view at each of the three levels of the criminal justice system, namely the law, the operation of the courts and the work of the police. At this late stage in the book we will do no more than suggest the analytic possibilities the structural consensus perspective opens up in these three areas. For the case of law itself we need only recall from Chapter 4 Gusfield's point about the purpose of the rhetoric associated with the notion of the 'killer-drunk' as found in appeal court judgments (p. 88). Quite apart from whatever utility such language has in expediting the operation of the courts or the apprehension of criminals, such declamations serve the societal symbolic function of marking moral boundaries by constructing and dramatizing the image of the 'evil one' in whatever the incarnation of the day is (Pearson 1983). As we argued in Chapter 8 much the same function is served by jury trials. What is worth noting here is that the public, ritual exiting from society of the embodied version of the hated image – namely the now-convicted person – is not matched by an equivalent public ritual of re-entry into society when his or her time is served. In terms of this approach the person is a prop of the ritual, and not the other way round. It is the occasion of public vilification that the society needs, not the reformation of the criminal. As for the police the approach helps to make sense of the observation that far from acting in ways that are designed to eradicate deviance, police 'behave in ways that are likely to ensure the persistence of deviance' (Sharrock 1984: 90). That is, as we saw in Chapter 6, the bulk of police work is taken up with keeping the peace rather than law enforcement, with arrest being the control device of last resort. Police seek to contain and regulate crime rather than to eliminate it. They develop working relationships with criminals for they are dependent on criminals for the information with which to do their work. Here the court system conspires to facilitate police operations by stigmatizing the convicted, assigning them to a school of crime (prison) and making it extremely difficult for them to resume normal life upon release. The police then seek out the 'known criminal' as suspect for the type of crime that they were known to have committed. After this, as we saw in Chapter 11, a life of crime may seem the only livable recourse. In these ways criminal justice arrangements work to guarantee a ready supply of recycled candidates for society's appetite for necessary deviance.

The second criticism, made by Roshier (1977), is one which challenges Durkheim's very concept of society. Thus, Roshier claims that rather than attempting to remove crime through a process of elevating people's consciousness and eventually threatening the very existence of society, logically it is possible to eradicate crime simply by removing the laws which are used as the resource for its identification.

Crime and the clarification of moral boundaries

Structural consensus theorists claim that crime can not only serve a maintenance function but also a clarification function with respect to moral boundaries. The key work in this area is Erikson's *Wayward Puritans* (1966). This study in historical sociology, grounded in a fusion of structural consensus and symbolic interactionist approaches, considers the part played by three events in the evolution of Puritan society in New England from the late sixteenth century on. These events are the antinomian crisis, the Quaker persecutions and the Salem witchcraft panic. Each of these, Erikson agues, resulted in a clarification of the moral boundaries of Puritan society. We shall illustrate this process with reference to the first of these, namely the antinomian crisis or, more colloquially, the case of Mrs Hutchinson.

Prior to their departure for New England the Puritans considered themselves and were considered by the established church as religious revolutionaries. They believed they were members of God's elect upon whom grace had been directly bestowed. Rather than following, therefore, a covenant of works through which believers were required to demonstrate to clerical intermediaries their worthiness of God's salvation, they adhered to a *covenant of grace*. This released them from the rules of establishment religious practice. However, such freedom was intolerable to the religious authorities, hence their eventual departure for New England where they could practise their faith as they saw fit.

After a while it seemed to the original settlers, and in particular to a Mrs Hutchinson, that the religious messages of the church leaders were more in accordance with the old covenant of works than the covenant of grace. No longer themselves in opposition the Puritan leaders were becoming conservative and similar to the established church back in Europe. The covenant of works was becoming attractive to them. Yet they dared not abandon the covenant of grace. The clergy attempted to solve this dilemma by 'resorting to the argument that *the state of grace was a condition for which one had to be prepared*; and, being peculiarly nearer to God, who better to prepare His chosen few than the clergy themselves?' (Box 1981: 34, original emphasis). However, Mrs Hutchinson declared that obedience to the clergy was irrelevant as far as God's grace was concerned, and many agreed with her. Soon, a majority of the local congregation preferred meeting at her house to meeting at the church. She not only instructed them in correct religious thinking, she also called into question the state of grace of the church leaders. Faced with this challenge the clergy impeached her and subsequently declared her guilty of 'casting doubt upon the authority of the church'. As Box puts it:

> By a raw display of power Mrs. Hutchinson had been declared guilty of 'Hutchinsonism', no more, and certainly no less. Her views were declared to be deviant views. Anyone uttering such views in the future, therefore, ran the risk of also being declared deviant. That was the outcome of the confrontation, and with that outcome the social boundaries of the New England Settlement had been clarified and decisively shifted.
>
> (Box 1981: 35)

'Hutchinsonism' was made authoritatively illegal through Mrs Hutchinson's ensuing spiritual trial. Her belief in her state of her own of grace was declared to be a delusion because 'God reveals Himself to no man (or woman)'. Mrs. Hutchinson then repented but the clergy thought her repentance was insincere, calling her a liar. On the basis of this label they excommunicated her, casting her out of the church.

Erikson argues that by publicly declaring what deviance was, the clergy had not only revealed their power but they had also clarified the moral boundaries of New England society. The meaning of the covenant of grace had been transformed and the clergy had gained in political as well as spiritual authority. Arguably, then, Puritan society as a whole benefited from this exercise in moral clarification, which contributed to its persistence and stability. Perhaps this might not have happened without Mrs Hutchinson's 'deviance'.

THE FUNCTIONS OF CRIME: THE STRUCTURAL CONFLICT PERSPECTIVE

We have already said in Chapter 3 that unlike the structural consensus view of functions as being performed with respect to the 'whole' society, the structural conflict perspective sees functions in relation to particular groups or classes within society. Thus, rather than 'law and order' serving the 'national' interest, they are seen to serve the interests of the ruling class (who may well try to represent their interests as the 'national interest'). This may be achieved directly for the capitalist class under the instrumentalist interpretation or more indirectly via the interests of the state under the structuralist interpretation. As we have tried to show throughout, this may be seen in several ways: (1) in the enactment of law, (2) in the administration of justice and (3) in the enforcement of law.

With respect to the enactment of law it has already been shown in Chapter 3 that it is easily demonstrated that the passage of laws is related to the political economic interests of the powerful within society rather than the interests of everyone in society. This is obviously so for the case of laws protecting private property, as we suggested in Chapter 8. These clearly do not benefit everybody equally; rather, they benefit only those possessing it. To this it may be objected that, in fact, most officially recorded acts of theft are perpetrated by working-class people on other members of the same class. This state of affairs is one which the 'left realists' have emphasized as a result of their 'crime surveys'. The implication is that 'something has got to be done about law and order', the laws are there for the benefit of working-class as well as bourgeois 'victims' and that the causes of this irritation to the social body must be the focus of criminological research. But, as Snider argues in the following passage, this position misses the point about how property laws protect capital.

> It is true that those who own the least may suffer more when what they have is stolen, because they are losing a much greater percentage of their worldly goods in this one transaction than a middle- or upper-class person, who has property in many different forms and locations, would be. The real basis for comparison here is not how much is lost per theft, but which class has more to lose? Which would be the most threatened if 50–80 percent of their wealth were to be confiscated, by land redistribution or by revolution? Only then is it obvious how much our present system of laws safeguards the institutions of private property, which allows the most privileged to preserve, protect, and pass on their vast enclaves of wealth.
>
> (Snider 1988: 312)

Moreover, as Spitzer (1975) argues, the ruling class is quite ready to tolerate intra-working-class victimization, for obvious reasons.

But it is also true for laws which are ostensibly 'inimical' or 'irrelevant' to ruling-class interests. Hepburn (1977), in a forceful rejoinder to those critics who argue that the existence of such laws demonstrates the weakness of the structural conflict perspective, reminds critics of an observation of Marx himself that, for example, labour laws designed to protect the interests of factory workers in fact in the long run serve the interests of the capitalist class through the cultivation of worker contentment and consent: the Factory Acts in the mid-nineteenth century 'represented the state protecting capitalists from themselves' (Caputo *et al* 1989: 9; Hall and Scraton 1981: 493). Such steps nevertheless leave the fundamental divisions of society intact. Goldthorpe *et al* (1978), for instance, have shown for the United Kingdom that even though over the course of this century absolute standards of living and levels of social mobility have increased for the mass of the population, when changes in occupational structure are allowed for there has been virtually no change in the relative positions of the social classes. As Goldthorpe and co-authors put it:

> In other words, one is led to believe that in the course of recent decades the overall extent of social fluidity in England and Wales, at least if thought of in terms of movement between class positions, has altered little. During a period in which, as we have observed, the occupational division of labour has been transformed and in which, it is generally supposed, major changes have also occurred in modes of 'social selection', there would appear to have been a somewhat remarkable degree of continuity in the underlying processes of intergenerational class mobility.
>
> (Goldthorpe *et al* 1978: 456)

Furthermore, such laws not only protect, they also regulate, thus ensuring the promotion of discipline in the work force and workplace. Laws regulating the activities of the capitalist class – for example, laws on fraud, embezzlement, insider trading, worker health and safety, combinations to restrict trade – can also be seen to promote rather than inhibit the interests of this class, by serving to protect it from the exposure that may be occasioned by the too-obvious exploitation by 'rogue' capitalists 'getting away with murder'. By enforcing the law against the 'deviant' members of the capitalist class – the Ivan Boeskys, Donald Trumps and others of similar notoriety – the state fosters the illusion of a society-wide social solidarity under the rule of law, thereby masking underlying material divisions and class interests.

Hepburn (1977) also argues that laws which apparently demonstrate the prowess of pressure groups to shape public morality – for example, in the area of sexual mores, drugs and alcohol, and gambling – in fact help to divert attention away from structural and material matters to moral and status concerns which have no impact on the underlying structural inequalities in society. They help to foster the illusion of democracy in capitalist society by making the political arena accessible to ordinary citizens, grassroots organizations and other relatively powerless groupings. The enactment of moral prohibitions makes little difference to basic economic inequalities though it may serve to criminalize problem populations and otherwise divide the working class on racial, status and otherwise moral lines. Again, this is a lesson which we drew from Comack's analysis of the origins of Canada's drug laws and from Snider's analysis of the reform of Canada's rape laws in Chapter 3. It is also a lesson which is given wider currency in Spitzer's (1975) 'Marxian' theory of deviance where he argues that those activities which are most subject to the process of criminalization are those which, as we saw in Chapter 7, are performed by various 'problem populations'. They comprise 'problems' because of their lack of integration and synchronization with the workings of capital.

The structural conflict conception of the functions of crime can also be seen in connection with the enforcement and administration of law, as examined in Chapters 7 and 8. Thus, both police and judicial processes can be analysed for the ways in which they serve not only to conserve current class divisions but also to perpetuate self-serving bureaucracies of legal authority. We have seen how, from this perspective, the law is enforced and administered inequitably, with the result that disproportionate numbers of lower-class and minority-group offenders are selected for criminal processing in the first place and, in keeping with their subordinate positions in the structures of dominance that comprise the ruling social relations, receive both softer and harsher sentences, compared to their more privileged and powerful counterparts, when convicted. It is also quite easily appreciated that 'crime' provides an essential material condition for the livelihoods of vast numbers of police, lawyers, judges, court workers, probation and parole officers, prison guards and governors, prison doctors and psychiatrists, locksmiths, safe makers, insurance companies and, of course, criminology professors.

Structural conflict theory also points to the 'functions' of the use of myths of crime and the failure to address the criminogenic social arrangements in crime control. Taken together, these produce a cumulative mystification of the social nature of crime which in turn serves to perpetuate current divisions of wealth, power and privilege in society. In earlier chapters we have examined some particular myths of crime, specifically in connection with drug and alcohol use. However, at this point we should state that the orientation of the criminal justice system in general is to crime as an individual problem. It is individuals who are seen as largely responsible for their criminal behaviour just as it is individuals who are tried, convicted and sentenced. As the current (1990) Ontario government campaign puts it, 'only *you* can stop drinking and driving'. It is a relatively easy matter, of course, to debunk this widely accepted view. Thus, crime, as we have shown in earlier programmes, is more appropriately viewed as a *social* phenomenon, that is, as one constructed through criminalizing acts of the legislators, the courts and the police. However, even though it is possible to point to the 'mistaken', 'misguided' and 'mythical' nature of the individualistic conception of crime, what is important for our purposes here is to appreciate the social functions of this belief. It serves to obscure and divert attention from the criminalizing character of the state itself. Inequalities of wealth, power, privilege, access to opportunities are all more or less accepted as the 'natural' facts of life. When individuals are blamed for what is called 'their own fault' these natural facts are left undisturbed and indeed are endorsed. The provision of social programmes to alleviate the worst consequences of industrial capitalism does not relieve the individual of the burden of responsibility for 'failure'. On the contrary, there is judged to be even less excuse for a person's criminality when 'you've never had it so good' (see Caputo *et al* 1989: 10). In short, the individualistic conception of crime is a particular instance of the prevailing individualistic ideology so central to the capitalist social system. Blame the individual offender and the system escapes blame. Meanwhile, those with most to gain from the system benefit.

PRACTISING CRIMINOLOGY

In this book we have recommended a radically sociological view of the subject matter of criminology. This has involved being prepared to distance ourselves from the concerns, presuppositions and questions that have traditionally motivated inquiry into crime and crime control both in the practical discipline of criminology and in the society at large. To practical and academic inquirers, inside and outside the criminal justice system, the overriding approach to the subject has been cast in terms of two questions, namely what causes crime, and what can be done to cure it (Eysenck and Gudjonsson 1989). We have seen that for socio-logical inquirers operating with this correctional or cause-and-cure approach this has meant interrogating the social environment for those criminogenic conditions of criminal behaviour in individuals. As against this point of view we have brought to bear three sociological perspectives that (1) share a conception of 'crimes', 'crime problems', 'criminals', 'crime causes' and 'crime cures' as irremediably constructed phenomena, but (2) differ markedly in the angles of vision they open up on this phenomenal field, and in the ways of practising criminology which they make possible.

To say that crime is 'constructed' is to say that it is inseparable from criminalization. There may be some amongst you who, having patiently journeyed with us to this place in the book, are feeling that we have somehow never got to the point. Frustrated, you may still be wondering when we are going to explain WHY people commit crimes. While we are tempted to say, 'please return to go' (Chapter 1), there is perhaps something that can be usefully said at this late stage of the proceedings. If it is the case that 'crime' is a status accorded some acts and not others at some times and not others and in some places and not others, and that those acts are engaged in to some degree by most people at least some of the time, then it is highly questionable whether there is anything special that needs to be explained about criminal acts. Presumably people engage in acts deemed criminal for the same reasons they engage in activities deemed 'legitimate': 'We are brought up to do them; they are fun; there is an economic advantage in doing them; they are the way we have always behaved; they are how we make our living; and so on' (Sharrock 1984: 99). However, even if this may be a useful thing to say, we should not be misled into thinking that the question of causes is one that is worth asking in the first place.

'There cannot be specific kinds of motivation to engage in deviant activities if there are no categories of activities which are inherently deviant' (Sharrock 1984: 99).

Whilst the three perspectives of symbolic interactionism, ethnomethodology and structural conflict theory and, indeed, as we have seen in this chapter, the structural consensus perspective, all share a view of crime as a product of criminalization, they offer different models of criminological practice. Each model provides a different focus, different insights and different ways of engaging with the social world. It is our view that attempts to contrive grand syntheses of these different approaches serve only to dilute their essential character, damaging their integrity and diminishing their analytic potential. For us they are essentially incommensurable, each providing its own unique vision. We do not subscribe to the view that those engaged in sociological inquiry have to swear allegiance to one view over all the others. Which model one adopts on any occasion of inquiry depends on the sort of question one wishes to address, what resources one has at hand and the theoretical and practical goals of inquiry one has. Structural conflict theory provides a powerful tool for engaging in critical inquiry in the interests of promoting major structural social change. Studies of global, societal and local political economy, for example, reveal just how criminalization, crime control and criminal activity are intimately connected both with one another and with the political and economic interests of the contending classes. Indeed, research conducted under the auspices of this approach has been self-consciously 'interventionist'. As Sim and co-authors indicate:

> While much of this work has developed directly from academic research and analysis it has retained an interventionist and applied emphasis. Critical criminologists have worked alongside community leaders, local politicians, union officials and church leaders in constructive attempts to pursue more accountable policing and to provide sensitive and appropriate police responses on the streets.
>
> (Sim *et al.* 1987)

Symbolic interactionism offers a critical appreciation of the organizational and interactional parameters and processes comprising the criminal justice system, and the possibility of empathetic understanding of the 'nature' of 'criminal' and 'control' actions and 'criminal' and 'control' subcultures. Finally, ethnomethodology permits us not only to conceive of criminalization as a product of situated courses of practical action and reasoning, but also reminds us of the locally embodied and accomplished character not only of 'crimes, courts and corrections' (Brannigan 1984) but of sociological and criminological inquiry itself.

Bibliography

Adler, P. A. (1985) *Wheeling and Dealing: An Ethnography of an Upper-level Drug Dealing and Smuggling Community*, New York: Columbia University Press.

Albert, M., Cagan, L., Chomsky, N., Hahnel, R., King, M., Sargent, L. and Sklar, H. (1986) *Liberating Theory*, Boston: South End Press.

Alexander, F. and Ross, H. (eds) (1952) *Dynamic Psychiatry*, Chicago: Chicago University Press.

Allen, H. (1987) 'Rendering them harmless: the professional portrayal of women charged with serious violent crimes', in P. Carlen and A. Worrall (eds) *Gender, Crime and Justice*, Milton Keynes: Open University Press.

Alschuler, A. (1968) 'The prosecutor's role in plea bargaining', *University of Chicage Law Review* 36 (1): 50–112.

Althusser, L. (1971) 'Ideology and ideological state apparatuses', in *Lenin and Philosophy*, London: New Left Books.

Amernic, J. (1984) *Victims: The Orphans of Justice*, Toronto: McClelland and Stewart-Bantam.

Amnesty International (1990) 'United States of America: the death penalty government survey finds patterns of racial disparities in imposition of death penalty', London: Amnesty International.

Anderson, N. (1923) *The Hobo*, Chicago: Chicago University Press.

Athens, L. (1980) *Violent Criminal Acts and Actors*, London: Routledge & Kegan Paul.

Atkinson, J. M. (1978) *Discovering Suicide: The Social Organization of Sudden Death*, paperback edn (1982), London: Macmillan.

Atkinson, J. M. and Drew, P. (1979) *Order in Court: The Organization of Verbal Interaction in Judicial Settings*, London: Macmillan.

Atkinson, J. M. and Heritage, J. C. (eds) (1984) *Structures of Social Action: Studies in Conversation Analysis*, Cambridge: Cambridge University Press; Paris: Maison des Sciences de l'Homme.

Atwood, M. (1972) *Survival: a Thematic Guide to Canadian Literature*, Toronto: Anansi Press.

Becker, H. S. (1953) 'Becoming a marihuana user', *American Journal of Sociology* 59: 235–242. (Reprinted in H. S. Becker (1963)).

Becker, H. S. (1963) *Outsiders: Studies in the Sociology of Deviance*, 2nd edn (1973), New York: Free Press.
—— (ed.) (1964) *The Other Side: Perspectives on Deviance*, New York: Free Press.
—— (1973) 'Labelling theory reconsidered', in *Outsiders*, 2nd edn, New York: Free Press.
Becker, H. S., Geer, B. and Hughes, E. C. (1968) *Making the Grade: The Academic Side of College Life*, New York: John Wiley.
Bell, D. (1960) 'The myth of crime waves: the actual decline of crime in the United States', in *The End of Ideology*, Glencoe, IL: Free Press.
Bell, L. (ed.) (1987) *Good Girls/Bad Girls: Sex Trade Workers and Feminists Face to Face*, Toronto: Women's Press.
Bendix, R. (1962) *Max Weber: An Intellectual Portrait*, revised edn, London: Heinemann.
Berger, P. L. (1963) *Invitation to Sociology*, Garden City, NY: Doubleday Anchor.
Berger, P. L. and Luckmann, T. (1966) *The Social Construction of Reality*, Garden City, NY: Doubleday Anchor.
Best, J. (ed.) (1989) *Images of Issues: Typifying Contemporary Social Problems*, New York: Aldine de Gruyter.
Bilmes, J. (1988) 'The concept of preference in conversation analysis', *Language in Society* 17: 161–181.
Bittner, E. (1967a) 'The police on skid row: a study of peace keeping', *American Sociological Review* 32 (5): 699–715. (Reprinted in W. B. Sanders and H. C. Daudistel (eds) (1976) *The Criminal Justice Process: A Reader*, New York: Praeger.)
—— (1967b) 'Police discretion in emergency apprehension of mentally ill persons', *Social Problems* 14 (3): 278–292. (Reprinted in O. Grusky and M. Pollner (eds) (1981) *The Sociology of Mental Illness: Basic Studies*, New York: Holt, Rinehart and Winston, and in Coulter (1990).)
—— (1980) *The Functions of the Police in Modern Society*, Cambridge, MA: Olegeschlager, Gunn, and Hain. (Originally published in 1970; partially reprinted in C. B. Klockars (ed.) (1983) *Thinking About Police: Contemporary Readings*, New York: McGraw-Hill.)
Blackwell, J. C. and Erickson, P. G. (eds) (1988) *Illicit Drugs in Canada: A Risky Business*, Scarborough, ON: Nelson Canada.
Blumberg, A. (1976) 'The practice of law as a confidence game: organizational co-optation of a profession', in W. B. Sanders and H. C. Daudistel (eds) *The Criminal Justice Process: A Reader*, New York: Praeger. (Originally published in 1967 in *Law and Society Review* 1 (1): 15–39.)
Blumer, H. (1956) 'Sociological analysis and the "variable"', *American Sociological Review* 21 (6): 683–690. (Reprinted in H. Blumer (1969).)
—— (1969) *Symbolic Interactionism: Perspective and Method*, Englewood Cliffs, NJ: Prentice-hall.
—— (1971) 'Social problems as collective behaviour', *Social Problems* 18: 298–306.
Bogen, D. and Lynch, M. (1989) 'Taking account of the hostile native: plausible deniability and the production of conventional history in the Iran–Contra Hearings', *Social Problems* 36 (3): 197–224.

Bogoch, B. and Danet, B. (1984) 'Challenge and control in lawyer–client interaction: a case study in an Israeli Legal Aid office', *Text* (special issue, 'Studies of legal discourse', edited by B. Danet) 4 (1–3): 249–275.

Bottomley, A. K. (1979) *Criminology in Focus: Past Trends and Future Prospects*, Oxford: Martin Robertson.

Bottomley, A. K. and Coleman, C. (1981) *Understanding Crime Rates: Police and Public Roles in the Production of Official Statistics*, Farnborough, Hants: Gower.

Box, S. (1981) *Deviance, Reality and Society*, 2nd edn, London: Holt, Rinehart and Winston. (Originally published in 1971.)

—— (1983) *Power, Crime, and Mystification*, London: Tavistock.

Box, S. and Hale, C. (1982) 'Economic crisis and the rising prisoner population in England and Wales, 1949–1979', *Crime and Social Justice* 16 (1): 20–35.

Brannigan, A. (1984) *Crimes, Courts and Corrections: An Introduction to Crime and Social Control in Canada*, Toronto: Holt, Rinehart and Winston of Canada.

Brannigan, A. and Levy, J. C. (1983) 'The legal context of plea bargaining', *Canadian Journal of Criminology* 25 (4): 399–420.

Brophy, J. and Smart, C. (eds) (1985) *Women-in-law: Explorations in Law, Family and Sexuality*, London: Routledge & Kegan Paul.

Brown, L. and Brown, C. (1973) *An Unauthorized History of the RCMP*, 2nd edn (1978), Toronto: James Lorimer.

Bunyan, T. (1976) *The Political Police in Britain*, New York: St. Martin's Press.

Burris, C. A. and Jaffe, P. (1986) 'Wife abuse as a crime', in R. A. Silverman and J. J. Teevan (eds) *Crime in Canadian Society*, 3rd edn, Toronto: Butterworths. (Originally published in 1983 in *Canadian Journal of Criminology* 25 (3): 309–318.)

Caputo, T. C., Kennedy, M., Reasons, C. E. and Brannigan, A. (1989) 'General introduction: theories of law and society', in T. C. Caputo *et al.* (eds) *Law and Society: A Critical Perspective*, Toronto: Harcourt Brace Jovanovich.

Carey, J. T. (1968) *The College Drug Scene*, Englewood Cliffs, NJ: Prentice-Hall.

Carlen, P. (1976) *Magistrates' Justice*, London: Martin Robertson.

—— (1983) *Women's Imprisonment: A Study in Social Control*, London: Routledge & Kegan Paul.

Carver, T. (1982) *Marx's Social Theory*, Oxford: Oxford University Press.

CBC (Canadian Broadcasting Corporation) Enterprises Radio-Canada (1989) 'Access to information', *Ideas* 15 February (transcript).

Center for Research on Criminal Justice (1975) *The Iron Fist and Velvet Glove: An Analysis of the U.S. Police*, Berkeley: Center for Research on Criminal Justice.

Centre for Contemporary Cultural Studies (1982) *The Empire Strikes Back*, London: Hutchinson.

Chambliss, W. J. (1964) 'A sociological analysis of the law of vagrancy', *Social Problems* 12 (1): 67–77.

—— (1976a) 'The state and criminal law', in W. J. Chambliss and M.

Mankoff (eds) *Whose Law? What Order? A Conflict Approach to Criminology*, New York: John Wiley. (Originally published in D. Glaser (ed.) (1974) *Handbook of Criminology*, Chicago: Rand McNally.)

—— (1976b) 'The saints and the roughnecks', in W. J. Chambliss and M. Mankoff (eds) *Whose Law? What Order? A Conflict Approach to Criminology*, New York: John Wiley. (Originally published in 1973 in *Society* 11 (11): 24–31; reprinted in E. Rubington and M. S. Weinberg (eds) (1987).)

Chomsky, N. (1975) 'Introduction', in C. Perkus (ed.) *COINTELPRO: The FBI's Secret War on Political Freedom*, New York: Monad.

—— (1987) *Pirates and Emperors: International Terrorism in the Real World*, Montreal: Black Rose Books.

—— (1988) *The Culture of Terrorism*, Montreal: Black Rose Books.

—— (1989) *Necessary Illusions: Thought Control in Democratic Societies*, Toronto: CBC Enterprises.

—— (1991a) *Deterring Democracy*, New York: Verso.

—— (1991b) '"What we say goes": the Middle East in the new world order', *Z Magazine* 4 (5) (May): 49–64.

Chomsky, N. and Herman, E. S. (1979) *The Political Economy of Human Rights*, 2 Volumes, Montreal: Black Rose.

Chunn, D. E. (1988) 'Maternal feminism, legal professionalism and political pragmatism: the rise and fall of Magistrate Margaret Patterson, 1922–1934', in W. W. Pue and B. Wright (eds) *Canadian Perspectives on Law and Society: Issues in Legal History*, Ottawa: Carleton University Press.

Churchill, W. (1991) 'Death squads in the U.S.: confessions of a government terrorist', *Z Magazine* 4 (5) (May): 103–108.

Churchill, W. and Van der Wall, J. (1988) *Agents of Repression: the FBI's Secret Wars Against the Black Panther Party and the American Indian Movement*, Boston: South End Press.

Cicourel, A. V. (1964) *Method and Measurement in Sociology*, New York: Free Press.

—— (1968) *The Social Organization of Juvenile Justice*, New York: John Wiley.

—— (1976) 'Introduction', in *The Social Organization of Juvenile Justice*, London: Heinemann.

Clark, L. M. G. and Lewis, D. J. (1977) *Rape: The Price of Coercive Sexuality*, Toronto: Women's Press.

Clemmer, D. (1940) *The Prison Community*, New York: Christopher Publishing House.

Cloward, R. A. and Ohlin, L. (1960) *Delinquency and Opportunity: A Theory of Delinquent Gangs*, Glencoe, IL: Free Press.

Cohen, A. (1955) *Delinquent Boys: The Culture of the Gang*, Glencoe, IL: Free Press.

Cohen, S. (1972) *Folk Devils and Moral Panics: The Creation of the Mods and Rockers*, 2nd edn revised 1980, Oxford: Martin Robertson.

—— (1985) *Visions of Social Control: Crime, Punishment and Classification*, Cambridge: Polity Press.

Cole, S. G. (1989) *Pornography and the Sex Crisis*, Toronto: Amanita.

Coleman, R. V. (1976) 'Court control and grievance accounts: dynamics of traffic court interaction', *Urban Life* 5 (2): 165–188.

Comack, E. (1985) 'The origins of Canadian drug legislation: labelling versus class analysis', in T. Fleming (ed.) *The New Criminologies in Canada*, Toronto: Oxford University Press.

Comack, E. and Brickey, S. (eds) (1991) *The Social Basis of Law: Critical Readings in the Sociology of Law*, 2nd edn, Halifax, NS: Garamond.

Conrad, P. and Schneider, J. W. (1980) *Deviance and Medicalization: From Badness to Sickness*, St Louis: C. V. Mosby.

Cook, S. J. (1969) 'Canadian narcotics legislation, 1908–1923: a conflict model interpretation', *Canadian Review of Sociology and Anthropology* 6 (1): 36–46. (Reprinted as Small (1978).)

—— (1970) 'Variations in Response to Illegal Drug Use', Toronto: Alcoholism and Drug Addiction Research Foundation, unpublished manuscript.

Corrado, R. R. (1987) 'Political crime in Canada', in R. Linden (ed.) *Criminology: A Canadian Perspective*, Toronto: Holt, Rinehart and Winston of Canada.

Cressey, D. R. (1953) *Other People's Money*, Glencoe, IL: Free Press.

Critchley, T. A. (1967) *A History of Police in England and Wales 900–1966*, London: Constable.

Cuff, E. C. and Francis, D. W. (1978) 'Some features of "invited stories" about marriage breakdown', *International Journal of the Sociology of Language* 18: 111–133.

Cuff, E. C. and Payne, G. C. F. (eds) (1979) *Perspectives in Sociology*, 2nd edn 1984, London: George Allen and Unwin.

Cuff, E. C., Francis, D. W. and Sharrock, W. W. (1990) *Perspectives in Sociology*, 3rd edn, London: Unwin Hyman.

Danet, B. and Bogoch, B. (1980) 'Fixed fight or free-for-all? An empirical study of combativeness in the adversary system of justice', *British Journal of Law and Society* 7 (1): 36–60.

Davis, M. and Ruddick, S. (1988) 'Los Angeles: civil liberties between the hammer and the rock', *New Left Review* 170: 37–60.

Davis, N. J. and Stasz, C. (1990) *Social Control of Deviance: A Critical Perspective*, New York: McGraw-Hill.

Dickson, D. (1968) 'Bureaucracy and morality: an organizational perspective on a moral crusade', *Social Problems* 16 (2): 143–156.

Dion, R. (1982) *Crimes of the Secret Police*, Montreal: Black Rose Books.

Douglas, J. D. (1967) *The Social Meanings of Suicide*, Princeton, NJ: Princeton University Press.

—— (ed.) (1971) *Crime and Justice in American Society*, New York: Bobbs-Merrill.

Douglas, M. (ed.) (1973) *Rules and Meanings: The Anthropology of Everyday Knowledge: Selected Readings*, Harmondsworth: Penguin.

Downes, D. and Rock, P. (1982) *Understanding Deviance: A Guide to the Sociology of Crime and Rule-Breaking*, 2nd edn 1988, Oxford: Oxford University Press.

Drew, P. (1978) 'Accusations: the occasioned use of members' knowledge of "religious geography" in describing events', *Sociology* 12 (1): 1–22.

Duncan, B. and Eglin, P. A. (1979) 'Making sense of the reliability and validity of official crime statistics: review and prospect', *Canadian Criminology Forum* 2 (1): 7–19.

Dunstan, R. (1980) 'Contexts for coercion: analysing properties of courtroom "questions"', *British Journal of Law and Society* 7 (1): 61–77.

Durkheim, E. (1951) *Suicide: A Study in Sociology*, New York: Free Press. (Originally published in French in 1897.)

—— (1964) *The Division of Labour in Society*, New York: Free Press. (Originally published in French in 1893.)

—— (1982) *The Rules of Sociological Method; and Selected Texts on Sociology and its Method*, London: Macmillan. (Originally published in French in 1895.)

Edwards, S. (1990) 'Violence against women: feminism and the law', in L. Gelsthorpe and A. Morris (eds) *Feminist Perspectives in Criminology*, Milton Keynes: Open University Press.

Eglin, P. A. (1979) 'Resolving reality disjunctures on Telegraph Avenue: a study of practical reasoning', *Canadian Journal of Sociology* 4 (4): 359–377.

—— (1980) 'Culture as method: location as an interactional device', *Journal of Pragmatics* 4: 121–135.

—— (1987) 'The meaning and use of official statistics in the explanation of deviance', in R. J. Anderson, J. A. Hughes and W. W. Sharrock (eds) *Classic Disputes in Sociology*, London: Allen and Unwin.

Eglin, P. A. and Hester, S. (1992) 'Category, predicate and task: the pragmatics of practical action [Review article on *Categorization and the Moral Order* by Lena Jayyusi]', *Semiotica* 88 (3–4), in press.

—— (eds) (forthcoming) *Identity, Interaction and Institution: Studies in Membership Categorization.*

Eglin, P. A. and Wideman, D. B. (1986) 'Inequality in professional service encounters: verbal strategies of control versus task performance in calls to the police', *Zeitschrift fur Soziologie* 15 (5): 341–362.

Embree, S. (1977) 'The State Department as moral entrepreneur: racism and imperialism as factors in the passage of the Harrison Narcotics Act', in D. F. Greenberg (ed.) *Corrections and Punishment*, Beverly Hills, CA: Sage.

Emerson, R. M. (1969) *Judging Delinquents: Context and Social Process in Juvenile Court*, Chicago: Aldine.

Ericson, R. V. (1981) *Making Crime: A Study of Detective Work*, Toronto: Butterworths.

—— (1982) *Reproducing Order: A Study of Police Patrol Work*, Toronto: University of Toronto Press in association with the Centre of Criminology, University of Toronto.

Ericson, R. V. and Baranek, P. (1982) *The Ordering of Justice: A Study of Accused Persons as Dependents in the Criminal Process*, Toronto: University of Toronto Press.

Erikson, K. T. (1962) 'Notes on the sociology of deviance', *Social Problems* 9 (4): 307–314. (Reprinted in Becker (1964) and Rubington and Weinberg (1987).)

—— (1966) *Wayward Puritans: A Study in the Sociology of Deviance*, New York: John Wiley.

Eysenck, H. J. (1964) *Crime and Personality*, 3rd edn 1977, London: Routledge & Kegan Paul.

Eysenck, H. J. and Gudjonsson, G. H. (1989) *The Causes and Cures of Criminality*, New York: Plenum.

Ferraro, K. J. (1989) 'Policing women battering', *Social Problems* 36 (1): 61–74.

Fishman, M. (1980) *Manufacturing the News*, Austin: University of Texas Press.

Fitzgerald, M. (1977) *Prisoners in Revolt*, Harmondsworth: Penguin.

Fleming, T. (ed.) (1985) *The New Criminologies in Canada: State, Crime, and Control*, Toronto: Oxford University Press.

Foucault, M. (1977) *Discipline and Punish: The Birth of the Prison*, London: Allen Lane.

Francis, D. W. (1987) 'The great transition', in R. J. Anderson, J. A. Hughes and W. W. Sharrock (eds) *Classic Disputes in Sociology*, London: Allen and Unwin.

Frank, A. G. (1981) 'After Reaganomics and Thatcherism, What? From Keynesian demand-management via supply-side economics to corporate state planning and 1984', *Contemporary Marxism* 4: 18–28, Winter.

Freidson, E. (1970) *Professional Dominance: The Social Structure of Medical Care*, New York: Atherton.

French Army-Surgeon (1972 (1898)) *Observations on the Esoteric Manners and Customs of Semi-Civilized Peoples; being a Record of Thirty Years' Experience in Asia, Africa, America and Oceania* (Documents on Medical Anthropology, Vol. 1: Untrodden Fields of Anthropology), Huntington, NY: Krieger.

Fritz, N. (1991) 'The Social Construction of Drinking Driving as a Social Problem', unpublished undergraduate thesis in sociology, Wilfrid Laurier University, Waterloo, ON.

Galliher, J. F. and Walker, A. (1977) 'The puzzle of the social origins of the Marihuana Tax Act of 1937', *Social Problems* 24 (3): 367–376.

Gamble, A. and Wells, C. (eds) (1989) *Thatcher's Law*, Cardiff: GPC Books.

Garabedian, P. (1963) 'Social roles and processes of socialization in the prison community', *Social Problems* 11: 139–152.

—— (1964) 'Social roles in a correctional community', *Journal of Criminal Law, Criminology, and Police Science* 55: 338–347.

Garfinkel, H. (1956a) 'Some sociological concepts and methods for psychiatrists', *Psychiatric Research Reports* 6: 181–195.

—— (1956b) 'Conditions of successful degradation ceremonies', *American Journal of Sociology* 61 (2): 420–424.

—— (1967) *Studies in Ethnomethodology*, Englewood Cliffs, NJ: Prentice-Hall. (Reprinted in 1984 by Polity Press.)

—— (1974) 'The origins of the term "ethnomethodology"', in Roy Turner (ed.) *Ethnomethodology: Selected Readings*, Harmondsworth: Penguin. (Originally published in R. J. Hill and K. S. Crittenden (eds) (1968) *Proceedings of the Purdue Symposium on Ethnomethodology*, Lafayette, IN: Purdue University Press.)

Garfinkel, H. and Sacks, H. (1970) 'On formal structures of practical actions', in J. C. McKinney and E. A. Tiryakian (eds) *Theoretical*

Sociology: Perspectives and Developments, New York: Appleton-Century-Crofts. (Reprinted in Coulter (1990).)

Gelsthorpe, L. and Morris, A. (eds) (1990) *Feminist Perspectives in Criminology*, Milton Keynes: Open University Press.

Giallombardo, R. (1966) *Society of Women: A Study of a Woman's Prison*, New York: John Wiley.

Giddens, A. (1971) *Capitalism and Modern Social Theory: An Analysis of the Writings of Marx, Durkheim and Max Weber*, Cambridge: Cambridge University Press.

Gladstone, J., Ericson, R. V. and Shearing, C. D. (eds) (1991) *Criminology: A Reader's Guide*, Toronto: Centre of Criminology, University of Toronto.

Glueck, S. and Glueck, E. (1950) *Unravelling Juvenile Delinquency*, New York: Commonwealth Fund.

—— (1956) *Physique and Delinquency*, New York: Harper.

Goff, C. and Reasons, C. E. (1978) *Corporate Crime in Canada*, Scarborough, ON: Prentice-Hall.

Goffman, E. (1961) *Asylums: Essays on the Social Situation of Mental Patients and Other Inmates*, Garden City, NY: Doubleday Anchor.

—— (1962) 'On cooling the mark out: some aspects of adaptation to failure', in A. M. Rose (ed.) *Human Behavior and Social Processes*, Boston: Houghton Mifflin. (Originally published in 1952 in *Psychiatry* 15: 451–463.)

Goldthorpe, J. H., Payne, C. and Llewellyn, C. (1978) 'Trends in class mobility', *Sociology* 12 (3): 441–468.

Gordon, P. (1987) 'Community policing: towards the local police state?', in P. Scraton (ed.) *Law, Order and the Authoritarian State*, Milton Keynes: Open University Press.

Grahame, K. M. (1985) 'Sexual harassment', in C. Guberman and M. Wolfe (eds) *No Safe Place: Violence Against Women and Children*, Toronto: Women's Press.

Gramsci, A. (1971) *Prison Notebooks*, London: Lawrence and Wishart.

Gray, H. (1989) 'Popular music as a social problem: a social history of claims against popular music', in J. Best (ed.) *Images of Issues*, New York: Aldine de Gruyter.

Green, M. (1986) 'A history of Canadian narcotics control: the formative years', in N. Boyd (ed.) *The Social Dimensions of Law*, Scarborough, ON: Prentice-Hall Canada. (Originally published in 1979 in *University of Toronto Faculty of Law Review* 37: 42–79.)

Greisman, H. C. (1984) 'Social meanings of terrorism: reification, violence, and social control', in J. D. Douglas (ed.) *The Sociology of Deviance*, Boston: Allyn and Bacon. (Originally published in 1977 in *Contemporary Crises* 1 (3): 303–318.)

Griffiths, C. T. and Verdun-Jones, S. N. (1989) *Canadian Criminal Justice*, Toronto: Butterworths.

Griffiths, C. T., Klein, J. F. and Verdun-Jones, S. N. (1980) *Criminal Justice in Canada: An Introductory Text*, Toronto: Butterworths.

Grosman, B. A. (1969) *The Prosecutor*, Toronto: University of Toronto Press.

Gusfield, J. R. (1981) *The Culture of Public Problems: Drinking Driving and the Symbolic Order*, Chicago: Chicago University Press.

—— (1989) 'Constructing the ownership of social problems: fun and profit in the welfare state', *Social Problems* 36 (5): 431–441.

Hagan, J. (1980) 'The legislation of crime and delinquency: a review of theory, method, and research', *Law and Society Review* 14 (3): 603–628.

—— (1985) 'The corporate advantage: a study of the involvement of corporate and individual victims in a criminal-justice system', in T. Fleming (ed.) *The New Criminologies in Canada*, Toronto: Oxford University Press. Originally published in 1982 in *Social Forces* 60 (4): 993–1022.)

—— (1991) *The Disreputable Pleasures: Crime and Deviance in Canada*, 3rd edn, Toronto: McGraw-Hill Ryerson.

Hagan, J. and Leon, J. (1977) 'Rediscovering delinquency: social history, political ideology and the sociology of law', *American Sociological Review* 42: 587–598.

Hale, S. M. (1990) *Controversies in Sociology: A Canadian Introduction*, Toronto: Copp Clark Pitman.

Halkowski, T. (1990) '"Role" as an interactional device', *Social Problems* 37 (4): 564–577.

Hall, J. (1952) *Theft, Law, and Society*, revised edn, Indianapolis: Bobbs-Merrill.

Hall, S. (1980) *Drifting Into a Law and Order Society*, London: Cobden Trust.

Hall, S. and Scraton, P. (1981) 'Law, class and control', in M. Fitzgerald, G. McLennan and J. Pawson (eds) *Crime and Society: Readings in History and Theory*, London and Henley: Routledge & Kegan Paul in association with The Open University Press.

Hall, S., Critcher, C., Jefferson, A., Clarke, J. and Roberts, B. (1978) *Policing the Crisis: Mugging, the State, and Law and Order*, London: Macmillan.

Hargreaves, D., Hester, S. and Mellor, F. (1975) *Deviance in Classrooms*, London: Routledge & Kegan Paul.

Harris, M. (1986) *Justice Denied: The Law versus Donald Marshall*, Toronto: Macmillan.

Hart, H. L. A. (1965) 'The ascription of responsibility and rights', in A. Flew (ed.) *Logic and Language*, first and second series, Garden City, New York: Doubleday Anchor. (Originally published in 1948/49 in *Proceedings of the Aristotelian Society*.)

Hart, H. L. A. and Honoré, A. M. (1962) *Causation in the Law*, Oxford: Clarendon Press. (Originally published in 1959.)

Hawkins, R. and Tiedeman, G. (1975) *The Creation of Deviance: Interpersonal and Organizational Determinants*, Columbus, OH: Charles E. Merrill.

Heffernan, E. (1972) *Making It In Prison: The Square, the Cool, and the Life*, New York: Wiley-Interscience.

Hepburn, J. R. (1977) 'Social control and the legal order: legitimated repression in a capitalist state', *Contemporary Crises* 1 (1): 77–90.

(Reprinted in W. K. Greenaway and S. L. Brickey (eds) (1978) *Law and Social Control in Canada*, Scarborough, ON: Prentice-Hall of Canada.)

Heritage, J. C. (1984) *Garfinkel and Ethnomethodology*, Cambridge: Polity Press.

Herman, E. S. and Chomsky, N. (1988) *Manufacturing Consent: The Political Economy of the Mass Media*, New York: Pantheon.

Herman, E. S. and O'Sullivan, G. (1989) *The 'Terrorism' Industry: The Experts and Institutions that Shape Our View of Terror*, New York: Pantheon.

Hester, S. (1991) 'The social facts of deviance in school: a study of mundane reason', *British Journal of Sociology* 42 (3): 443–463.

—— (1992) 'Recognising references to "deviance" in referral talk', in R. Sieler and G. Watson (eds) *Text in Context: Contributions to Ethnomethodology*, Beverly Hills, CA: Sage.

Hilbert, R. A. (1989) 'Durkheim and Merton on anomie: an unexplored contrast and its derivatives', *Social Problems* 36 (3): 242–250.

Hill, C. (1975) *The World Turned Upside Down: Radical Ideas During the English Revolution*, New York: Viking.

Hinch, R. (1985) 'Marxist criminology in the 1970s: clarifying the clutter', in T. Fleming (ed.) *The New Criminologies in Canada*, Toronto: Oxford University Press.

—— (1987) 'Cultural deviance and conflict theories', in R. Linden (ed.) *Criminology: A Canadian Perspective*, Toronto: Holt, Rinehart and Winston of Canada.

Hippchen, L. J. (1977) 'Biochemical research: its contribution to criminological theory', in R. F. Meier (ed.) *Theory in Criminology: Contemporary Views*, London: Sage.

Hobbs, D. (1988) *Doing the Business: Entrepreneurship, the Working Class, and Detectives in the East End of London*, Oxford: Clarendon Press.

Hogarth, J. (1971) *Sentencing as a Human Process*, Toronto: University of Toronto Press in association with the Centre of Criminology, University of Toronto.

Hooton, E. A. (1939) *Crime and the Man*, Cambridge, MA: Harvard University Press.

Houston, S. E. (1978) 'Victorian origins of juvenile delinquency: a Canadian experience', in W. K. Greenaway and S. L. Brickey (eds) *Law and Social Control in Canada*, Scarborough, ON: Prentice-Hall of Canada. (Originally published in 1972 in *History of Education Quarterly* 12: 254–280.)

Hughes, D. (1982) 'Control in the medical consultation: organizing talk in a situation where co-participants have different competence', *Sociology* 16 (3): 359–376.

Hunt, J. (1987) 'Normal force', in E. Rubington and M. S. Weinberg (eds) *Deviance*, 5th edn, New York: Macmillan. (Originally published in 1985 in *Urban Life* 13 (4): 315–341.)

Hylton, J. (1981) 'The growth of punishment: imprisonment and community corrections in Canada', *Crime and Social Justice* 15 (1): 18–28.

Ignatieff, M. (1978) *A Just Measure of Pain: The Penitentiary in the Industrial Revolution, 1750–1850*, New York: Pantheon.

Ignatieff, M. (1983) 'State, civil society and total institutions: a critique of recent social theories of punishment', in S. Cohen and A. T. Scull (eds) *Social Control and the State*, New York: St Martin's Press. (Originally published in M. Tonry and N. Morris (eds) (1981) *Crime and Justice: An Annual Review of Research* 3: 153–191, Chicago: University of Chicago Press; excerpts reprinted in R. P. Saunders and C. N. Mitchell (eds) (1990) *An Introduction to Criminal Law in Context*, 2nd edn, Toronto: Carswell.)

Irwin, J. K. (1970) *The Felon*, Englewood Cliffs, NJ: Prentice-Hall.

Irwin, J. K. and Cressey, D. R. (1962) 'Thieves, convicts and inmate culture', *Social Problems* 10: 142–155.

Jacobs, J. B. (1974) 'Street gangs behind bars', *Social Problems* 21 (3): 395–409.

Jayyusi, L. (1984) *Categorization and the Moral Order*, London: Routledge & Kegan Paul.

Jefferson, G. (1978) 'Sequential aspects of storytelling in conversation', in J. N. Schenkein (ed.) *Studies in the Organization of Conversational Interaction*, New York: Academic.

Jenness, V. (1990) 'From sex as sin to sex as work: COYOTE and the reorganization of prostitution as a social problem', *Social Problems* 37 (3): 403–420.

Johnson, J. M. (1981) 'Program enterprise and official cooptation in the battered women's shelter movement', *American Behavioral Scientist* 24 (6): 827–842.

—— (1989) 'Horror stories and the construction of child abuse', in J. Best (ed.) *Images of Issues*, New York: Aldine de Gruyter.

Kinsey, R., Lea, J. and Young, J. (1986) *Losing the Fight Against Crime*, Oxford: Basil Blackwell.

Kitsuse, J. I. (1962) 'Societal reaction to deviant behavior: problems of theory and method', *Social Problems* 9 (3): 247–256. (Reprinted in Rubington and Weinberg (1987).)

Kitsuse, J. I. and Cicourel, A. V. (1963) 'A note on the uses of official statistics', *Social Problems* 11 (2): 131–139. (Reprinted in J. M. Bynner and K. M. Stribley (eds) (1979) *Social Research: Principles and Procedures*, London: Longman in association with the Open University Press.)

Kleck, G. and Sayles, S. (1990) 'Rape and resistance', *Social Problems* 37 (2): 149–162.

Klein, J. F. (1976) *Let's Make a Deal: Negotiating Justice*, Lexington, MA: D. C. Heath.

Klockars, C. B. (1979) 'The contemporary crises of Marxist criminology', *Criminology* 16 (4): 515.

Kretschmer, E. (1925) *Physique and Character: An Investigation of the Nature of Constitution and of the Theory of Temperament*, 2nd edn 1936, London: Kegan Paul, Trench, Trubner.

Kuttner, R. E. (1985) 'The genocidal mentality – Phillip II of Spain and the Sultan Abdul-Hamid II', *Omega: Journal of Death and Dying* 16 (1): 35–42.

Law Reform Commission of Canada (1978) *Report 10: Sexual Offences*, Ottawa: Supply and Services Canada.

Lea, J. and Young, J. (1984) *What Is To Be Done About Law and Order?*, Harmondsworth: Penguin.

Lemert, E. M. (1948) 'Some aspects of a general theory of sociopathic behavior', *Proceedings of Pacific Sociological Society* 16 (1): 23–29.

—— (1951) *Social Pathology*, New York: McGraw-Hill.

—— (1964) 'Social structure, social control, and deviation', in M. B. Clinard (ed.) *Anomie and Deviant Behavior: A Discussion and Critique*, New York: Free Press.

—— (1967) *Human Deviance, Social Problems and Social Control*, 2nd edn 1972, Englewood Cliffs, NJ: Prentice-Hall.

—— (1974) 'Beyond Mead: the societal reaction to deviance', *Social Problems* 21: 457–468.

—— (1976) 'Responses to critics: feedback and choice', in L. A. Coser and O. N. Larsen (eds) *Uses of Controversy in Sociology*, New York: Free Press.

Lenton, R. L. (1989) 'Parental discipline and child abuse', unpublished doctoral dissertation, Department of Sociology, University of Toronto.

Lombroso, C. (1972) *The Criminal Man*, Montclair, NJ: Patterson Smith. (Reprint of 1911 English translation of 1896–97 Italian edition.)

Los, M. (1990) 'Feminism and rape law reform', in L. Gelsthorpe and A. Morris (eds) *Feminist Perspectives in Criminology*, Milton Keynes: Open University Press.

Luckmann, T. (ed.) (1978) *Phenomenology and Sociology: Selected Readings*, Harmondsworth: Penguin.

Lukes, S. (1975) *Emile Durkheim: His Life and Work: A Historical and Critical Study*, Harmondsworth: Penguin. (Originally published in 1973.)

Lundman, R. J. (1980) *Police and Policing: A Sociological Introduction*, New York: Holt, Rinehart and Winston.

Lynch, M. (1982) 'Closure and disclosure in pre-trial argument', *Human Studies* 5 (4): 285–318.

MacAndrew, C. and Edgerton, R. (1969) *Drunken Comportment: A Social Explanation*, Chicago: Aldine.

McBarnet, D. J. (1981) *Conviction: Law, the State and the Construction of Justice*, London: Macmillan.

McCarthy, J. D. and Zald, M. (1973) 'The trend of social movements in America: professionalization and resource mobilization', Princeton: General Learning Press.

McGillivray, A. (1990) 'Battered women: definition, models and prosecutorial policy', in R. P. Saunders and C. N. Mitchell (eds) *An Introduction to Criminal Law in Context*, 2nd edn, Toronto: Carswell. (Originally published in 1987 in *Canadian Journal of Family Law* 6 (1): 15–45.)

MacKinnon, C. A. (1987) *Feminism Unmodified: Discourses on Life and Law*, Cambridge, MA: Harvard University Press.

McMullan, J. L. and Ratner, R. S. (1983) 'State, labour, and justice in British Columbia', in T. Fleming and L. A. Visano (eds) *Deviant Designations: Crime, Law and Deviance in Canada*, Toronto: Butterworths.

Malette, L. and Chalouh, M. (eds) (1991) *The Montreal Massacre*, Charlottetown, PEI: Gynergy.

Mandel, M. (1983) 'Imprisonment, class and democracy in contemporary Canadian capitalism', Toronto: Osgoode Hall Law School, mimeo.

Mander, C. (1985) *Emily Murphy: Rebel*, Toronto: Simon and Pierre.

Mann, E. and Lee, J. A. (1979) RCMP vs. The People: Inside Canada's Security Service, Don Hills, ON: General Publishing.

Manning, N. (ed.) (1985) *Social Problems and Welfare Ideology*, Aldershot: Gower.

Marx, K. (1970) 'Preface', in *A Contribution to the Critique of Political Economy*, Moscow: Progress. (Originally published in German in 1859.)

Marx, K. and Engels, F. (1970) *The German Ideology: Part One* . . . , New York: International Publishers. (Originally written in German in 1845/46.)

Matthews, R. and Young, J. (eds) (1986) *Confronting Crime*, London: Sage.

Matza, D. (1969) *Becoming Deviant*, Englewood Cliffs, NJ: Prentice- Hall.

—— (1990) *Delinquency and Drift*, New Brunswick, NJ: Transaction Publishers. (Originally published by John Wiley in 1964.)

Maynard, D. (1982a) 'Person-descriptions in plea bargaining', *Semiotica* 42 (2–4): 195–213.

—— (1982b) 'Defendant attributes in plea bargaining: notes on the modeling of sentencing decisions', *Social Problems* 29 (4): 347–360.

—— (1984) *Inside Plea Bargaining: The Language of Negotiation*, New York: Plenum.

—— (1988) 'On narratives and narrative structure in plea bargaining', *Law and Society Review* 22: 101–133.

Mead, G. H. (1934) *Mind, Self and Society*, Chicago: University of Chicago Press.

Mehan, H. (1979) *Learning Lessons: Social Organization in the Classroom*, Cambridge, MA: Harvard University Press.

Melossi, D. and Pavarini, M. (1981) *The Prison and the Factory: Origins of the Penitentiary System*, London: Macmillan.

Meltzer, B. N., Petras, J. W. and Reynolds, L. T. (1975) *Symbolic Interactionism: Genesis, Varieties and Criticism*, London: Routledge & Kegan Paul.

Menninger, K. (1969) *The Crime of Punishment*, New York: Viking.

Merton, R. K. (1938) 'Social structure and anomie', *American Sociological Review* 3: 672–682. (Reprinted in *Social Theory and Social Structure*, enlarged edn 1968, New York: Free Press; and in R. A. Farrell and V. L. Swigert (eds) (1978) *Social Deviance*, 2nd edn, Philadelphia: Lippincott.)

Miliband, R. (1969) *The State in Capitalist Society*, London: Weidenfeld and Nicholson.

Miller, C. (1991) 'The Problem of Drinking and Driving: A Social Construction', unpublished undergraduate thesis in sociology, Wilfrid Laurier University, Waterloo, ON.

Mills, C. W. (1940) 'Situated actions and vocabularies of motive', *American Sociological Review* 5 (6): 904–913. (Reprinted in D. Brisset and C. Edgley (eds) (1975) *Life as Theater: A Dramaturgical Sourcebook*, Chicago: Aldine.)

—— (1956) *The Power Elite*, New York: Oxford University Press.

Mitchell, A. (1985) 'Child sexual assault', in C. Guberman and M. Wolfe (eds) *No Safe Place*, Toronto: Women's Press.

Mitchell, C. N. (1991) 'Narcotics: a case study in criminal law creation', in J. Gladstone, R. V. Ericson and C. D. Shearing (eds) *Criminology: A Reader's Guide*, Toronto: Centre of Criminology, University of Toronto.

Morden, J. R. (1989) 'Letter: spy service evolves', *Globe and Mail* 19 December.

Murphy, E. F. (1922) *The Black Candle*, Toronto: Thomas Allen. (Reprinted in 1973.)

Nagel, I. (1981) 'Sex differences in the processing of criminal defendants', in A. Morris with L. Gelsthorpe (eds) *Women and Crime*, Cropwood Conference Series No. 13, University of Cambridge: Institute of Criminology.

Norrie, A. and Adelman, S. (1989) '"Consensual authoritarianism" and criminal justice in Thatcher's Britain', in A. Gamble and C. Wells (eds) *Thatcher's Law*, Cardiff: GPC Books.

O'Barr, W. M. (1982) *Linguistic Evidence: Language, Power, and Strategy in the Courtroom*, New York: Academic Press.

O'Dowd, L., Rolston, B. and Tomlinson, M. (1980) *Northern Ireland: Between Civil Rights and Civil War*, London: CSE Books.

Parker, G. (1983) *An Introduction to Criminal Law*, 2nd edn (3rd edn 1987), Toronto: Methuen.

Parsons, T. (1951) *The Social System*, Glencoe, IL: Free Press.

Payne, G. C. F. (1976) 'Making a lesson happen: an ethnomethodological analysis', in M. Hammersley and P. Woods (eds) *The Process of Schooling*, London: Routledge & Kegan Paul in association with the Open University Press.

Pearson, G. (1983) *Hooligan: A History of Respectable Fears*, London: Macmillan.

Perkus, C. (ed.) (1975) *COINTELPRO: The FBI's Secret War on Political Freedom*, New York: Monad.

Pfohl, S. J. (1977) 'The "discovery" of child abuse', *Social Problems* 24 (3): 310–323. (Reprinted in J. D. Douglas (ed.) (1984) *The Sociology of Deviance*, Boston: Allyn and Bacon.)

Pfuhl, E. H. (1980) *The Deviance Process*, New York: Van Nostrand.

Piliavin, I. and Briar, S. (1964) 'Police encounters with juveniles', *American Journal of Sociology* 70: 206–214, September. (Reprinted in W. B. Sanders and H. C. Daudistel (eds) (1976) *The Criminal Justice Process: A Reader*, New York: Praeger.)

Platt, A. M. (1969) *The Child Savers: The Invention of Delinquency*, 2nd edn 1975, Chicago: University of Chicago Press.

Platt, A. M. and Coooper, L. (1974) *Policing America*, Englewood Cliffs, NJ: Prentice-Hall.

Plummer, K. (1979) 'Misunderstanding labelling perspectives', in D. Downes and P. Rock (eds) *Deviant Interpretations*, London: Martin Robertson.

—— (ed.) (1991) *Symbolic Interactionism – Volume I: Foundations and History; Volume II: Contemporary Issues*, Brookfield, VT: Edward Elgar.

Pocket Criminal Code (of Canada) (1982), Agincourt, ON: Carswell.

Pollner, M. (1974a) 'Mundane reasoning', *Philosophy of the Social Sciences* 4 (1): 35–54. (Reprinted in Coulter (1990).)

—— (1974b) 'Sociological and common-sense models of the labelling process', in Roy Turner (ed.) *Ethnomethodology: Selected Readings*, Harmondsworth: Penguin.

—— (1975) '"The very coinage of your brain": the anatomy of reality disjunctures', *Philosophy of the Social Sciences* 5: 411–430.

—— (1978) 'Constitutive and mundane versions of labelling theory', *Human Studies* 1: 269–288.

—— (1979) 'Explicative transactions: making and managing meaning in traffic court', in G. Psathas (ed.) *Everyday Language: Studies in Ethnomethodology*, New York: Irvington.

——(1987) *Mundane Reason: Reality in Everyday and Sociological Discourse*, Cambridge: Cambridge University Press.

Pollock, F. and Maitland, F. W. (1968) *The History of English Law*, volume 2, Cambridge: Cambridge University Press.

Pomerantz, A. (ed.) (1988/89) 'Special section: the Dan Rather/George Bush episode on CBS News (papers by Pomerantz, Schegloff, Clayman and Whalen, Nofsinger)', *Research on Language and Social Interaction* 22: 213–326.

Prins, H. (1980) *Offenders, Deviants or Patients?*, London: Tavistock.

Prus, R. C. and C. R. D. Sharper (1991) *Road Hustler: Grifting, Magic, and the Thief Subculture*, expanded edn, New York: Kaufman and Greenberg. (*Road Hustler* originally published in 1977 by Lexington Books.)

Psathas, G. (ed.) (1973) *Phenomenological Sociology: Issues and Applications*, New York: Wiley-Interscience.

Quinney, R. (1970) *The Social Reality of Crime*, Boston: Little, Brown.

—— (1974) *Critique of Legal Order*, Boston: Little, Brown.

Radzinowicz, L. (1962) *In Search of Criminology*, Cambridge MA: Harvard University Press.

Ratner, R. S. and McMullan, J. L. (1985) 'Social control and the rise of the "exceptional state" in Britain, the United States, and Canada', in T. Fleming (ed.) *The New Criminologies in Canada*, Toronto: Oxford University Press.

Reasons, C. E., Ross, L. L. and Paterson C. (1981) *Assault on the Worker: Occupational Health and Safety in Canada*, Toronto: Butterworths.

Reid, S. T. (1985) *Crime and Criminology*, 4th edn, New York: Holt, Rinehart and Winston.

Reiman, J. H. (1979) *The Rich Get Richer and the Poor Get Prison*, New York: Wiley.

Reinarman, C. (1988) 'The social construction of an alcohol problem: the case of Mothers Against Drunk Drivers and social control in the 1980s', *Theory and Society* 17 (1): 91–120.

Roberts, L. W. (1979) 'Rocking the cradle for the world: the new woman and maternal feminism, Toronto, 1877–1914', in L. Kealey (ed.) *A Not Unreasonable Claim*, Toronto: Women's Educational Press.

Rock, P. (1986) *A View From the Shadows: The Ministry of the Solicitor General*

of Canada and the Making of the Justice for Victims of Crime Initiative,
Oxford: Clarendon Press.
Rose, E. (1982) 'The ethno-inquiries and Marxist premises', *Sociolinguistics Newsletter* 13 (1): 24–26.
Rose, V. M. (1977) 'Rape as a social problem: a byproduct of the feminist movement', *Social Problems* 25 (1): 75–89.
Roshier, R. (1977) 'The functions of crime myth', *Sociological Review* 25: 309–324.
Ross, H. L. (1982) *Deterring the Drinking Driver: Legal Policy and Social Control,* Lexington, MA: D. C. Heath Lexington Books.
Rothman, D. J. (1971) *The Discovery of the Asylum,* Boston: Little, Brown.
Rubington, E. and Weinberg, M. S. (eds) (1987) *Deviance: The Interactionist Perspective,* 5th edn, New York: Macmillan.
Rusche, G. and Kirchheimer, O. (1939) *Punishment and Social Structure,* New York: Columbia University Press.
Rushton, J. P. (1989) 'Evolutionary biology and heritable traits (with reference to Oriental–White–Black differences)', paper given at the Annual Meeting of the American Association for the Advancement of Science, San Francisco CA, January.
Sacks, H. (1967) 'The search for help: no one to turn to', in E. Shneidman (ed.) *Essays in Self Destruction,* New York: Science House.
—— (1972a) 'An initial investigation of the usability of conversational data for doing sociology', in D. N. Sudnow (ed.) *Studies in Social Interaction,* New York: Free Press. (Reprinted in Coulter (1990).)
—— (1972b) 'Notes on police assessment of moral character', in D. N. Sudnow (ed.) *Studies in Social Interaction,* New York: Free Press. (Reprinted in W. B. Sanders (ed.) (1974) *The Sociologist as Detective,* New York: Praeger, and in Coulter (1990).)
—— (1974) 'On the analyzability of stories by children', in Roy Turner (ed.) *Ethnomethdology: Selected Readings,* Harmondsworth: Penguin. (Originally published in J. J. Gumperz and D. Hymes (eds) (1972) *Directions in Sociolinguistics: The Ethnography of Communication,* New York: Holt, Rinehart and Winston; reprinted in Coulter (1990).)
—— (1989) 'Harvey Sacks – Lectures 1964–65' (edited by Gail Jefferson with an introduction/memoir by E. A. Schegloff), *Human Studies* 12 (3–4): 211–393.
Sacks, H. and Schegloff, E. A. (1979) 'Two preferences in the organization of reference to persons in conversation and their interaction', in G. Psathas (ed.) *Everyday Language: Studies in Ethnomethodology,* New York: Irvington.
Sacks, H., Schegloff, E. A. and Jefferson, G. (1974) 'A simplest systematics for the organization of turn-taking in conversation', *Language* 50 (4): 696–735. (Reprinted in J. N. Schenkein (ed.) (1978) *Studies in the Organization of Conversational Interaction,* New York: Academic Press.)
Sanders, W. B. (1976) 'Pumps and pauses: strategic use of conversational structure in interrogations', in W. B. Sanders (ed.) *The Sociologist as Detective: An Introduction to Research Methods,* 2nd edn, New York: Praeger.

Sanders, W. B. (1977) *Detective Work: A Study of Criminal Investigations*, New York: Free Press.

Sargent, N. (1990) 'Law, ideology and corporate crime: a critique of instrumentalism', in R. P. Saunders and C. N. Mitchell (eds) *An Introduction to Criminal Law in Context*, 2nd edn, Toronto: Carswell. (Originally published in 1989 in *Canadian Journal of Law and Society* 4: 39–75.)

Saunders, R. P. and Mitchell, C. N. (eds) (1990) *An Introduction to Criminal Law in Context*, 2nd edn, Toronto: Carswell.

Scarman Report (1981) London: HMSO.

Scheff, T. J. (1968) 'Negotiating reality: notes on power in the assessment of responsibility', *Social Problems* 16 (1): 3–17.

Schegloff, E. A. (1968) 'Sequencing in conversational openings', *American Anthropologist* 70 (4): 1075–1095. (Reprinted in J. J. Gumperz and D. Hymes (eds) (1972) *Directions in Sociolinguistics: The Ethnography of Communication*, New York: Holt, Rinehart and Winston, and in J. Fishman (ed.) (1972) *Advances in the Sociology of Language, Volume 2: Selected Studies and Applications*, The Hague: Mouton, and in Coulter (1990).)

Schegloff, E. A., Jefferson, G. and Sacks, H. (1977) 'The preference for self-correction in the organization of repair in conversation', *Language* 53 (2): 361–382. (Reprinted in G. Psathas (ed.) (1990) *Interaction Competence*, Washington, DC: International Institute for Ethnomethodology and Conversation Analysis, and University Press of America.)

Schur, E. (1962) *Narcotic Addiction in Britain and America: The Impact of Public Policy*, Bloomington, IN: Indiana University Press.

—— (1973) *Radical Non-Intervention: Rethinking the Delinquency Problem*, Englewood Cliffs, NJ: Prentice-Hall.

Schutz, A. (1967) 'Concept and theory formation in the social sciences', in *Collected Papers 1: The Problem of Social Reality*, The Hague: Martinus Nijhoff.

Schwendinger, H. and Schwendinger, J. (1975) 'Defenders of order or guardians of human rights?', in I. Taylor, P. Walton and J. Young (eds) *Critical Criminology*, London: Routledge & Kegan Paul. (Originally published in 1970 in *Issues in Criminology* 5: 123–157.)

Scott, M. B. and Lyman, S. (1968) 'Accounts', *American Sociological Review* 33 (1): 46–62. (Reprinted in D. Brisset and C. Edgley (eds) (1975) *Life as Theater: A Dramaturgical Sourcebook*, Chicago: Aldine.)

Scraton, P. (1985) 'The State v The People: An Introduction', *Journal of Law and Society* 12 (3): 251–266.

—— (1987a) 'Unreasonable force: policing, punishment and marginalization', in P. Scraton (ed.) *Law, Order and the Authoritarian State*, Milton Keynes: Open University Press.

—— (ed.) (1987b) *Law, Order and the Authoritarian State: Readings in Critical Criminology*, Milton Keynes: Open University Press.

—— (1990) 'Scientific knowledge or masculine discourses? Challenging patriarchy in criminology', in L. Gelsthorpe and A. Morris (eds) *Feminist Perspectives in Criminology*, Milton Keynes: Open University Press.

Scull, A. T. (1972) 'Social control and the amplification of deviance', in

R. A. Scott and J. D. Douglas (eds) *Theoretical Perspectives on Deviance*, New York: Basic Books.

—— (1984) *Decarceration: Community Treatment and the Deviant: A Radical View*, 2nd edn, Cambridge: Polity. (Originally published in 1977.)

Sharrock, W. W. (1974) 'On owning knowledge', in R. Turner (ed.) *Ethnomethodology: Selected Readings*, Harmondsworth: Penguin. (Reprinted in Coulter (1990).)

—— (1977) 'The problem of order', in P. Worsley (ed.) *Introducing Sociology*, 2nd edn, Harmondsworth: Penguin.

—— (1979) 'Portraying the professional relationship', in D. C. Anderson (ed.) *Health Education in Practice*, London: Croom Helm.

—— (1984) 'The social realities of deviance', in R. J. Anderson and W. W. Sharrock (eds) *Applied Sociological Perspectives*, London: George Allen and Unwin.

Sharrock, W. W. and Anderson, R. J. (1986) *The Ethnomethodologists*, Chichester: Ellis Horwood, and London: Tavistock.

Sharrock, W. W. and Watson, D. R. (1984) 'What's the point of "rescuing motives"?', *British Journal of Sociology* 35 (3): 435–451.

Shaver, F. M. (1985) 'Prostitution: a critical analysis of three policy approaches', *Canadian Public Policy* 11 (3): 493–503. (Reprinted in R. P. Saunders and C. N. Mitchell (eds) (1990) *An Introduction to Criminal Law in Context*, 2nd edn, Toronto: Carswell.)

Shearing, C. D. (1982) 'Private security in Canada', in C. L. Boydell and I. A. Connidis (eds) *The Canadian Criminal Justice System*, Toronto: Holt, Rinehart and Winston of Canada. (Abridged from W. T. McGrath and M. P. Mitchell (eds) (1981) *The Police Function in Canada*, Toronto: Methuen.)

—— (1983) 'Cops don't always see it that way', in T. Fleming and L. Visano (eds) *Deviant Designations: Crime, Law and Deviance in Canada*, Toronto: Butterworths.

Sheldon, W. H. (1949) *Varieties of Delinquent Youth: An Introduction to Constitutional Psychiatry*, New York: Harpers.

Silberman, C. E. (1980) *Criminal Violence, Criminal Justice*, New York: Vintage.

Silverman, R. A. (1980) 'Measuring crime: a tale of two cities', in R. A. Silverman and J. J. Teevan (eds) *Crime in Canadian Society*, 2nd edn, Toronto: Butterworths.

Sim, J. (1987) 'Working for the clampdown: prisons and politics in England and Wales', in P. Scraton (ed.) *Law, Order and the Authoritarian State*, Milton Keynes: Open University Press.

Sim, J., Scraton, P. and Gordon, P. (1987) 'Introduction: crime, the state and critical analysis', in P. Scraton (ed.) *Law, Order and the Authoritarian State*, Milton Keynes: Open University Press.

Skolnick, J. H. (1966) *Justice Without Trial: Law Enforcement in Democratic Society*, 2nd edn 1975, New York: John Wiley.

Small, S. J. (1978) 'Canadian narcotics legislation, 1908–1923: a conflict model interpretation', in W. K. Greenaway and S. L. Brickey (eds) *Law and Social Control in Canada*, Scarborough, ON: Prentice-Hall of Canada. (Reprint of Cook (1968) with an 'Author's Postscript'.)

Smandych, R. (1985) 'Marxism and the creation of law: re-examining the origins of Canadian anti-combines legislation, 1890–1910', in T. Fleming (ed.) *The New Criminologies in Canada*, Toronto: Oxford University Press.

Smart, C. (1990) 'Feminist approaches to criminology or postmodern woman meets atavistic man', in L. Gelsthorpe and A. Morris (eds) *Feminist Perspectives in Criminology*, Milton Keynes: Open University Press.

Smith, D. E. (1977) 'Women, the family and corporate capitalism', in M. Stephenson (ed.) *Women in Canada*, revised edn, Don Mills, ON: General Publishing. (First edition 1973.)

—— (1978) '"K is mentally ill": the anatomy of a factual account', *Sociology* 12 (1): 23–53.

—— (1990) *The Conceptual Practices of Power: A Feminist Sociology of Knowledge*, Boston: Northeastern University Press.

Smith, G. W. (1988) 'Policing the gay community: an inquiry into textually-mediated social relations', *International Journal of the Sociology of Law* 16: 163–183.

Snider, D. L. (1985) 'Legal reform and social control: the dangers of abolishing rape', *International Journal of the Sociology of Law* 13 (4): 337–356.

—— (1988) 'The criminal justice system', in D. Forcese and S. Richer (eds) *Social Issues: Sociological Views of Canada*, 2nd edn, Scarborough, ON: Prentice-Hall Canada. (First edition 1982.)

—— (1990) 'The potential of the criminal justice system to promote feminist concerns', in S. S. Silbey and A. Sarat (eds) *Studies in Law, Politics and Society: A Research Annual* 10: 143–172, Greenwich, Conn: JAI Press.

Snider, D. L. and West, W. G. (1980) 'A critical perspective on law in the Canadian state: delinquency and corporate crime', in R. J. Ossenberg (ed.) *Canadian Society: Power and Conflict*, Toronto: McClelland and Stewart. (Reprinted in T. Fleming (ed.) (1985) *The New Criminologies in Canada*, Toronto: Oxford University Press.)

Spector, M. and Kitsuse, J. I. (1987) *Constructing Social Problems*, Chicago: Aldine. (Originally published by Benjamin/Cummings in 1977.)

Spitzer, S. (1975) 'Toward a Marxian theory of deviance', *Social Problems* 22 (5): 638–651. (Reprinted in R. A. Farrell and V. L. Swigert (eds) (1978) *Social Deviance*, 2nd edn, Philadelphia: Lippincott.)

—— (1979) 'The rationalization of crime control in capitalist society', *Contemporary Crises* 3: 187–206, April.

Spitzer, S. and Scull, A. (1977) 'Social control in historical perspective: from private to public responses to crime', in D. F. Greenberg (ed.) *Corrections and Punishment*, Beverly Hills, CA: Sage.

Stamp, J. (1929) *Some Economic Factors in Modern Life*, London: P. S. King and Son.

Stark, T. J. (1991) *Cold War Blues: The Operation Dismantle Story*, Hull, Que: Voyageur.

Stoddart, K. (1982) 'The enforcement of narcotics violations in a Canadian city: heroin users' perspectives on the production of official statistics', *Canadian Journal of Criminology* 24 (4): 425–438. (Reprinted in Rubington and Weinberg (1987), and in Blackwell and Erickson (1988).)

Strong, P. M. (1979) 'Sociological imperialism and the profession of medicine: a critical examination of the hypothesis of medical imperialism', *Social Science and Medicine* 13A: 199–216.

Stryker, S. (1980) *Symbolic Interactionism: A Social Structural Version*, Menlo Park, CA: Benjamin/Cummings.

Sudnow, D. N. (1967) *Passing On: The Social Organization of Dying*, Englewood Cliffs, NJ: Prentice-Hall.

—— (1976) 'Normal crimes: sociological features of the penal code in a public defender office', in W. B. Sanders and H. C. Daudistel (eds) *The Criminal Justice Process: A Reader*, New York: Praeger. (Originally published in 1965 in *Social Problems* 12 (3): 255–276; also reprinted in Rubington and Weinberg (1987).)

Sutherland, E. H. (1939) *Principles of Criminology*, 3rd edn, Philadelphia: Lippincott. (First edition 1924.)

—— (1949) *White Collar Crime*, New York: Dryden Press.

Sutherland, E. H. and Cressey, D. R. (1978) *Criminology*, 10th edn, Philadelphia: Lippincott.

Sykes, G. M. (1958) *The Society of Captives*, Princeton, NJ: Princeton University Press.

Tarling, R. (1982) 'Unemployment and crime', *Research Bulletin No. 14*, London: Home Office.

Taylor, I., Walton, P. and Young, J. (1973) *The New Criminology: For a Social Theory of Deviance*, London: Routledge & Kegan Paul.

Taylor, L. (1972) 'The significance and interpretation of replies to motivational questions: the case of sex offenders', *Sociology* 6 (1): 23–39.

Tepperman, L. (1977) *Crime Control: The Urge Toward Authority*, Toronto: McGraw-Hill Ryerson.

Tierney, K. J. (1982) 'The battered women movement and the creation of the wife beating problem', *Social Problems* 29 (3): 207–220.

Turk, A. T. (1969) *Criminality and Legal Order*, Chicago: Rand McNally.

—— (1976) 'Law as a weapon in social conflict', *Social Problems* 23 (3): 276–292.

Turner, R. (1969) 'Occupational routines: some demand characteristics of police work', paper given at the Annual Meeting of the Canadian Sociology and Anthropology Association, Toronto, June.

Valpy, M. (1989) 'Spying by police a frightening thing', *Globe and Mail* 22 November (with second article on 23 November).

Valverde, M. (1991) 'Feminist perspectives on criminology', in J. Gladstone, R. V. Ericson and C. D. Shearing (eds) *Criminology: A Reader's Guide*, Toronto: Centre of Criminology, University of Toronto.

Van Maanen, J. (1978) 'The asshole', in P. K. Manning and J. Van Maanen (eds) *Policing: A View from the Street*, New York: Random House.

Vold, G. B. (1958) *Theoretical Criminology*, London: Oxford University Press.

Walker, G. A. (1990) *Family Violence and the Women's Movement: The Conceptual Politics of Struggle*, Toronto: University of Toronto Press.

Ward, D. A. and Kassebaum, G. G. (1965) *Women's Prison: Sex and Social Structure*, Chicago: Aldine.

292 A sociology of crime

Watson, D. R. (1976) 'Some conceptual issues in the social identification of "victims" and "offenders"', in E. C. Viano (ed.) *Victims and Society*, Washington, DC: Visage Press.

—— (1978) 'Categorization, authorization and blame-negotiation in conversation', *Sociology* 12 (1): 105–113.

—— (1983) 'The presentation of victim and motive in discourse: the case of police interrogations and interviews', *Victimology* 8 (1): 31–52.

—— (1990) 'Some features of the elicitation of confessions in murder interrogations', in G. Psathas (ed.) *Interaction Competence*, Washington, DC: International Institute for Ethnomethodology and Conversation Analysis, and University Press of America.

West, C. (1984) *Routine Complications: Troubles With Talk Between Doctors and Patients*, Bloomington, IN: Indiana University Press.

West, D. J. (ed.) (1969) *Criminological Implications of Chromosome Abnormalities*, Cambridge: Institute of Criminology.

Whalen, J., Zimmerman, D. H. and Whalen, M. R. (1988) 'When words fail: a single case analysis', *Social Problems* 35 (4): 335–362.

Wheeler, S. (1967) 'Criminal statistics: a reformulation of the problem', *Journal of Criminal Law, Criminology, and Police Science* 58: 317–324.

Whitaker, R. (1987) *Double Standard: The Secret History of Canadian Immigration*, Toronto: Lester and Orpen Dennys.

Whyte, W. F. (1943) *Street Corner Society: The Social Structure of an Italian Slum*, 2nd edn 1955, Chicago: University of Chicago Press.

Wieder, D. L. (1974) *Language and Social Reality: The Case of Telling the Convict Code*, The Hague: Mouton.

Wilkins, J. L. (1970) 'Producing suicides', *American Behavioral Scientist* 14: 185–201.

Wilkins, L. T. (1964) *Social Deviance: Social Policy, Action and Research*, London: Tavistock. (Excerpted as 'The deviance-amplifying system', in R. A. Farrell and V. L. Swigert (eds) (1978) *Social Deviance*, 2nd edn, Philadelphia: Lippincott.)

Williams, R. (1983) *Keywords: A Vocabulary of Culture and Society*, revised edn, London: Fontana Flamingo.

Wilson, J. Q. and Herrnstein, R. J. (1986) *Crime and Human Nature*, New York: Touchstone.

Wilson, T. P. (1970) 'Normative and interpretive paradigms in sociology', in J. D. Douglas (ed.) *Understanding Everyday Life: Toward the Reconstruction of Sociological Knowledge*, Chicago: Aldine.

Winch, P. (1970) 'Understanding a primitive society', in B. R. Wilson (ed.) *Rationality*, Oxford: Basil Blackwell. (Originally published in 1964 in *American Philosophical Quarterly* 1: 307–324; reprinted in P. Winch (1972) *Ethics and Action*, London: Routledge & Kegan Paul.)

Wise, S. and Stanley, L. (1987) *Georgie Porgie: Sexual Harassment in Everyday Life*, London: Pandora Press.

Woolgar, S. and Pawluch, D. (1985) 'Ontological gerrymandering: the anatomy of social problems explanations', *Social Problems* 32: 214–227.

Wowk, M. (1984) 'Blame allocation, sex and gender in a murder interrogation', in S. Wise and L. Stanley (eds) *Men and Sex: A Case Study in 'Sexual Politics'*, Oxford: Pergamon.

Young, J. (1971a) *The Drugtakers*, London: Paladin.

—— (1971b) 'The police as amplifiers of deviancy', in S. Cohen (ed.) *Images of Deviance*, Harmondsworth: Penguin.

—— (1979) 'Left idealism, reformism and beyond: from new criminology to Marxism', in National Deviancy Conference and Conference of Socialist Economists, *Capitalism and the Rule of Law*, London: Hutchinson.

—— (1986) 'The failure of criminology: the need for a radical realism', in R. Matthews and J. Young (eds) *Confronting Crime*, London: Sage.

Zimmerman, D. H. and Pollner, M. (1970) 'The everyday world as a phenomenon', in J. D. Douglas (ed.) *Understanding Everyday Life: Toward the Reconstruction of Sociological Knowledge*, Chicago: Aldine. (Also in H. Pepinsky (ed.) (1970) *People and Information*, New York: Praeger, and reprinted in Coulter (1990).)

Name index

Subject index

72–3, 208–17
murder 71, 170–2, 176–7, 185–6;
and the insanity defence 81–3,
85, 90
mystification 176–7, 179
myths of crime 113–16, 268

narcotics legislation 22, 27
natural attitude 217
naturalistic research 113
negligence 71, 79–80, 170–1
neo-colonialism 20, 50, 141, 152,
166, 175, 182
neutralization, techniques of 191
newspaper headlines 119–30
normal crimes 218–20
Northern Ireland 57–8, 63, 164

objective crime *see* mundane
reason
'October crisis' 169
official statistics 9–10, 23, 105–8,
197, 216
Oka 57
organizational demand
characteristics (exigencies,
imperatives) 79, 197–202
overcrowding, in prisons 244

particularized knowledge 133
passive recipiency 136
patriarchy 20, 22, 43, 67–8, 141,
152, 166, 172–3, 175, 179, 182,
185–7
persuasion 139
phenomenology 16, 72, 193
plea bargaining, negotiation 17,
176–80, 190–202, 218–22
police, policing 35, 62–3, 117–40;
and mundane reason 128–30;
and plea bargaining 199–200;
and symbolic interactionism 9,
11, 91–116, 197; and use of
'excessive force' 153–4; and use
of normal force 100–4;
assessment of moral character
130–1; communal 141, 143–7;
community 142, 153, 154–7;
contemporary 152–65; culture

91–116; ethnomethodology of
17, 117–40; modern 141, 147,
149–52; on skid row 131–4;
peace-keeping 131–4; politically
problematic populations and
142, 157–63, 165, 175; private
147–8; slave 141–3; structural
conflict perspective on 21, 26,
141–65; *see also* Royal Canadian
Mounted Police
police interrogation 17, 134–40
political economy 17, 20, 47–8,
58, 233, 243
pornography 40
positivism 7–10, 23, 216
post-prison stigmatization 252–3
post-structuralism 22
power 18–20, 51, 204; elite 21
practising criminology 269–71
preference organization 136,
228–9
primary deviance 19, 111
principled justification 104
prisons 230–58; development
231–9; functions of 239–40;
prison crisis 243–7; social
control within 240–3;
subcultures 247–57; women's
prison 240–3
private property 48, 58, 142,
147–8, 171, 174
production: factors of 48; forces
of 47–8, 58, 141, 143, 147;
means of 48–9, 58, 174; mode
of 58–50, 52, 58, 143, 145–6,
149; relations of 47–8, 58, 141,
143, 147, 163; social 48
professional dominance thesis
202–7
prostitution 25, 32, 39, 41. 65, 66,
187, 197
psychological theories of crime 5
punishment 26, 119

Quebec 164, 167, 169

race, racism (conflict,
discrimination, problem) 2, 18,
20, 24, 33, 50, 57–62, 107, 155,